MR CHARMING

MR CHARMING

THE LIFE AND CRIMES OF FELIX VOSSEN

MICHAEL HARRISON

AMBERLEY

To Fiona, Nick, Ellie and Ciara

First published 2019

Amberley Publishing
The Hill, Stroud
Gloucestershire, GL5 4EP

www.amberley-books.com

ISBN 978 1 4456 7793 4 (hardback)
ISBN 978 1 4456 7794 1 (ebook)

British Library Cataloguing in Publication Data.
A catalogue record for this book is available from the British Library.

Typesetting by Aura Technology and Software Services, India. Printed in the UK.

CONTENTS

1

ARREST AND DETENTION

It is nearing five o'clock on a cold, bright afternoon in February 2016 and the low winter sun casts a pale shadow down the length of Avenue de Peris y Valero. There is nothing very remarkable about this particular avenue, a nondescript thoroughfare close to the centre of Valencia populated with pizza joints, mobile phone shops, low-rise apartment buildings and the inevitable graffiti-strewn hoardings that scar much of this Spanish coastal city. But there is something unusual about the well-dressed, bespectacled stranger with the designer stubble standing at the junction of Peris y Valero and a narrow side street, Carrer del Cap Jubi, in his three-quarter length brown leather coat and boating shoes. He is engaged for some reason in animated discussion with an unkempt-looking Cuban man.

As the four-strong police motorcycle patrol cruises by, its attention is drawn to this rather odd couple. Realising they are being observed, the two men turn and begin to walk smartly away in the opposite direction. The officers, who are identifiable as members of Spain's Policia Nacional from the gold and red crown insignia on their navy-blue uniforms, dismount and challenge the pair, asking for their identity papers. The Cuban is allowed to go on his way after he produces his passport and insists he is simply en route to collect his young daughter from school.

But brown leather coat is not so plausible. And the less convincing he becomes, the more he arouses the suspicion of the motorcycle patrol. He maintains that he had only stopped to ask for directions and is in a hurry to reach an appointment. He says he is on business but then describes himself as a tourist. He speaks in English, giving his name as James, but he talks with a heavy German accent. He claims his identity papers are back at his apartment but refuses to say where that is. And he is very nervous. At this point, the officers decide to search James. They escort him to the side of the pavement and up some nearby steps leading to an apartment block. There, they instruct him to remove his coat. Stuffed into its inside pockets they discover almost EUR6,000 in cash in large denomination notes, along with a Greek driving licence, French passport and Italian identity card – each one bearing the same photograph but a different name.

James decides it is time to flee. But as he attempts to make his escape, two of the officers grab him around the waist and shoulders. As they tumble down the steps wrapped around each other his glasses fall to the ground and are crushed beneath the wrestle of bodies. Dishevelled and subdued, his vision blurred, James is arrested and put in handcuffs. The officers ask him why he attempted to escape but he does not reply.

Ordinarily, a suspect picked up on the street in such circumstances would be taken by the arresting officers to the nearest police station. But because of the large amount of cash and forged documents in James's possession, the patrolmen decide it is more appropriate to hand this suspect over to the UDYCO, Spain's drugs and organised crime squad. After a short wait, he is bundled into a blue 'Z' type police car emblazoned with the Spanish flag and taken to UDYCO headquarters, a 15-minute ride across town in Carrer de Ramon y Cajal.

There, he is interrogated for more than an hour and made to empty out his pockets. Among his possessions is a set of keys with, by luck or carelessness, an address label attached to them. The police congratulate themselves on their discovery and laugh incredulously to one another at the schoolboy error committed by their otherwise taciturn and uncommunicative suspect.

That same evening, a two-man team of UDYCO officers is despatched to the address they have found. When they search the apartment, they discover two more forged identity documents – Greek and Dutch passports – further large quantities of cash consisting of 82,000 Swiss francs and £13,000, together with 11 mobile phones, six laptops and 244 grams of what appears to be cocaine along with the paraphernalia for processing and packaging the drug. On further examination, the white powder turns out to be decorator's filler of the type used to repair cracks in plaster walls though police have little doubt its real purpose is to adulterate cocaine for the purposes of then dealing the drug.

The police make one other crucial discovery: a genuine passport in the name of Felix Burghardt Norbert Vossen, born Germany, 11 April 1974. Armed with his true identity, the officers return to UDYCO headquarters and conduct a rapid search of their computer database. They establish that the man they have in custody is a great deal more than a common or garden back street drug dealer: he is the subject of an International Extradition

Order issued by Swiss prosecutors 11 months earlier in March 2015 in connection with financial and economic crime.

Felix Vossen, scion of a wealthy German textile empire, has been on the run for almost a year after disappearing from his London flat, leaving investors in his various Zurich-domiciled investment and asset management companies owed £45 million. In addition to the Swiss warrant, he is being sought by police in Britain and Germany and is also a subject of interest to the FBI.

A man of many parts – day trader, investment guru, technology fanatic and London film producer – this is the story of how a charming, immensely complicated and chameleon-like sociopath with a name reminiscent of a James Bond villain systematically defrauded his family and many of his closest friends out of very large sums of money over a 12-year period.

For some, the money consisted of inheritances and property windfalls, for others it represented their live savings and retirement pots. In some cases, it was wealth accumulated by selling successful businesses, in others it was money scraped together to launch new business ventures. Vossen did not discriminate when it came to selecting his targets. Some of his victims were old and some were young. Some were successful entrepreneurs, but some were pensioners and grandmothers. A few had only recently met Vossen, but most were very close friends of many years standing, in some cases more than a decade. Some were professional colleagues, some were sexual partners and others were family members. The largest single victims of Vossen's fraud were his now-estranged parents, Norbert and Cornelia Vossen. But he also hollowed out whole extended families and groups of inter-connected friends. He even cheated and stole from his godfather.

Many of his victims have survived and moved on, albeit chastened and changed forever by the experience: the amount he stole from them was significant but not life-threatening. Others have been less fortunate – left destitute, penniless and near-homeless. But they are all connected by a cruel and common thread: Vossen used their friendship and their trust to defraud them.

Vossen's fraud was at heart a good old-fashioned 'Ponzi' scheme, so named after Charles Ponzi, an Italian-born fraudster from the 1920s who swindled American investors out of $20 million through a scheme which involved buying International Postal Reply Coupons at discounted prices, exchanging them for full-price airmail stamps, then selling the stamps and pocketing the difference. Investors were persuaded to part with their money with the promise of 100 per cent profits after 90 days. At its height, the fraud was reputedly making Ponzi $250,000 a day. But it also earned him a 14-year jail term. Ponzi has had many imitators since then, the most celebrated being Bernie Madoff who is now serving 150 years in jail for defrauding thousands of investors in his US securities business.

The defining characteristic of Ponzi schemes is that they promise to generate super returns for each new investor, not from genuine trading activity but from the money contributed by the next investor. To stay aloft, such schemes require a constant flow of fresh blood in the shape of new investors or further investments from existing members. When these dry up or initial subscribers seek to get their money out, the Ponzi invariably unravels.

Most Ponzi schemes collapse within a year or two as it becomes increasingly difficult to keep alive the illusion that real and legitimate returns are being generated. Unusually, Vossen's Ponzi survived for a very long time – as did Madoff's - as regulators either missed evidence of wrongdoing or neglected to investigate properly and lending banks failed to spot what was going on under their collective corporate noses. As with Madoff, it is also probable that Vossen's investment scheme began at least as a genuine activity, in his case purportedly trading in and out of technology stocks on the US Nasdaq securities market.

There, the similarities end. The Ponzi run by Madoff was enormous by comparison with Vossen's. Madoff's $65 billion scheme sucked in 4,800 investors who between them lost an estimated $18 billion. Vossen's scheme ensnared a much more modest 33 victims that we know of while the face value of total investments was of the order of £30 million.

Madoff used his reputation on Wall Street and his apparently stellar returns to attract new investors, very few of whom will have been known to him. Vossen, by contrast, used a combination of personality, intimacy and absolute trust to reel in his victims. Behind that veneer of friendship and fidelity, however, lay duplicity and profound, premeditated deceit. As James Ramsden, QC, put it when Vossen's distraught investors went to the High Court in London shortly after he fled to obtain a worldwide order freezing his assets: 'It is an odd case. It is a very odd case. Those of us sitting at the front of the court have never seen anything quite like this before, save that [Mr Vossen] does have characteristics of somebody who is a pathological liar.'

Vossen, Mr Ramdsen went on, was 'an extremely charming, urbane, self-effacing, delightful individual for whom you have an instinctive sense of trust and that is the currency on which he is trading. He is an intriguing character and possibly that was part of his attraction ... he was exciting, and he was promising exciting returns on these investments. He was seen as bright, as innovative, all the things that a convincing fraudster needs.'

Hearing the case, Mr Justice Lewis put it more bluntly: 'I have no feel for this person at all.'

Quite why his investors failed to see behind the mask and quite how they suspended judgement and ignored the first rule of investment – that if something looks too good to be true then it probably is too good to be true – will haunt them forever.

But investors were not the only ones to be hoodwinked by Vossen. So were successive accountants and lawyers, none of whom raised a red flag. Nor, more significantly, did Vossen's three principal banks – UBS, Credit Suisse and Barclays - ever appear to question his probity or financial dealings despite subsequent evidence that he had used these three financial bastions to launder money over many years.

Managing and apparently investing his friends' money was only part of what Vossen did. His other persona was as a successful film producer. His credits included the remake of *The Sweeney*, starring Ray Winstone, and *I, Anna*, a 2012 noir thriller starring Charlotte Rampling, Gabriel Byrne and Hayley Atwell. At the time of his disappearance, he was producing the Toni Collette and Drew Barrymore vehicle *Miss You Already*, a womance about two life-long friends facing up the challenges of childbirth and cancer. It was ironically apt subject matter: Vossen's favourite default position whenever he found himself trapped in an awkward conversation with an investor asking for a statement of account or, worse still, their money back was to switch the conversation to his own health or that of his family, one of whom was invariably in the early stages of treatment for one imaginary cancer or another.

Vossen undoubtedly used some of his investors' money to finance his passion for film. But he also relentlessly and assiduously used his film connections and his ability to move freely amongst the Hollywood glitterati to burnish his credentials and increase his appeal to would-be investors. It was Vossen's equivalent of a virtuous circle, although there was precious little that was honourable about his behaviour.

So, who were Vossen's victims? Some are rich – though not as rich now as they were before they met their nemesis. But none are famous. They are Everyman. They are you and me. They are IT consultants, advertising men and film producers. They are sports journalists and yoga teachers and financial traders. They are orthodontists and architects and estate agents. And they are housewives and pensioners.

One of Vossen's oldest friends and earliest investors, Steven Walters, a commercials film editor, describes him thus: 'Felix was kind, intelligent and a joy to be around. Through all the years of friendship, dinners, even holidays, I never questioned his sincerity. He came across as a caring, animal-loving new tech fan that we'd all come to know and love. He once shed a tear at a dinner party because his unwell goldfish had just passed away. That greatly impressed the ladies.'

Walters was owed £2.2 million when Vossen disappeared off the radar.

One of the very last investors to trust Vossen with his money was David Benziger, a Swiss architect and property developer now living in Hong Kong. He lost $100,000. 'I only met the man in the flesh twice, but I really thought we had become good friends,' says Benziger.

They were as shocked and stunned as anyone when Vossen went on the run, sending a lachrymose text message of apology to his long-time girlfriend Sophia Rafaat, a model and former television presenter, and leaving instructions for a removals company to shred every document in his Jermyn Street flat. He then took a Swissair flight to Zurich and cleared out his offices there too. That day is emblazoned in the memories of Vossen's investors: it was Tuesday, 3 March 2015 – by coincidence the same day that Charles Ponzi had been born 133 years earlier.

Thirteen months later, April 26, 2016, and Vossen is once again on board a Swissair flight back to Zurich: this time from Madrid and under very different circumstances. He is accompanied by two plain clothes Swiss police officers who are extraditing him back to Switzerland. After landing on Swiss soil, he is immediately re-arrested and taken to the prison adjacent to Zurich airport, Flughafen Gessangis. Vossen is held there for 13 months before being indicted on charges of fraud, money laundering and forgery. Finally, he is to face justice and his victims.

There is one man, however, who is not among that group of victims. He is a London-based script writer and successful investor in his own right called Danny Moynihan. Moynihan came very close to giving Vossen his money and even went to view his trading operations in Jermyn Street and downtown Zurich. But Moynihan was struck by how little infrastructure there appeared to be – either technological or human - to support a business which allegedly had £250 million of funds under management. He carried out some background checks of his own with banking contacts in Zurich and finally concluded he did not know enough about Vossen to trust him with his money. Nor could he verify Vossen's track record or fund performance to his satisfaction.

When Moynihan called Vossen to tell him he had decided not to invest, he joked: 'For all I know, you could be the next Bernie Madoff.' Vossen laughed uproariously down the phone in his booming German baritone.

2

THE MAKING OF A FRAUDSTER

Felix Vossen was born on 11 April, 1974 in Gütersloh, a small industrial town in North Rhine Westphalia, some 60 miles from the German-Dutch border. Socially conservative and a stronghold of Angela Merkel's CDU party, the region is home to a fifth of Germany's population and built its fortune on coal and steel. When those two traditional industries went into decline Gütersloh found other ways of generating wealth. Today it is best-known as the home of two different German icons – the media conglomerate Bertelsmann and the domestic appliance manufacturer Miele, both of which are family-owned. However, until the early 1990s, the third biggest private employer in the town was a textiles manufacturer called Vossen, the company that gave the world the terry towelling bathrobe. To this day it remains one of the brand's most popular exports with some six million terry towelling products sold each year in 43 countries.

The eldest of four children born to Norbert and Cornelia Vossen, Felix lived a very comfortable life thanks to the success of the family firm. The business was founded in 1925 by his grandfather Burkhardt Vossen. As a young man Burkhardt had visited Britain on holiday shortly after the end of the First World War. During the trip he discovered how popular terry towelling had become. Although the technique for producing the distinctive material had originally been discovered accidentally by a Turkish weaver, who mistakenly wove loops instead of smooth fabric on his hand loom, the invention was expropriated by a passing Englishman who took the idea back home with him and industrialised it.

Burkhardt returned to Gütersloh, convinced there was a similar business opportunity to be had in Germany, provided he could make the product affordable. Once home, he promptly enrolled to study textile technology at a technical college in the nearby town of Bielefeld, using any spare time he had to visit the modern textile mills in France and Czechoslovakia to observe the latest weaving techniques. It was only natural, then, that when Burkhardt left college he should open a small weaving mill in Gütersloh. The first terry material was spun from his loom on 6 May, 1925 and made into towelling. But Burkhardt also had a hunch that its warmth and softness would appeal in more ways than that, and so he also fashioned his first bathrobe.

Initially, the little mill on Neuenkirchener Strasse employed just five workers. In the early years Burkhardt did not have enough money to rent, much less own, a house and so he lived in a small room inside the mill. However, as terry towelling grew in popularity so Burkhardt's little mill also expanded in size and by the time that war broke out in Europe in 1939 he was employing some 400 people and making handsome profits. The war brought a halt to production and so Burkhardt had to start from scratch again in 1945, initially with a workforce of just 40 people. But his pre-war connections stood him in good stead and very quickly Vossen ramped up production, aided by its Swiss-designed colour weaving machines which improved efficiency four-fold and by Burkhardt's own keen commercial sense and eye for new export markets. Vossen thus became a perfect example of the Mittelstand, that vast legion of small and medium-sized firms on which the might of the modern-day German economy was famously built. Despite a serious fire in 1963 which burned down the company's main manufacturing facility and stopped production for two months, the business continued to grow and prosper over the next two decades.

Led by Vossen, Gütersloh had become known as one of Germany's most important textile centres. At its height in the mid-1980s, the town employed some 6,000 textile workers, many of them migrants who had arrived in the region from Syria to supplement the local labour force.

By the time Felix was born, Vossen had outgrown its Mittelstand status to become a genuinely big business with a workforce which peaked at 3,500. The company was making profits to match and it was using those profits to expand internationally. Gütersloh and a sister production facility in the nearby town of Warburg were no longer able to meet demand, even though Vossen was bussing workers in from the surrounding countryside to man its weaving and printing machines. So the company began producing its bathrobes and towels in Hungary, Austria and Mauritius.

Life was good for Vossen's loyal workforce while the company itself was as much a fixture of Gütersloh as the River Dalke which runs through it and pumpernickel, a heavy sweet ryebread typically served with Westphalia ham for which the town is renowned. Whilst they had not quite achieved the same standing in Gütersloh as the Miele family or the Mohns, who owned Bertelsmann, the Vossens were without doubt up there and jostling for position. They were serious contenders.

Felix and his three siblings – a brother also called Norbert and two twin sisters, Christina and Isobel – looked forward to the day when they would inherit the family business. Felix, by common consent, held a special place in his grandfather's affections. When the old man died in 1981 – the same year that his younger brother was born - two of the possessions that the seven-year-old Felix inherited were his grandfather's wrist watch and his wedding ring, which he still owns and wears to this day. Following the death of Burkhardt, responsibility for running the company passed to Felix's father, Norbert Senior, one of Burkhardt's three children.

Horst Wormann, who joined Vossen in 1943 as an apprentice weaver on DM25 a month and rose to become manager of the Gütersloh site, says: 'Felix was Burkhardt's favourite grandchild. There was no question of that. Felix would come to the factory with his father and his grandfather would play with him, rolling around the floor and tickling him. Sometimes Norbert would say to me, "I can't work out who Felix's father is, me or Burkhardt".'

Although his parents were ambitious for their eldest son, Vossen seems to have grown up in a family where there was very little emotional expression. 'It was not a household which went in for hugs,' Vossen would later tell friends. He portrayed his parents as strict and unemotional and claimed that as a young boy he was closest to his paternal grandfather Burkhardt.

After primary school, Felix was initially sent to one of Gütersloh's two secondary schools – Evangelische Stiftisches

Gymnasium, a 20-minute walk from the family home. Founded in 1851 by the Protestant movement, Evangelische Stiftisches boasts one of Germany's most famous trombone choirs and pupils are taught trilingually in German, English and French. As a faith school (motto: Glory to God Alone), it is self-governing and non-fee paying. In the year that Felix first went to the school, Bertelsmann endowed an impressive media and arts department at the school.

Although Evangelisches Stiftisches was to prove perfectly satisfactory for his siblings, Felix's parents chose for some reason to remove him from the school after a short period there. And so, when he reached the age of 12, Felix was sent instead to the Lyceum Alpinum Zuoz, a prestigious international boarding school set in spectacular alpine landscape a two-minute walk from the slopes of the Swiss ski resort of St Moritz.

It was an unusual thing to do. Most German children – whatever their family wealth and background – are educated in the state system. To do otherwise suggests either an ostentatious and slightly vulgar display of wealth or that the child in question is not that bright.

In any event, the Alps is where Felix went. There, according to the school's prospectus, he would be imbued with the 'Spirit of Zuoz' and taught the values of 'individual creative endeavour, integrity, reliability and life-long friendship'. Pupils at Zuoz were encouraged to live by a simple creed: 'a healthy mind in a healthy body'. The end product would be one more 'cosmopolitan, responsible citizen of the world' of the type Zuoz had been turning out for almost a century. Back in the 1980s when Vossen first arrived at Alpinum Zuoz, the school catered for both boarders and day pupils who lived in the local valley.

But, wherever they came from, Alpinum Zuoz's pupils were regarded as special and treated accordingly.

Today, in keeping with its exclusive cachet, Zuoz limits student numbers to 300 and boasts a student-teacher ratio of four to one. Among the ten reasons for attending the school listed on the Zuoz website are its remote location, 320 days of sun a year and its very active alumni network – its former pupils include Ferdinand Piech, chairman and major shareholder in the luxury car maker Porsche, the actor George Gotz and Lichtenstein's head of state, Prince-elect Hans Adam II.

The wealth being generated from the Vossen textiles business was comfortably enough to enable them to pay the boarding fees of Sf80,000 (£64,000) a year. They also hoped that, alongside a privileged education, attending Alpinum Zuoz would allow Felix to rub shoulders with other boys and girls who would one day become not just the movers and shakers of the Swiss-German business world, but members of a global elite.

Rolf Zehnder, 79, one of Vossen's former teachers, told the German radio broadcaster NDR that his parents only sent Felix to Alpinum Zuoz reluctantly. They were resigned to doing so, however, because they were determined he would receive a first-class education and were concerned that the demands of running the family business would not leave them with sufficient time to dedicate to their son.

Vossen had only been at Alpinum Zuoz for a couple of days when he suffered an accident. He lost one of his front teeth jumping into the school's swimming pool. It was a false tooth that the young Vossen had to have fitted after he accidentally walked into a lamp post whilst gazing at a girl on the other side of the road, or so he told his friends. Another pupil, Ralph Weber, who had arrived at Alpinum Zuoz from Johannesburg a year earlier, was the best swimmer in the school and was therefore instructed by the governor to dive down into the pool and retrieve the missing tooth, which he successfully did. It was the beginning of a friendship between the two boys which lasted for the entire duration of their time in the Swiss Alps. Vossen and Weber joined the same small class of 15 boys and girls and also went on to become room-mates for a year.

'It was a weird introduction but we actually had a good year together,' recalls Weber. 'We had a very similar sense of humour and so there was lots of laughing. He wasn't the most social person but then neither was I at that time so we formed a good friendship. There were only four boarders in our set because the rest of the class was made up of day pupils who came from the local valley so we came to rely upon one another. It was quite an intense relationship. We knew everything about each other because we were together twenty-four hours a day.'

Weber remembers a boy who was 'charming, eloquent and a good listener'. But, he adds, Vossen rationed that charm. 'He had a hierarchical system. He wasn't like that with everyone, especially the day pupils. It was essential if you were a boarder to have good relations with the day pupils in order to survive and get things like newspapers brought up to the school from St Moritz. Felix got on well with some of them, and had good connections with the girls, but most of the day pupils hated him, particularly the guys. I think he came over to them as arrogant and snobbish.'

Weber and Ralph Zehnder both testify to Vossen being a good athlete but not a big team player. 'He wasn't interested in games like soccer or hockey but he was a very good runner,' says Weber. 'He was very fast.'

He was also fascinated with the movie industry, even at that young age. 'He received regular magazines about films and he knew the names of all the stars and directors,' says Weber. 'There was a magazine called *Cinema* which he subscribed to. You could open it and ask him to name the director of any film and he would tell you. I don't think his parents were very happy about this because it became clear to them at a certain point that Felix was not going to take over the running of their business. Shortly before I left the school he told me he had no interest in doing that because he was more interested in movies.'

Vossen's pre-occupation with movies may partly explain why he never quite lived up to the school's hyberbole and certainly did not demonstrate any great academic prowess. According to a former rector at the school Felix was 'a good average'. 'I did not remember him as a star pupil but he never made any problems.'

But did Vossen exhibit any incipient signs of the fraudulent character that he was to become? Zehnder noted that the young Vossen had 'a certain craftiness' about him. And Weber remembers Vossen importing a variety of Chinese medicines and pills from the US, which he thought might be steroids, which Vossen tried unsuccessfully to sell to his fellow pupils. 'Nobody was really interested in buying them from Felix, but he was always looking for a business opportunity,' recalls Weber.

As their time together wore on, however, Weber became more circumspect about Vossen, finally deciding he was a 'chiseller who took advantage of people and situations' and cautioning fellow pupils not to lend money to him.

Something clearly went wrong for Vossen towards the end of his school time in the Swiss Alps. He left the Alpinum Zuoz at 16 without taking the Swiss Matura or German

Arbitur – the equivalent of English A Levels – placing him amongst the one per cent of Zuoz students who failed to progress to a top university after their time in the Swiss Alps. Vossen would later tell friends in London that he suffered at boarding school and lost the desire to learn. Although he had been proud to attend such a prestigious institution, Vossen had nevertheless endured some terrible times at Alpinum Zuoz, he claimed.

Weber says Vossen's professed unhappiness with his schooldays may have had something to do with the strict regime to which he was obliged to submit. 'His teachers were very rigid in their educational style and it was not a very liberal place,' he says. 'For me, it was the right structure but for Felix it meant he did not have enough freedom. He was always looking to find some loophole in the system, some way of getting out of school.'

Like Vossen, Weber also left Alpinum Zuoz prematurely – though in Weber's case it was because the money to fund his education ran out after the death of his father. Shortly after leaving the school, and despite his misgivings about Vossen, Weber decided to team up with his erstwhile room-mate one last time. That was when Weber got his first and only real taste of Vossen's capacity for deceit and ability to separate his friends from their money.

Vossen had gone to Bergamo in northern Italy to visit some friends who worked at a distribution facility that the family owned in the town. Weber was invited to join them with the promise that he could stay with Vossen and his friends. 'I arrived late in the evening and was told that I couldn't stay at the friends' house after all and would have to book into a hotel,' he says. 'I stayed in Bergamo for a week and paid for literally everything. Every time I asked Felix if he could pay, he said he didn't have any money on him.'

When they left Bergamo, the two boys travelled to St Moritz where they stayed at the Carlton, an historic five-star hotel overlooking the lake with palatial architecture, a spa and rooms starting at almost £600 a night. 'The concierge knew Felix for sure because he greeted us saying 'Hello Mr Vossen, so nice to see you, we have a nice room for you'. The agreement was that Vossen would pay for the stay in the Carlton because Weber had stood the bill when they were in Bergamo. When the time came to pay, Vossen's credit card bounced and so Weber was obliged to call his mother to ask her to bail them out.

The two boys had a tremendous row and Weber ended his friendship there and then, vowing never to see him again. 'It was a five-star hotel so it was a lot of money,' says Weber. 'But it wasn't so much that. I was fed up that he hadn't kept to his word. It would have been OK if he'd said, "I'm sorry Ralph, I've fucked up, I don't have the money." But he insisted that we stayed at the hotel and then didn't think it was a bad thing that he didn't have the money to pay the bill. He didn't seem to mind at all. I thought that's not how I want to carry on, I couldn't trust him any longer. You think you have a good relationship and you think that you know someone and then suddenly you realise that's not the case and you don't know why.'

While Vossen was wasting his time in the Swiss Alps, the trajectory of the family firm had begun to alter course, at first quite slowly but then, later, in a series of rapid moves which ultimately took the business in a downward and terminal direction. Norbert Senior had become managing director of the company in 1972. He eventually took full control of the business when his father died nine years later. Now in charge, he reasoned that if Vossen was to prosper in the face of growing competition from low-cost Asian and east European competitors, it needed to spread its wings beyond Gütersloh. So, Vossen began to loosen its ties with its home town. It opened the production site in Mauritius and shifted more production to Hungary. It also bought out a company called Frottana in eastern Germany which produced finished textiles under the Moeve brand, using raw materials sourced from Vossen. Vossen was able to supply not just its own needs but those of other manufacturers because the old man Burkhardt had wisely invested in his own spinning mill in Gütersloh to coincide with the company's silver jubilee in 1950. But its biggest investment was to build a sister production facility to Gütersloh in Jennersdorf in Austria which began production in the early 1960s.

By 1975 Vossen had become the biggest towelling manufacturer in Europe. In a brochure produced to commemorate and celebrate the company's fiftieth anniversary, Vossen spoke of Burkhardt's achievements and vision for the business. 'New aims are pending. Now and in the future his son Norbert will achieve them in the true tradition of his father,' it proclaimed.

That Norbert was cut from very different cloth to his father Burkhardt, there is no doubt. Burkhardt was old-style, patriarchal, paternalistic and omnipresent. The villa he lived in, the same one in which Felix was brought up, was a stone's throw from his work. That was handy given Burkhardt's penchant for rising early and paying unscheduled visits to the factory. In keeping with this paternalistic instincts, he funded the pensions of former employees out of his own pocket. He also bought up land surrounding the factory, selling or letting it out to employers at peppercorn rates so they could build their own homes. When Burkhardt was alive, managers and employees would be invited to the family home when the old man threw one of his regular parties. When he died, the family's maid discovered that he had made provision for her – gifting her an apartment in which she lived with her sister until dementia struck and she was forced to move into a nursing home.

When Norbert took over the reins, all that changed. Horst Wormann, the long-serving Gütersloh site manager, probably knows more about the company than any man alive. Now aged 90, he lives with his wife close to the centre of Gütersloh in a neat three-bedroomed house that he bought in the mid-1950s with the help of his mentor and benefactor Burkhardt Vossen. Wormann has a lot of time for the company's founder. A year after he joined the company in 1943 he was conscripted into the German army and sent by Hitler to the Russian front where he was captured and held prisoner-of-war until 1945. On his release, he returned to Gütersloh and re-joined Vossen. Although he had trained as a weaver, he instead joined a small team working directly under Burkhardt Vossen. When he retired in 1989 he was presented with a special key to all of the company's facilities, including the family's private wine cellar, such was the trust and respect in which he was held. Even after his retirement, he stayed on the Vossen payroll as a consultant.

So, he is a Burkhardt fan through and through. After Norbert took over, Wormann says he never went to the family home again. Norbert and Cornelia were intent, however, on maintaining the Vossen family's social standing in Gütersloh. Cornelia ran a wife's club for the spouses of the owners of the town's other big companies – Miele, Bertelmsmann, the food producer Oettker and Henkel, a detergents and consumer goods conglomerate in the mould of Unilever. 'They hung out socially, but Cornelia would also bring the wives on site and I would give them a tour of the facilities to demonstrate the quality of Vossen goods,' says Wormann.

Norbert's management style also differed dramatically from that of his father. 'Burkhardt was ever present. Nobody was safe from him day or night,' remembers Wormann. 'He would show up at the factory unexpectedly or come back from holidays two days early. His own operations team had to start work at 5.30am, the same time as Burkhardt.'

Wormann says with evident pride:

> When Norbert took over, he did not start work until 8am because it was important for him always to have breakfast with the family. He was a big family man. Nothing much changed in the beginning. Burkhardt had a lot of technical knowledge but Norbert did not have that. He bought a lot of machines that I advised him against buying because they were not suitable for our needs. When I retired, Norbert gave a speech and described me as one of the most uncomfortable men he had ever employed because nobody could fool me. His wife Cornelia took responsibility for product design but we had a lot of arguments because I said we could not produce these designs at the right quality. Burkhardt was always straight forward when it came to quality. He said if we can't produce to the right quality let's not do it. With Norbert, the focus switched more to the design side.

The Vossen family was not shy about associating itself with the product or indeed the contribution successive generations had made to the brand, whilst simultaneously denying that the business was run mainly to provide employment for family members. In one brochure produced around 1990, the entire family can be seen promoting the product. There, on one page, are Norbert and Cornelia holding bundles of brightly-coloured terry towelling, here on another is a young Felix flanked by his twin sisters and, overleaf a double-page spread depicting the Vossen brand's 'ambassador', Norbert Junior, modelling the entire Vossen range. The text is almost as illuminating as the artwork in its hyperbole.

> Vossen is undoubtedly a family business. The management, however, is largely entrusted to non-family members. Senior management positions are accorded on the basis of performance and professionalism, not nepotism. Just as the third Vossen generation will bring fresh impetus for the future, so the Vossen Group, following its success in Germany and Europe, will also have to adjust to new international markets. We see ourselves as citizens of the world and the fall of ideological borders and political frontiers will offer us new opportunities with new countries and peoples.

Little did the Vossen workforce know then that the company would never live to see the day when it would be passed over to the stewardship of a third generation. Nor did anyone in Gütersloh seem unduly worried about the slow eastwards drift of the company's manufacturing operations. Alarm bells did not even ring when the Vossen family finally uprooted themselves from Gütersloh in 1992, selling their villa and relocating to a new home close to the company's sister factory in Austria. It was, however, a double snub which did little to endear the family to its workforce or the wider community in Vossen's spiritual home, despite Norbert's promise that Gütersloh was safe and would remain an important centre of production.

Wormann says:

> We weren't concerned at the time because we were increasing production capacity everywhere to meet demand. That's why we needed a second production facility in Austria. We wanted to increase production in Gütersloh as well but we couldn't find enough staff. We were expanding so quickly. The economy was booming, there were other companies like Bertelsmann, Miele, Claas taking on staff and we had to bus workers into Gütersloh from surrounding towns.

What Wormann and others did notice, however, was that the more Vossen expanded and diversified, the more stretched its finances became as it took on loans to finance its various acquisitions and investments. It is the classic Mittelstand business model that banks work hand in hand with the owners of medium-sized private family enterprises, sometimes becoming shareholders as well as creditors. However, at Vossen, the balance of power between the company and its banks began to tilt in favour of the latter.

'Burkhardt used to say if a banker came to see us at Vossen, they needed to hold the door open for him because he was calling the shots,' says Wormann. 'Slowly but surely that changed after Norbert took over. He began to hold the door open for the bankers.'

It was only much later that the workforce realised what was really happening to Vossen and to Gütersloh. Hans Werner Heissmann-Gladow, an official with the IG Metall trades union, takes up the story. At the end of the 1980s Vossen still had

1,000 employees in the town. By the time Heissmann-Gladow took on responsibility for negotiating with the company in 1995, that number had shrunk to 400. He says that in the preceding two years, Vossen had sought to cut costs, first by extending the working week by two and a half hours without extra pay and then by slicing three days from the annual holiday entitlement. To do this, it needed to make changes to the binding labour agreement that was in place with the union. The union refused to play ball, and so, according to Heissmann-Gladow, Norbert went to employees individually to ask them to sign new employment contracts.

The following year, there was another stand-off between management and unions after Vossen attempted to push through a fresh redundancy programme which involved cutting the workforce by more than 10 per cent.

Vossen's loyal but shrinking workforce did everything they could to keep the firm solvent, working overtime and at full capacity. Alas, their efforts and Norbert's restructuring of the business were not enough to save it, and on 10 December, 1996, the Vossen textiles group filed for bankruptcy. A few months later, the company's slimmed-down production site in Gütersloh closed with the loss of the remaining 200 jobs. The administrators of the company's insolvency searched in vain for new investors to inject fresh capital into the business and keep it going in its current form. Eventually, parts of the business were bought out of insolvency by the Austrian firm Linz which took full control of the business in 2004.

The bankruptcy and subsequent insolvency proceedings dragged on for the best part of a decade. But to this day, they are still a source of anger, frustration and dispute in Gütersloh.

Heissmann-Gladow contends that there was never any intention of keeping Vossen in business as a going concern once the administrators had been called in.

> Normally when you file for insolvency, the objective is to keep the company going. There was no intent by Norbert Vossen to keep the company going. Vossen had strategically planned to run Gütersloh into the ground.
>
> There was a workers' council with co-determination rights to be consulted about all decisions and plans which affect the workforce. But management did not work closely enough with it in order to create a long-term plan to save the company. They played games. There was an intent to make Vossen bankrupt. The company did not need to go down.

What caused further outcry was the way that the family's private wealth appeared to have been ring-fenced from the financial woes of the company they were running. Heissmann-Gladow cites numerous pieces of evidence to support this.

A complicated group structure meant that the Gütersloh and Jennersdorf sites were kept under separate ownership. When the business went under, Jennersdorf was placed into administration 14 days before Gütersloh. Gütersloh in turn was weighed down with significant debts in the form of receivables which it owned to the Jennersdorf company.

Those debts were guaranteed by a family holding company, Burkhardt Vossen AG. However, about 18 months before the bankruptcy, the contract under which those debts were guaranteed was cancelled. The only asset that the weaving mill in Gütersloh had to pay off creditors was a property in Berlin valued at DM3 million.

The Gütersloh company had also held the licences for a number of brands under which Vossen traded, including Moeve, Frottana and a brand called Flamingo. According to Heissmann-Gladow, Norbert Vossen sold off these brand rights to a consortium of Swiss banks for DM2 million.

A year prior to filing for bankruptcy, Norbert Vossen set up an arrangement to pay the salary of his managing director into a special blocked bank account that was beyond the reach of administrators for a guaranteed period of 10 years.

Nor were administrators able to seize the family home, set on the outskirts of Gütersloh close to the city's botanical gardens, to help pay off creditors. The three-acre site was valued at the time at DM5 million but that, too, was owned separately. After the Vossens had left Gütersloh, part of the grounds were sold off to another family, the Stichlings, who owned a kitchen manufacturing business. They used the land to build a pair of houses for their two daughters.

At the height of the crisis, with the Vossen empire collapsing and the workforce unsure of their jobs or their future, a shipment of textile materials arrived at the Belgian port of Antwerp, destined for the weaving mill in Gütersloh. Because administrators had already been called in, the consignment never left the port but was instead auctioned off for a fraction of its true value. Vossen, according to Heissmann-Gladow, attempted to sue the Gütersloh company for the loss of the shipment but failed in his lawsuit.

After the bankruptcy filing, the union wrote to Norbert Vossen demanding his resignation from the Gütersloh company, which the workforce pinned to the door of his office. The Austrian state in which the Jennersdorf company was located agreed to provide financial guarantees so that it could buy back the Vossen brands that had been sold to the Swiss banking consortium and carry on trading. But only on the proviso that Norbert Vossen stood down from that company too.

The union subsequently commissioned a legal report into the Vossen family's stewardship of the business which was handed over to federal prosecutors. But no action was taken.

Looking back, Heissmann-Gladow says:

> At the time of the bankruptcy, the reaction of the workforce in Gütersloh was actually quite muted. They were hopeful they could continue working for the company based on the assumption that Norbert was a reliable as Burkhardt. They didn't realise the business was being intentionally wound up. They weren't prepared for the kind of tactics that Norbert Vossen used.
>
> When I heard what Felix Vossen had done, my first reaction was that the apple does not fall far from the tree.

Horst Wormann also still believes that the company could have been saved. He has created a beautifully-produced history of the firm, bound in royal blue terry towelling fabric and containing all manner of documentation detailing the firm's 71-year existence including maps, architects' drawings, site plans, photographs and testimonials.

Reading from it, he says: 'Burkhardt had a motto: "Sparing in words, dynamic in actions, convincing in performance." Had his son followed that motto the company would still be alive today.'

'I could see it coming by the way they managed their people and led their staff. Myself and one of my colleagues predicted that if they went on as they did, the firm would go down in ten years. It took Norbert 15 years.'

On 2 February, 2001 – some five years and two months after the administrators were called in – the bulldozers finally arrived to raze to the ground what was left of the sprawling Vossen factory site in Gütersloh. Today it is a mixed industrial, commercial and retail park. The only remaining visible trace that the company ever existed is a street sign welcoming you to Vossen Strasse. It is a cul-de-sac.

Following the collapse of the firm, Norbert junior took charge of one of the production sites of its Moeve subsidiary which was hived off from the rest of the business prior to the bankruptcy of the parent company. He still works there today.

It seems that even in the good times when the business was thriving, Felix was never regarded by his parents as heir apparent, the son who would one day take over the running of the family firm. Horst Wormann recalls a conversation he once had with Norbert about the possibility of Felix succeeding him. 'We talked about his kids. He said that as a parent, the best you can do is give them a good education but what they do with it is up to them. They didn't force him to become involved in the company. It was never a topic of conversation that Felix would or should take over the company. He was not present anyway because he was at school in Switzerland.'

Unlike his younger brother, who often appeared in the company's advertising brochures modelling the Vossen range and who would go on to join the business, Felix had never shown any appetite for following in his father's footsteps. He preferred instead to develop his interests in computer technology and the film industry. His father was fond of telling colleagues that Felix 'had other talents'.

Interviewed in 2013 by the German online business publication *Wirschafts Woche*, Norbert Junior participated in a quick-fire round of questions and answers. In response to the question: 'Shares or gold?' Norbert replied: 'Don't put all your eggs in one basket.' It was prescient advice that would, had he but known it, have best been directed at his elder brother's investors.

Today, Norbert and Cornelia divide their time between their homes in Austria and Switzerland, where they have an apartment on Lake Geneva, and a cattle ranch in Argentina, trying to forget about the fresh shame that their eldest son has heaped upon the family name. Since his arrest and detention, they have never once visited him in prison, although Vossen's siblings did make the journey to Gessangis, the airport prison where he was initially held on remand, during his time there.

Linz, the present-day owner of the Vossen company, also saw fit to distance itself from the family name, to prevent any damage to its corporate reputation. Following the news that Vossen had absconded owing investors £45 million, the Austrian conglomerate issued a press release stating: 'The Vossen company was sold in 1996 and has been a wholly owned subsidiary of Linz Textil AG, an Austrian textile company, since 2004. Since then, Vossen GmbH & Co has had no business or other relationship with the Vossen family.'

As well as bringing shame to the family name, Felix also tarnished the carefully-constructed image of his alma mater, Alpinum Zuoz. Other than Ralph Weber, none of his contemporaries at the school are ready to talk about him and the Zuoz Club, the alumni association for former pupils, rather wishes it could airbrush Felix Vossen from its year books. It is as if Zuoz Club members have signed a collective non-disclosure agreement or sworn an oath of *omerta* which prevents them from speaking publicly about any former member. Asked to comment on Vossen and whether he had exhibited any incipient signs of criminality during his time at the school, the former president of Zuoz, Dogan Taskent, would only say: 'It is very unfortunate to read such news about one of our members. But I am very proud to inform you that the rest of our members, approximately 2,499 of them, are making a great contribution to the economy and humanity.'

The current president, Dr Nicole Kollas, who runs a management training consultancy in the German city of Baden, says simply: 'The Zuoz Club is a private club. We do not disclose any information.'

The citizens of Gütersloh have not closed ranks, nor do they appear to be suffering from any collective shame brought down on their heads and that of the town by its most famous and errant export. Stephan Recklin, a reporter on the daily regional newspaper *Westfalen Blatt,* reported on the original collapse of the Vossen company and has been following the tale of Felix Vossen's fraud since he went on the run. 'The local reaction has been less one of shock and embarrassment and more one of amusement, he says. 'How could the scion of one of the town's best-known families have done what he did? And was his fate another example of a fault line that ran through the family?'

Despite the collapse of the firm and Felix's own personal failure to graduate from Alpinum Zuoz with flying colours, his parents continued to fund his education. After quitting boarding school, Vossen came over to England where he began an International Baccalaureat at a school in Oxford. He then went on to study for a degree in business studies – known in German as a BWL – and then spent time undertaking a law apprenticeship in Madrid, working at a legal practice which specialised in representing German clients. Whether he stayed the course at any of these institutions is unclear.

Vossen's time in Madrid gave him a taste for the Iberian way of life. He moved back to the Spanish capital in his early twenties and, bankrolled once again by his parents, set up a small computer business trading and dealing in Apple products. The venture went bust and Vossen was left owing his parents, and a number of other creditors, considerable sums of money. According to former friends, it was this episode that precipitated the estrangement of Vossen from his parents, a separation that appears to have lasted until they were reconciled a decade later. Whenever he was asked about his siblings, Felix had a habit of depicting his younger brother Norbert as the black sheep of the family, the prodigal son who was forever testing the patience and pockets of his parents. In reality, he was describing himself.

By the time Vossen left Spain following his early and unsuccessful foray into computer retailing he was 26 and had almost certainly developed a cocaine habit – an addiction that was to become more acute as time went by and he established his twin-track career in London as film producer and financial trader. However, he very rarely smoked and almost never drank, preferring diet coke and Red Bull. Pressed to a champagne toast of some success or another, he would feign a sip and then cradle his glass for the rest of the evening. As for food, he was a prodigious meat eater. He entertained guests with beef fillet which he claimed was flown over to London from the family's cattle ranch in Argentina. But Vossen never touched vegetables, with the exception of potatoes.

He had become a snappy dresser, though somewhat in the style of Eurotrash, with a particular love of expensive leather shoes and strongly-scented aftershave. He was vain and weight-obsessed and he was also fastidious to the point of being anally retentive. He could not bear it if his shoes had the slightest mark on them. Brand new shirts would be worn once, laundered, folded and then put back into the packaging in which they had arrived.

Friends recall how his apartment would be so spotlessly clean, pristine and un-lived in as to be mildly unsettling. Vossen employed a cleaner on a daily basis and visitors would be encouraged to take off their shoes before entering. He had a habit of finishing a meal quickly and then clearing away the plates and spraying down the table with cleaning products whilst those dining with him continued to eat. He was obsessed by the latest toys that technology had to offer. He owned a mini-Dyson for any crumbs that fell from the table and would plump up the cushions as soon as anyone stood up from his immaculately presented sofas. His bathroom and WC looked for all the world as if they had never been used and were awaiting their first customer. A new oven in one of his apartments still had the packaging material inside it months after it had been installed. In short, Vossen craved perfection and wanted to create the illusion of perfection in everything he did.

In the same way that he controlled his living environment, he also controlled his emotions – for the most part. Outwardly charming, confident and calm, the mask would occasionally slip when Vossen was with colleagues or girlfriends. One colleague says: 'He was nearly always incredibly complimentary to me but in a few instances I saw his fierce temper and couldn't believe he was the same person. His anger was irrational and came seemingly out of the blue. He was like a pressure cooker holding in the anger.'

Vossen was also undoubtedly bright. He had an enquiring mind and the capacity to absorb and retain voluminous amounts of information which he then delighted in playing back to whichever audience was before him. Although he had no medical training, he prided himself on his self-taught knowledge of all things medicinal. He enjoyed nothing more than for friends and colleagues to approach him for advice about health and lifestyle.

He was also something of a polyglot enabling him to defraud people in several different languages. In addition to English and his native German, Vossen also spoke French, Italian and Spanish.

Before arriving at dinner parties, he would make a point of doing a little homework on his fellow guests. Armed with some small but telling personal fact about them, he would use the information to engage them in conversation and impress them. He would regard it as a failure if he departed from such social events without having spoken to all those present and having converted at least one of them into his new best friend.

Although he had girlfriends, his friends were never quite sure of his sexuality. One, Jake Sinclair, recounts how the long and generous hugs he would give his male friends at the end of an evening went on too long for comfort. Another, Jon Peterson, thought Vossen was 'totally asexual'. 'He was into man hugs and sometimes he would over-hug,' says Peterson. 'I remember a few occasions on which he would come bounding up, hug me and kiss me on the cheek, totally over the top for a Swiss German. It was almost as if he knew in his head that he had done something wrong and this was his way of relieving his guilt.'

A former friend describes Vossen's need for affirmation and human contact – often late at night or at weekends – which led to him making telephone calls which would last for hours and leave the ears of his listener throbbing. His voice on the phone also seemed deeper and more piercing than in face-to-face conversation, which made other friends wonder whether there was some kind of voice enhancer attached to the mouthpiece. To cap it all, Vossen appeared incapable of bringing those conversations to a close. 'He would finally sign off by saying 'darling, darling, darling, darling, love you, love you, love you, bye, bye, bye-bye, byeeee, darling, darling, byeee!', says a friend.

'I felt that deep down he was so lonely and unsure. He desperately wanted re-assurance. He couldn't stay the distance and that made him angry and frustrated.'

Mandy Collins, another early investor, remembers that Vossen rarely wanted to speak to women and always seemed more comfortable in the presence of men. 'I sort of thought he didn't like women all that much or didn't have a huge amount of respect for them. I thought that might be because he was a closet gay and just preferred the company of men.'

There was a strange symbiosis between Vossen and his victims. They keened to his company, but equally there is no doubt that he too was desperate to be wanted by them.

He hated swearing but, in private, a darker side to Vossen would emerge that put the worst profanity into the shade. Wherever he went, he was accompanied by his collection of soft toys and stuffed animals, all with their own pet names. They were always by his bedside. At night time they would take centre stage, characters in grisly little tableaux in which Vossen would act out violent fantasies involving rape and murder, according to one of his former girlfriends. 'He did not sleep well, probably with all the lies on his mind. He would talk in his sleep and toss and turn.

I used to take Night Nurse and put ear plugs in to sleep or sleep in a different room if we went away,' she adds.

He had also developed an affectation which involved speaking in child-like voices, especially on the telephone. He would answer a call in a strange kiddy voice, say something cruel and then instruct his badly-behaved and imaginary children to hand back the receiver. These children had gone to bomb-making school or possessed GCSEs in bio-terrorism and were prone to doing bad things, for example murdering prostitutes. One girlfriend remembers Vossen speaking mainly in child tongues when they were alone. She found the habit intensely frustrating until she realised that if she too pretended to be a child she could relate to him on a deeper level and communicate things that could not be said in normal conversation.

For Vossen, it was one more persona – an identity to adopt and to be used to protect the inner man. One of his close friends describes him thus:

> When he suddenly became interested in Pilates I would go to his apartment once a week early in the morning to teach him. The spotlessness of the bathrooms always frightened me. I could never imagine how he lived like that. He was a total anal retentive. But he loved cats and was always looking after other people's.
>
> His desire for, and his giving of, affection was just so childlike. The length of his hugs was indeed intense but I also thought he needed those hugs so much. I felt that deep down he was so lonely and unsure. He desperately wanted reassurance. Setting himself up in the film industry, for instance, gave him a great identity for a while but then that started to challenge him, leaving him feeling empty. He would tell me how frustrated he was at the whole

> process, how you had to discuss things over and over again before making decisions. He found it draining. It felt as if he could not keep it up because his sense of self was so absent and because this was just another identity he was playing out, from such a very non-existent core. He couldn't stay the distance. I don't think he had any real emotional savvy. It was all a game to him because he was so damaged and empty inside.

This, then, is the portrait of the complicated and complex man who would come to play a more significant part in the lives of his friends, lovers and colleagues than any of them could possibly have imagined.

The Felix Vossen that arrived in London at the turn of the millennium was a man of many parts. But the one thing that he could no longer lay claim to being was a glowing advertisement for the motto of his alma mater: 'Fair Play'.

3

THE FRAUD BEGINS

Vossen arrived in London in 1999. The dot.com bubble was fully-inflated and yet to burst and the capital city was expanding at an unprecedented rate, economically and demographically. Tony Blair's New Labour government seemed to capture perfectly the zeitgeist of the coming millennium. Not only had it embraced the business community but it had forged a bond with the leading lights of the Britpop movement. Things could only get better for Britain and things could only get better for Felix Vossen. He was determined to make the most of what London had to offer – socially, culturally and, most especially, financially.

His first foray into British business life was, however, as far removed from his twin passions of stock market investing and computer technology as it was possible to get. He opened a sandwich bar in Bond Street Underground Station on Oxford Street along with a business partner by the name of Alexander. Like Vossen, Alexander was a German émigré who had chosen to settle in London after graduating from the European Business School in Regent's Park.

The partnership did not last very long: Vossen and Alexander had one row too many and decided to go their separate ways. But not before Vossen had met and struck up a relationship with one of Alexander's friends – a Colombian-born socialite and party animal called Mickey de Fernandez-Paz. An immigrant himself, Fernandez-Paz had arrived in the UK two decades earlier, initially living in Cambridge where he established a fashion boutique called Cinque. He then relocated to London where he moved into a house in Chelsea and landed himself a job as manager of L'Equipe Anglaise, an ultra-fashionable members club in Marylebone. The club stayed open until six in the morning and was frequented by the likes of Jack Nicholson, Leonardo di Caprio, the Rolling Stones, Oasis and Kate Moss when they were in town. But it was also the haunt of minor aristocracy and celebrity businessmen such as Richard Branson and the property magnates the Tchenguiz brothers. Fernandez-Paz divided his time between L'Equipe Anglaise and the Sloane Ranger set who frequented the bars and nightclubs of the King's Road when they were not playing tennis or croquet as the mood took them at the Hurlingham Club.

For Felix Vossen, a young man on the make and on the take, Fernandez-Paz was the perfect conduit to the social set he wanted to join and L'Equipe Anglaise represented the ideal entry point.

Today, Fernandez-Paz remains a fully paid-up member of the Chelsea set: the week before Prince Harry and Meghan tied the knot he was to be found acting as one of the ushers at the marriage of another member of the aristocracy to a glamorous American bride – that of Frederick Hervey, 8th Marquess of Bristol, to the Boston art consultant Meredith Dunn at the Brompton Oratory. The Hervey family are uncomfortably and tragically familiar with the worlds of celebrity and drugs – Frederick's two sisters Lady

Victoria and Lady Isabella epitomised the It Girl era of the late 1990s while his two half-brothers Nicholas and John both died after succumbing to cocaine addiction.

According to Fernandez-Paz, Vossen was no stranger to drugs either in those early days when they first met. And the company he kept could, on occasion, be far from salubrious. 'He knew all the drug dealers in the area. They called him boss,' says Fernandez-Paz.

> I think he was subsidising them – lending them money to buy drugs in return for a cut of the dealing proceeds or free cocaine. Sometimes Felix was stoned 24 hours a day. He would go on three or four-day drug binges and often there would be what seemed to be hookers hanging around his flat.
>
> I think he was involved with the mafia, with crooks. He was borrowing money and laundering money for these crooks and he used to spend it on hookers and cocaine. He also had a thing for boys, too. He was a bit bi-sexual.
>
> One day I went to see him at his flat and two hookers were just arriving. He wanted me to stay and pay for sex but I made my excuses and said no.

Other friends also suspected Vossen paid for sex. 'He once made a joke about ordering in a prostitute,' says one friend. 'At the time it appeared a weird thing to say. When I didn't respond, he instantly changed tack and never mentioned anything similar again.'

Fernandez-Paz also remembers something else about Vossen. 'He was on the phone all the time. Even in those days, he would carry two or three mobile phones with him. He was elusive. I always had a feeling that there was something going on. He was a very tricky customer.'

It was only after Vossen's disappearance that investors would discover his long-standing penchant for throwing extravagant, noisy drug-fuelled parties that occasionally got so out of control that neighbours would call the police.

Despite his misgivings about his new friend's lifestyle and morals, Fernandez-Paz was happy to introduce Vossen to his London social set. 'Everyone he knew, he knew through me. He knew I had powerful friends and was well connected in London society. He was always asking me to introduce him to people.'

One of those people was a budding young journalist called Nadia Rafaat, who at the time was going out with Fernandez-Paz. Nadia was working for *The Hill*, a lifestyle magazine that featured everything you needed to know about Notting Hill and the surrounding area from its arts and cultural scene to property market and nightlife. It was the same year that the Richard Curtis film *Notting Hill* was released, starring Hugh Grant and Julia Roberts. Nadia, according to Fernandez-Paz, also had the looks and body of a movie star. 'She was a very pretty girl. A blonde. She looked like Kylie Minogue,' he says. 'She looked like a model, she was quite a head turner. I said she had the nicest bum in Chelsea.'

It was to be another connection that would prove immensely important for Vossen. Shortly after meeting Nadia, Vossen began a relationship with Sophia Rafaat, her fashion model sister. Sophia would become Vossen's soul mate-cum-muse cum-live-in girlfriend and a central figure in his life for the next 15 years.

The Rafaat sisters came from a relatively wealthy and privileged background. They were both born in London to an Egyptian father and an Irish mother. The family was completed by two brothers. Both parents were in the medical profession – he was a doctor and she a nurse. The father was a highly respected member of society back in his native Egypt, where he had the ranking of a 'pasha' – one of the highest accolades the country can bestow, akin to a British peerage. Despite their pedigree, the two daughters decided their future careers lay elsewhere than medicine. Whilst Nadia was making her way in the media world, Sophia took up a place at King's College to study philosophy after leaving school. Half way through her course, however, she was talent spotted in the street one day by a scout working for a modelling agency. And so, Sophia left university before completing her degree to launch a career on the catwalk.

Together Felix and Sophia made for a glamorous and engaging couple – he with his boyish good looks, flowing auburn locks and penchant for expensive clothes; she with her bright and enquiring mind, vivacious personality and model's figure. Vossen was soon investing some of Rafaat's earnings from modelling. She, in turn, introduced Felix to some of her modelling friends and he began investing small amounts on their behalf too.

At the time, Vossen was living in a dingy ground floor flat on Hogarth Road, just off the Earl's Court Road, an area of the city best known for its itinerant Australian backpackers and twin exhibition centres. It was somewhere to negotiate if you wanted to get from the rather smart Holland Park to the even smarter Cheyne Walk.

Sophia meanwhile had moved into a small flat on the King's Road, opposite the local Waitrose. Vossen was apt to sofa surf between the two apartments. Felix and Sophia began to spend a lot of time with Sophia's sister and Fernandez-Paz who, at that time, were living close by in Olympia. Fernandez-Paz recalls that Vossen struggled to make a favourable impression on Sophia's mother. 'I don't think she was very fond of Felix. I don't think she trusted him,' he says. But the two sisters and their respective boyfriends were fast becoming a fixture. 'At first we spent a lot of time together, the four of us. We would cook together like a family,' says Fernandez-Paz. 'Felix used to say to me "I want to be like you, only much better". I think he meant he wanted to be as popular with people as I was only more so and much more successful. I just laughed at him. I thought at first he was a nice guy, that's why I put him together with Sophia. She was single when she met Felix.'

By now, Vossen had become a regular visitor to L'Equipe Anglaise where he networked furiously with his fellow club members. Even though he did not appear to have any obvious source of income, he nevertheless always seemed to have enough cash on him to stand his round and buy drinks for his new-found friends – an ability Fernandez-Paz now puts down to his drug-dealing activities.

Fernandez-Paz was intrigued by Vossen but he does not have favourable memories of the apartment. 'He lived there on his own. It was smokey and there was a mess everywhere. The place was like a pig sty, it was terrible. Magazines and videos lying everywhere. He was not a very tidy person. He used to smoke all the time. I think because he did so many drugs and he was always snorting and sniffing.'

Remarkably, however, Vossen appeared able to keep this sordid existence separate from his other life – with Sophia and her Chelsea set friends. It was a manifestation of Vossen's ability to compartmentalise his life and prevent the disparate aspects of his existence from colliding with one another. It was also another example of Vossen's capacity for re-inventing himself. The dissolute, sexually promiscuous, undisciplined and untidy Vossen that Fernandez-Paz describes is a very far cry from the fastidious, anally-retentive, health geek he was to become.

Perhaps it was in part thanks to the civilising influence of Sophia. Once he and Sophia had become a regular item, Vossen quickly began to move up in the world. He left the drug-fuelled environs of Earls Court behind and relocated to an apartment in Maida Vale, a stone's throw from the pretty, gaily-painted house boats that line the banks of Little Venice and the Regent's Canal. Fernandez-Paz began to see less of him too. However, he ascribes that to one particularly unsettling encounter he had with Vossen. Although Vossen had successfully kept his other life of drugs and prostitutes secret from Sophia and the rest of the Rafaat family, Fernandez-Paz felt he had a duty to warn them about the kind of man they had taken to their bosom. 'My relationship with Felix started to deteriorate when I told Nadia that this guy is not good news for your sister,' he says. 'He is a phantom, a ghost, you don't know him. He's a Jekyll and Hyde figure. I said this to Nadia and she went and told her sister and then Sophia told Felix what I had said. He came to see me and said "how dare you say that to Sophia". That's when he threatened me. He grabbed me by the throat and said if you say that one more time I will kill you.'

Although Maida Vale was a better neighbourhood than Earls Court, Vossen's flat at 9, Warrington Gardens, W9 was still a relatively modest billet. Nevertheless, it was from here that Vossen launched his life of crime. He began by operating from his bedroom, sat at a simple Ikea desk and surrounded by the paraphernalia of fraud – a library of books on finance and a sophisticated-looking array of computer terminals and trading screens which seemingly enabled him to make a good living from betting on the financial markets.

Meanwhile Sophia's career was taking off too after she was approached to take part in a Channel 4 documentary about the modelling business. It gave her a taste for the small screen and convinced her that television would be a more fulfilling industry to work in than fashion. 'The producer of the programme said I had a natural on-screen presence and encouraged me to give it a try,' she later told *The Guardian* in a 2004 interview. 'He introduced me to the producer of bid-up.tv who gave me a screen test. It lasted about 30 minutes and I spent much of it laughing, but for reasons unknown to me the producer really liked me and asked me to come on board as a presenter.'

From there she went on to present *Auctionworld* on Sky Digital, the *Lottery Live* draw on BBC1 and a couple of documentaries – *The Sexiest Videos Ever* and *Before They Were Famous*.

Back in Maida Vale, friends of the couple had begun to visit her boyfriend's makeshift office, drawn by reports of his fabulous ability to spot stock market winners and turn base metal into gold. There they would invariably be treated to a demonstration of Vossen's apparent Midas-like abilities and investment prowess as he sat at his desk, screens flickering and fingers dancing across the keyboards, monitoring share prices, buying low and then selling high before the market turned.

Vossen's investment strategy was as simple as it was beguiling: he claimed to be a day trader in American technology stocks on the Nasdaq exchange. He would start each day with a float which he would invest hour by hour. He claimed he put in a 12–15 hour shift each day and rarely took holidays. He would start work at 6am to study the 'form' for his investments, begin trading when the Nasdaq opened at 2.30pm UK time and then continue trading until it closed at 9pm UK time. He kept a stop watch on his desk to time his trades and determine how long he would remain in a given stock. Altogether, it created an impression of someone who was at the top of their game, trading in a calculated, mechanical and unemotional fashion.

Sometimes he would buy and sell shares in only the big stocks – Apple, Hewlett-Packard, Cisco, Dell and the like. At other times, he would show investors how he executed a 'chaser' manoeuvre – tracking shares in companies that supplied the Silicon Valley technology giants. When, for instance, Apple shares rose, the price of these 'chaser stocks' would rise too. Many big institutional investors employed automatic trading programmes, meaning that they would sell when the price hit a certain level. Vossen, however, would hold his nerve, wait for the shares to bounce and then sell out for an even bigger profit.

Along with his finance books and computer terminals, visitors to Vossen's Maida Vale flat were also struck by the chaotic paper mountains that lay everywhere – an indication, perhaps, that Vossen was engaged in at least some genuine trading in those early days and not just fraud. Visitors to his subsequent offices would be struck by just how clinical and uncluttered they were, almost as if he no longer needed to keep any paper records of his activity.

Film editor Steven Walters, one of the earliest investors, recalls visiting the Maida Vale flat not long after meeting Vossen.

> He showed me this 'chaser' programme, involving a company that supplies Dell. He said when Dell shares go up, its shares will rise too. He then said that when the price reaches a certain level it will drop because a lot of investors will have instructed their brokers to sell. But the price will come back again. I watched him make £65,000 in six minutes. If it wasn't a genuine trade, then it certainly looked like one.

Vossen claimed investor money was 100 per cent safe because he cashed in his positions at the end of each trading day and put his entire fund into US Treasury bonds overnight before accessing it again the following day.

It is important to remember the environment in which Vossen operating. A great many more individuals had become familiar with investing in stocks and shares – thanks in large part to the phenomenon of privatisation, a process which had considerably widened, though not necessarily deepened, share ownership in the UK. But memories were also still fresh of the collapse in world stock markets in 2000 when the dot.com bubble had burst and many investors, institutional and retail alike, lost their shirts. So there was a good deal of scepticism and nervousness that traditional stock brokers necessarily knew best. Although investors wanted decent returns – or at least superior returns to those that could be achieved by leaving their money on deposit at the bank or invested in government gilts – they also yearned for safety. Vossen appeared to offer the perfect combination of the two.

It was also significant that Vossen was not dealing with professional investors – or even keen, amateur retail investors – who might have stopped to wonder at his proposition. Rather, his clients were his friends and, although many of them were smart, savvy and very capable in their own chosen fields of endeavour, none of them would profess to be stock market experts.

***

Vossen's earliest victims were to be three women from the same family – Angela Shaw, now a grandmother in her late seventies, and her two daughters, Elizabeth and Grace. Of the three,

Angela would become in many ways his most tragic victim. The Shaw family met Vossen in 2003. He was introduced to the family by Sophia who had forged a close friendship with Elizabeth Shaw. At the time Elizabeth was working for a small Spanish company that made a living publishing socio-economic country reports. She later went on to become a documentary film maker and then a yoga teacher. Together, she and Sophia became part of a group of twenty-something creatives that included de Paz and Nadia who frequented L'Equipe Anglaise. Elizabeth says:

> Sophia was a great friend of one of my best friends and so we started to meet socially. That's how I got to know Felix. I was being paid offshore and being paid well and excited by the fact that I was making decent money. He said 'I can help you' and that's how it all started. I invested first and then I told my mum about Felix. He was so bright and charming and convincing. I was swept in.

One of Vossen's favourite means of cementing friendships and strengthening the bonds of loyalty with his victims was to shower them with small acts of kindness – dinners, theatre tickets, hampers from Fortnum & Mason and the like – and sometimes not so small acts of kindness such as airline upgrades and gifts of brand new iPads and iPhones. In the case of the Shaws his gift was to become the son, the brother and the protector they never had.

Angela, who had been born in Kent, was evacuated during the Second World War during which time she and her family were moved twice. She was educated at a convent school and went on to study in Paris. Her peripatetic young life gave her a taste for travel and as she grew into adulthood, she went to live first in the Middle East and then in Mexico, where she met her husband. After a spell living in the US and Bermuda with their two small daughters, they moved back to London so that their girls could be educated at the French Lycée in Kensington and Angela could take a Masters in Psychotherapy at City University. But the marriage ended acrimoniously in 1996 and without any divorce settlement. It was also a period that coincided with the death of her parents. 'I lost husband and a home and two parents in the space of four years. That was a big trauma in my life,' she says. 'I had amazing support from my family to get me through the trauma, but I suppose you could say I had become a reasonably vulnerable human being because of everything that had happened to me.'

Enter Felix Vossen. Elizabeth takes up the story:

> Felix came to us like a knight in shining armour in many ways. My parents' divorce had been very messy and the three of us – my mum, my sister and me – were on our own. Felix offered to look after us and we needed that. He was a saviour really. He was just such a loveable sort of person. He told me that he loved me all the time. My mum would spend hours on the phone chatting to him and he'd tell her that if he hadn't been going out with Sophia then I would be his ideal girlfriend. Did he say that to charm her and charm me? Probably.

Angela recalls the courtship thus:

> I met him, and he was charming. He was always a joy to meet – so welcoming and warm and huggy. I felt very open towards him, always pleased to see him. I needed him, and he was clever, he was

> effervescent and optimistic. He was going to look after me in my old age. He might have been the son I never had.

Angela was living in South Wimbledon at the time. Despite being left without any maintenance, she had kept their flat in Kensington. She also possessed a flair for spotting property bargains and so began to re-build her life and her finances by buying, renovating and selling houses. She was also riding the crest of the London property boom in the late nineties and early noughties.

Vossen had never owned a property himself. Indeed, as it turns out, he did not own much of anything: when he went on the run, it transpired that even the furniture in his apartment was rented. But he tapped into Angela's zeal for playing the property market, as he would tap into the passions and professional interests of other investors as a means of insinuating himself into their lives and then ensnaring them. Angela says:

> It was 2003 and I was living in South Wimbledon. At that time Felix only had two or three clients, model friends of Sophia's. I needed to invest for my future and not be dependent on my daughters, and he was offering the most extraordinary returns. I went to look at his screens and he showed me where he was trading. He was a friend of the family, so I didn't have any reason to be suspicious about his abilities.

Vossen claimed that his fund was already worth tens of millions of pounds and that he would only take on high net worth individuals as clients – those who had a minimum of £250,000 to invest. But there would always be exceptions to that rule. So, in Elizabeth's case, he accepted an initial investment of £7,000.

Angela likewise began conservatively. She says: 'He said he'd like to try with a small investment for me and see how that goes and then perhaps go on to invest my savings.' So, she gave Vosssen £45,000 of her life savings and earned an 8 per cent return in six months. Vossen paid her back all the money, plus the interest her pot had accumulated. 'I decided this was amazing,' she says.

Delighted with the result, and re-assured that Vossen was bona-fide, Angela decided he could be trusted with much larger sums. So, when she sold her Kensington flat in late 2003 for just over £1m, she paid off her mortgage, gifted her daughters a £200,000 share of the proceeds, and gave the remainder – some £450,000 – to Vossen. Angela would go on to invest a total of £1.1 million with her substitute son.

For the next few years, Angela and her daughters were able to live comfortably off the returns Vossen appeared to be generating on their investments. Angela, according to the sporadic investment summaries she would receive from Vossen, was making 10 per cent a year on her investments, part of which she took as income, part of which remained invested in what she thought was an ever-growing retirement pot.

Elizabeth, meanwhile, had invested her share of the Kensington house sale with Vossen and was earning a 12 per cent return worth £22,000 a year – enough to allow her to pursue her passion for documentary film making. She had also become engaged to Matthew Allen, a sports journalist whom she had met while studying for a masters' degree at the London School of Journalism. The couple married in 2010. So close was their relationship with Vossen and his girlfriend, that Sophia would become godmother to their first son. Curiously, however,

Vossen never showed up at either Elizabeth's engagement party or her wedding to Matthew – something which hurt her badly.

Elizabeth had also taken up Pilates in a serious way and when Vossen discovered this he too became a devotee. And so, she settled into a routine of visiting him once a week early in the morning to teach her good friend how to get the most out of this form of exercise.

Her husband, Matthew, saw Vossen less often – a couple of times a year at parties or dinners with other friends and once in the South of France when they were staying with Angela in a rented villa and Vossen came out to visit, overlapping with Matthew and Elizabeth by two or three days.

While his early investors sat back and reaped the rewards of Vossen's apparently phenomenal investment returns, so the man himself continued to go up in the world. By 2005 he had taken on a further four clients – all of them close friends – and boasted that his fund was worth £150 million. One of them was Ricardo Morales Garidele, an old friend of Sophia and Elizabeth Shaw and another member of the L'Equipe Anglaise set. Garidele met Vossen in 2004 and made two separate investments of £240,000 and $240,000 after being shown fake investment performance charts indicating his money would earn an annual return of up to 20 per cent. Indeed it did grow handsomely in value – by 2015, his fund stood at a similarly illusory £2.6 million.

As befitted his rising status, Vossen left the Maida Vale flat he shared with Sophia a year later and re-located to Jermyn Street in the heart of London's clubland, the St James's district. If he had wanted to pick a location dripping with English heritage and smelling of money, old and new, then he could scarcely have selected a better location than Jermyn Street – home to

Fortnum & Mason, the country's most venerable shirt-maker Turnbull & Asser, London's best-known fish restaurant Wilton's and Tramp, one of the world's most exclusive members' clubs and the haunt of celebrities, socialites, aristocrats and royalty for half a century. It was all part of an elaborate façade designed to make Vossen's investors feel even more safe and secure in his hands. It also served, of course, as the perfect base for Vossen's own retailing forays and his love of made-to-measure attire.

His first address there was 107 Jermyn Street, a five-storey apartment building above the shirt-maker and tailor T. M. Lewin (founded 1898) and next door to the corporate headquarters of the oil and gas giant BG Group. Vossen would take tea with investors in Fortum and Mason before inviting them up to his lair – 'a proper split-level pile, gorgeous, eight screens, designated telephone lines, emergency back-up generator in case the mains supply went down while he was trading,' recalls Steven Walters.

Visitors to Vossen's home were invariably struck, however, by how pristine and unlived-in it appeared to be, almost as if it were a show house. It was not uncommon for them to be asked to remove their shoes before stepping inside, while the sofa looked as though it had never been sat on.

In addition to Jermyn Street, Vossen had also opened an office in the centre of Zurich at Waaggasse 4 in March, 2007. Nestling in the shadow of one of Zurich's most famous landmarks, Fraumunster Abbey, founded in 853AD by King Ludwig II as a Benedictine convent for female members of the aristocracy, Waaggasse 4 was the registered address of Vossen's principal companies, VCP Investment Advisers AG, VCP Asset Management and VCP Analytics. Zurich's very own Savoy Hotel and Bar sits around the corner and the building shares an address with the

Zurich Grasshoppers Club. He also claimed to have a second office in the city on the fourth floor of Bellevue Haus am See – a swish building overlooking Lake Zurich.

Along with his view of the lake, Vossen also claimed to have a boat moored on it. A number of his investors were keen sailors, or at least enthusiastic users of luxury yachts. Vossen's ownership of an expensive boat therefore served two useful purposes. First, it gave him a common interest, a shared passion which he could leverage to get ever closer to his victims. He enjoyed nothing more than appearing to inhabit their worlds and live their lives. Second, a yacht was just the sort of accoutrement that the outside world would expect a self-made and highly successful businessman to possess. As with most other things in Vossen's life, the yacht was, of course, a pretence. And occasionally when he was boasting about it, he would find himself getting caught out.

One investor who was himself an avid yachtsman recalls such an occasion.

> It was when he was still seeing Sophia, we were at a dinner in London with the two of them and Felix mentioned that he had a boat on the lake in Zurich. Sophia said that wasn't true, Felix didn't have a boat. He looked a bit sheepish and admitted that he hadn't told her about it. Later, when we went to visit him in Zurich he made excuses as to why he couldn't take us to see the boat, so to this day we have no idea whether it really existed.

Another investor, who would subsequently become Vossen's girlfriend, recounts how she went to Zurich many times with him and yet he never wanted to show her his boat. She also tells a very similar tale of how Vossen was at a dinner party and the host unexpectedly asked him when they were going to be taken out on Vossen's boat. Again there was an embarrassed silence until Vossen leaned over to Sophia and apologised for not having told her about his new possession. As with so many aspects of Felix Vossen's life, he often found it difficult to remember what story he had told to which person and which lie he would therefore need to employ to explain away the previous deceit.

Boat or not, Vossen's little investment empire was continuing to grow exponentially and, to cope with that expansion, he took on three members of staff in Zurich – Robert Gassner, Natalie Casanova and Jennifer Keller. They were model employees, they politely replied to emails from investors and they diligently sent out statements of account when requested. But Gassner, Casanova and Keller were never available to speak to on the telephone for the simple reason that they did not exist. They were all fictional creations of Felix Vossen. Perhaps this is why girlfriends who visited Zurich with him were not allowed to glimpse his office there. Vossen preferred instead to collect his mail from a PO box.

He also re-assured his parents and other investors that he was registered with and regulated by the Swiss financial watchdog FINMA – again a complete fiction. As far as his parents were concerned, their prodigal son turned financial genius was generating returns of 20 per cent on the money they had invested with him and was managing a fund worth in excess of $250 million.

Notwithstanding these trappings of wealth and success, Angela Shaw says that with the benefit of hindsight the tell-tale signs that Vossen's Ponzi scheme was beginning to run out of road had started to become apparent. His record-keeping had become erratic and she had to badger him constantly for statements of her account. But the Shaw family were carried along by the fiction that Felix was an investment guru and seduced by the returns he appeared to be generating and the tremendously powerful bond of kinship that had developed between them.

It was to cost them even more dearly. By 2013, Elizabeth and her husband Matthew had decided to sell up in London and re-locate to Brazil where he had secured a job to cover the build-up to the World Cup the following year. They were both still in their thirties and their young son had not yet reached school age. Why not spend some time in South America, developing their careers and experiencing a new and exciting environment? If all went well, then the Rio Olympics two years later would offer further work opportunities.

They put Matthew's Notting Hill flat on the market and made a £480,000 profit on the sale. The money was effectively everything they had in the world and almost all of it went into Vossen's investment funds. Court indictment papers show that Matthew and Elizabeth transferred £350,000 in March 2013 into Vossen's VCP Asset Management account at Zurcher Kantonalbank in Zurich and a further £100,000 in June 2014 – just nine months before his disappearance. Vossen had re-assured them that not only was their money safe but that he would make it grow quite handsomely, presenting them with charts which showed his fund stood at $350 million and over the past ten years had been making compound annual returns of 10 per cent on average. Matthew says:

> Elizabeth and I talked about it. At first, I didn't want to put all our eggs in one basket. It's not my world and I don't have the mindset for finance or figures. I said to friends in the City he's either a crook

> or a genius. But I went along to see him and was won over by his odd, easy charm. He was funny and self-deprecating and warm. I saw his computer screens and he talked me through his graphs.
>
> For me the main areas of re-assurance were that he said he invested in American tech – Apple, Twitter that kind of thing. He said he only ever kept his money in US bonds, so it could not be lost. The really big one was that my mother-in-law had taken her money out two or three times.
>
> I had friends telling me they weren't sure about it. A very good friend of mine who worked for a hedge fund suggested I just put half of it in. That was on my mind, but Felix said if you put this much in we can put you into this fund where you get a higher return. It all seemed to be going so well and we were getting paid dividends. He said I'll have the whole lot back to you in three months plus 12 per cent. It was so stupid, I didn't ask for details.

At about the same time as Vossen was draining Matthew and Elizabeth of their savings, he was about to part Elizabeth's mother from the remainder of her retirement pot. Angela had moved to a small village in West Sussex in 2008 where she had bought and lovingly restored what was in her words 'a miserable wreck of a house'.

In the spring of 2014, she reluctantly decided to sell. She had just lost her long-time companion, a bearded collie called Henry, her elder daughter was in Brazil and her younger one had emigrated to Puerto Moreles on the Caribbean coast of Mexico with her partner and their young son. They had very little income, so Angela decided to buy a house there where they could all live.

The sale of the house in West Sussex netted £910,000. Angela says: 'I recall Felix saying "You can't just leave all that money sitting in the bank, you're not getting any interest on it at all. Let me put it in a short-term technology fund". He was full of enthusiasm for some new investments that were all to do with the launch of the new Apple iPhone. He said that was where the money was.'

So, after paying off her debts and keeping a little aside for emergencies, she gave him the remaining £660,000 in two instalments, the last of which – £250,000 – disappeared from her bank account and into the Vossen black hole four days after Christmas, 2014. Whether Angela knew it or not, the money went not into Vossen's main investment fund account but into his film financing business Exponential Media Ventures. Either way, it was the last she ever saw of any of her money.

'I couldn't believe that he could betray me like that taking my last money knowing I was already 74 and couldn't just go back to work and start my life over again,' Angela says today. 'He knew all that and he knew how much I relied on that money for my retirement. How could he do that? Whatever emotional disorders he had, how could he be that cruel?'

Scarcely a day goes by that Elizabeth Shaw is not also wracked with regret at having introduced her mother and then her husband to Vossen. She sobs as she remembers: 'The whole sorry thing about my life is that I introduced so many people to Felix. That is what is so sickening, especially my mum. I don't understand why this had to happen to my mum at her time of life. She is just overwhelmed a lot of the time. I just try to be there for her.'

But it does not end there. Impressed by the returns Vossen was achieving for his mother-in-law, Matthew introduced his own mother, Christine Allen, to the German wunderkind.

Christine's husband, a director of a glass engraving business, had been possessed of a much more conservative approach to savings and investment. But he had died in 2010. Two years after her husband's death, Christine sold the ten-bedroomed house in Norfolk that they had shared for 35 years and began looking for a home for the £500,000 she had made from the sale. Matthew says,

> This was money for the rest of her life, but she's a natural gambler so when we started talking about Felix and how he'd made Elizabeth's mum a vast amount of money she immediately got very excited.
>
> I told Felix and mum came with me to meet him at his Jermyn Street flat. She was charmed by him and thought he was great. He hooked her in by recognising pretty quickly that what she really wanted to do was buy another big house. He told her 'Jenny, you're well on the way to that house, what do you want in it, a swimming pool?' All that kind of thing.

Vossen showed Christine the same impressive charts he had displayed to her son. She invested her entire wealth with Vossen in March 2013. Within a year her £500,000 had grown to £663,000 according to the 'account balance confirmation' she received from one of Vossen's imaginary staff. In reality, it had not appreciated in value at all. In fact, it had disappeared elsewhere, used either to fund Vossen's lifestyle or pay off more persistent and demanding investors. Christine never saw a penny of her money again. 'She put in absolutely everything, she's that kind of person, and has now been left in real trouble,' says Matthew.

Between them, the extended Shaw and Allen families invested £3.35 million with Vossen over a period of 11 years. At the point of his disappearance, they thought their collective pot had grown in value to £4.1 million. In fact, it was worth precisely nothing.

The one small saving grace for Matthew and Elizabeth was that they managed to recover some of their money from Vossen before the balloon went up. The couple received £110,000 back in quarterly dividends over the two-year period that Vossen had the money from their London house sale.

Others would not be so fortunate.

4

THE FRAUD DEEPENS

Shortly before Vossen began to wrap his tentacles around the Shaw family, he was introduced to a Surrey-based investor called Roger Phillips. Vossen met Phillips in 2002 at a party in London hosted by a power couple who were mutual friends of the two men. He was the owner of a recruitment agency; she worked for the BBC. Phillips would go on to become Vossen's biggest single victim, after his parents. He would also be the only investor to attend court in Zurich when Vossen finally went on trial for his crimes.

Phillips had made his fortune in property, building up a successful chain of estate agents before selling out to a larger competitor and retiring at the age of just 32. A significant chunk of the proceeds from the sale of his business disappeared into Vossen's investment funds.

An astute businessman, Phillips was initially wary of Vossen, even though the two men and their girlfriends had holidayed together in the Caribbean on board Phillips's yacht early on in their relationship. He therefore set a trap for Vossen to test whether he could get his money out as easily as he could put it in. The sale of his estate agency business had turned Phillips into a millionaire many times over. Towards the end of 2002, he took one of those millions and gave it to Vossen, but then asked for it back a short while later. 'In the early days I was always suspicious of how trustworthy he was, so I tested him by asking him to give me back my initial £1 million investment. He duly returned it', says Phillips. 'I was also repaid with interest.'

Satisfied that Vossen was honest and above board, the friendship between the two men burgeoned and, as it went from strength to strength, they made a point of meeting regularly for lunch, first in Maida Vale and then later at Fortnum & Mason, across the road from Vossen's apartment-cum-office. Phillips was further reassured by Vossen that in the event of something happening to him, his affairs would be looked after by one of three people: Oliver Plummer, a trustee based in London, and his two Swiss advisers, the lawyer Severin Roelli and accountant Michael Conrad. Between them, they would make sure investors' money was safely returned.

According to the indictment drawn up by Swiss prosecutors charging Vossen with fraud, forgery and money laundering, Phillips invested an initial $1 million with Vossen in September, 2004. He went on to invest a further £3.3 million with Vossen between then and 2013, transferring six-figure sums to Vossen on a regular basis on the not unreasonable assumption that the returns he was achieving outmatched anything Phillips could hope to earn by leaving his money on deposit with a bank or even playing the buoyant UK property market. By the end of 2014, Phillips 'account balance' stood at a very healthy but wholly illusory £10.6 million.

Phillips, like every other investor, was taken in by Vossen's easy charm and his apparently boundless generosity. He tells the story of how he was holidaying in Antibes in the South of France with Vossen and a couple of other investors in Vossen's funds – Steven Walters and Jon Peterson, another highly successful self-made businessman and property developer.

'One day Vossen invited us to spend a day cruising in the Mediterranean on an 80-foot yacht that he said he'd borrowed from some friends,' recalls Phillips. 'In fact, he had hired the boat and had paid for the hire using the funds he had stolen from me. Turns out he chartered it with my money and I was paying for the cruise.'

In the same way that Vossen used his relationship with Elizabeth Shaw to draw other family members into his orbit, so he exploited his close friendship with Roger Phillips and Steven Walters to recruit other investors. Phillips and Walters had met one another in the 1980s through a shared Brighton connection and went on to become good friends.

A year after Phillips had met Vossen, he introduced him to another friend, Jon Peterson, while the three men were on holiday together in the Caribbean.

He also introduced husband and wife Charles and Phoebe Huntley, two former investment bank executives, to the man who would become their nemesis.

Walters, in turn, provided Vossen with his entrée to seven others who were to become investors: his own long-time business partner and girlfriend, Mandy Collins; Mandy's mother and father, Bill and Mavis Baker; Peter Leinster, the director of a London advertising agency, and his wife Jane; Jake Sinclair, a television and commercial advertising film director; and Stewart Gregory, another commercial film maker. 'The clever thing about

Felix was that I'd introduce him to someone and the next thing I knew they'd invested with him,' says Walters. 'I had no idea they were going to invest with Felix and we never discussed our investments but one day they would say to me "Thanks for the introduction to Felix, it's all going very well". To this day I'm not sure how any of them still speak to me.'

Peterson puts it like this:

> We were knocked down step by step. We were seduced by what he did but we were also confused. Roger Phillips was a good road map for us. He was quite cautious, quite sceptical and quite untrusting so he was a good compass point. Felix was a genius at meshing us together but at the same time maintaining secrecy. Over a friendship lasting many years we never discussed Felix or our investments in any great detail. Looking back, it was most peculiar.
>
> It was an unwritten rule that although we all knew Felix we didn't talk about [our investments with him] or the quantum. It was top secret, so we didn't know who within the group were and were not investors.

The technique was quite deliberate on Vossen's part. He did not want investors talking to him about their investments, which is why he blurred the lines between the professional and the personal, cultivating their friendship at all times. And he certainly did not want investors talking to one another about their investments. He wanted to keep alive the illusion in each investor's mind that they had been individually selected and invited to be part of an uber-exclusive club.

The technique he used to get inside investors' bank accounts was firstly to get inside their lives and then inhabit their world.

Peterson says that he was hesitant initially. 'I wasn't immediately taken by him, charming as he was,' he says. 'Nonetheless, he was quite intriguing and unusual.'

But as time went by Vossen grew on him and Peterson came to see him as a trusted confidante.

> I would very much class him as a friend. My wife used to say 'Oh are you going off to see your boyfriend again?' She was very irked by the amount of time I could find to take calls from Felix or go and have a quick coffee with him in Jermyn Street. I think a lot of the wives were irritated that he had such a hold over their husbands.
>
> He was chameleon-like. He was totally fascinated with a concessions business I had and all my other businesses. He told me his brother had a concessions business and he'd put me in touch with people in Hong Kong that he knew. He also became an expert in property and started talking in square metres and committed development rights.
>
> If someone shows great interest in your world it panders to your ego. He was very adroit at tuning into other people's worlds but not giving much away about his own. It was always a one-way street. He would always turn the conversation around. He would talk about films or his sister Christina's brain tumour.

So entwined did Vossen become with the Petersons, that at one point he announced he was getting married to Sophia and that he wanted their daughter to be bridesmaid. As with so much else in Felix Vossen's world, it was a fantasy, if not pure fabrication. The wedding never took place.

Peterson invested an initial $500,000 with Vossen in April 2005, paying the money into his personal Credit Suisse account in St Moritz, according to court documents. He did not invest again until 2011, when he made a transfer of £350,000. That was followed by a further £1.2 million in the following two years. In total, Vossen took £1.95 million from Peterson on the promise that he would earn his friend returns of 6–18 per cent on the money. He was one of the lucky ones who succeeded in getting most of his initial capital back from Vossen. Nevertheless, he was still labouring under the misapprehension that the value of his investment account on the day Vossen went on the run was £1.47 million.

As with the Shaws, there were, on reflection, incidents that should have rung alarm bells. Around 2010, the Petersons sold a large house they owned to a minor Russian oligarch and, at Vossen's suggestion, put £500,000 of the proceeds into one of the short-term investments in technology stocks that he had begun to market. 'For some reason and unbeknown to me, my wife called Felix a short while later and told him she wanted all the money back because something was not quite right,' says Peterson. A week later, the £500,000 had been returned.

Many of Vossen's investors recount similar sliding-door moments when life could have turned out very differently for them – and for him.

In 2005, the same year that Peterson first began to entrust his money with Vossen, another group of family victims came on the scene: Charles and Phoebe Huntley and Charles's mother, Gail. As with his other victims, Vossen appeared in no hurry to take their money, preferring to cultivate their friendship and deepen the bonds of trust. 'Initially, he was reluctant to let us invest,' says Charles as he relaxes on the deck of his Sussex home looking out onto the marina below. 'He said it was a closed fund but as

I was a mate he would get me in. I went to his offices to see his set up and he said he was doing some trading as I watched. But in retrospect, I'm sure it was just a simulation exercise. He said he was managing a fund worth $350m and did his trading at the end of the day and he showed me what his trading patterns were. It was all incredibly plausible but, as I now realise, it was not real. He was a piece of work.'

The route Vossen chose to reach the hearts of the Huntleys was culinary in nature. But, again, it was a pretext and a fake one at that. 'On a couple of occasions, Felix gave us an extravagant present in the form of a hamper from Fortnums," says Charles. 'In return we would give him a present at Christmas of a home-baked cake. He sent a text picture showing he'd eaten the whole cake in a day. For someone with such an apparent love of food it seemed odd that he did not cook himself.'

Huntley was never quite as taken with Vossen as many others. 'I regarded him as a friend but I wouldn't say a good friend,' he says. 'He'd come to a few parties at our place. If I met him for dinner in London it would be to talk about the business side of things, but it would be a social occasion as well.'

Nevertheless, when the Huntleys did decide to take the plunge in 2007, they invested big. Charles, a wiry 56-year-old with short greying hair and a sailor's tan, had stashed away plenty of cash during a career in IT, first with British Airways and then Bank of America. His wife, Phoebe, had also enjoyed a successful career working in human resources for another bulge-bracket bank, Deutsche Bank. So, when the couple decided to step off the financial treadmill and take early retirement to indulge their passion for sailing properly, there was plenty of spare cash sloshing around and looking for a home.

Vossen also told the Huntleys, falsely, that most of his investors were Swiss and that only four of them were based in the UK. The Huntleys clearly knew that Roger Phillips was one of those investors as he had introduced them initially to Vossen.

Before they finally invested, Vossen assured them that in an emergency – such as his untimely death – he had made arrangements with his accountant in Zurich, Michael Conrad of Riedi Bemi Theus, to wind up his funds and return all monies to investors. Again, a complete falsehood. Nevertheless, re-assured about both his trading strategy and their ability to retrieve their money should anything unpleasant befall Vossen, the Huntleys took out their chequebooks.

Between 2007 and 2013 Charles and Phoebe put £660,000 into Vossen's various investment funds, court documents show. Charles invested a further £150,000 and $365,000 on behalf his mother, Gail. In August 2013, a few months before the Huntleys made their final investment, handing over a cheque for £100,000, they visited Vossen's plush offices in Zurich. The Huntleys had received regular communications over the years from his three staff, Gassner, Keller and Casanova, and were looking forward to meeting them and finally putting faces to names. When they arrived, Vossen apologised to them for the fact that none of his staff were actually present as it was the middle of summer and they were all away on holiday. In all the time that their money was in the care of Vossen, they never saw any company or group accounts, only what purported to be their personal statements.

In the year prior to Vossen's disappearance Charles had had to deal with a double loss – the death of his mother and his brother in the space of 12 months. But he and Phoebe were looking forward to putting family grief behind them and using some of the pension pot they had invested with Vossen to realise their long-held dream of a round-the-world sailing trip on board their newly-bought 60-foot yacht. After all, they thought their investment of a little over £1m had mushroomed to £2.2 million. That dream died the day Vossen disappeared. In order to keep afloat financially, the first thing that went was the boat.

'He was a very privileged individual and he came from a rich family,' Huntley says today. 'He was clearly the black sheep of the family, not his younger brother. I don't believe he ever made any money out of trading. When he sold himself to us as a successful trader that was just self-aggrandisement. He liked the glamour of it, found he wasn't very good at it but still went out and promoted himself as a trader to maintain the delusion. I think he was just very keen to be liked.'

Steven Walters was hooked from the day in late 2003 that he met Vossen at Roger Phillips's country pile in Surrey. Within six months he was sitting in Vossen's office, watching him execute a fictitious trade and putting his signature on one of his meaningless Investment Management Agreements.

Court records show that over a four-year period starting in April 2004, almost £700,000 was invested with Vossen in the name of Steven Walters. The deposits were always lodged in Vossen's personal account at the St Moritz branch of Credit Suisse. Until that fateful day in March 2015, the pot had seemingly grown in value to £2.6 million.

Steven and his then partner Mandy ran a successful production company working TV commercials into their finished form. Steven also made money from the London housing market as he moved up the property ladder, the profits of which would be invested with Vossen. 'Felix never had to rely on due diligence, he just got very close to people,' says Mandy.

Walters's first investment came about through an act of apparent generosity on Vossen's behalf. He had invested £100,000 in an American online gambling and lottery company but was having difficulty selling the shares. He asked Vossen for advice and Vossen said he would take care of it. 'A few months later, Felix said it was all sorted, he'd got the money out and would invest it for me,' says Walters.

Reassured, Walters said yes and when the statement of account showed the investment growing at up to 16 per cent a year, more money was sent Vossen's way.

Vossen made sure he kept his relationship with Walters well lubricated with lunches and drinks that he would pay for out of his own pocket. 'He'd never let you pay in a restaurant,' Walters remembers. 'He'd sneak off just before the end of the meal and when you got ready to leave you'd discover he'd settled the bill.'

Meanwhile, Vossen was continuing to do Steven and Mandy favour after favour. In 2007, he lent Walters £120,000, supposedly out of his own resources, to pay the deposit on a house they couple were moving into. He explained that Walter's investments were tied up in a special short-term fund yielding particularly attractive returns that could not be touched. As soon as possible, the loan was repaid to Vossen. 'How stupid was that?' says Mandy. 'We thought everything was above board. It was all about trust. But we now know it was all psychological, it was all just a game. He totally knew how to play people.'

By now, Vossen's friendship with Walters had blossomed into a fully-fledged bromance, much like his relationship with Jon Peterson and the bond he would go on to forge with other men, sometimes to the surprise and occasional consternation of their wives and partners. Mandy Collins puts it like this: 'Steven had become really good friends with Felix. I didn't have very much to do with him. I always thought he was a bit odd but Steven had total trust in him.' Walters says:

> Looking back I can safely say the only signs something was up was that he was often late with statements and payments. He always had excuses – it was a bank holiday, a family member or employee was unwell. Stupidly, you let him get away with it. With anyone else you'd smell a rat. But he was one of my dearest friends and I trusted him.

And that is how Mandy Collins's parents, Bill and Mavis Baker, came to invest with Vossen too. They had already heard Walters waxing lyrical about the German wunderkind and how talented, kind and generous he was – the latest example being the £120,000 house loan that Vossen has just provided. 'My parents asked us how we could afford to buy the house and so Steven told them about the loan from Felix. I was always quite nervous about introducing him to my parents.'

Bill had had a varied career before he and his wife set up a security company. By 2006 they had retired and had £215,000 to invest. Although it was beneath the £250,000 minimum that investors were supposed to have if they wanted to join Vossen's exclusive club, he agreed to make an exception in their case and thanked Mandy for the introduction. 'So, immediately, you were starting off the relationship enormously grateful that he'd even considered your recommendation,' she says.

Her father might have been thankful but Mandy and her sceptical mother were less impressed. 'He charmed my dad, but he didn't charm my mum,' says Mandy.

> She couldn't stand him and always maintained that he was a liar. There were some women he just couldn't charm and she was one of them. Intelligent women want a straight answer and the problem with Felix was that he couldn't provide a straight answer. When he called my parents he'd always want to speak to my dad because my mum would ask him difficult questions he did not want to answer.
>
> It was always really difficult to get regular reports from Felix. There were supposedly contingency plans in case he got run over by a bus about what would happen and which banks you were supposed to contact. The only person who ever followed up to test that was my mum who rang all the banks, but they wouldn't speak to her. She concluded it was all rubbish but by that time Felix had charmed my dad. They were smart people running a business which turned over millions, but he fooled them.

Despite Mavis's misgivings, the Bakers handed over the money in three tranches between May 2007 and December 2013. However, being astute, they stipulated that Vossen pay them a quarterly dividend of £2,500 each. As a result, they got a substantial proportion of their original investment back over the years. Even so, the last statement of account they received showing that their their fund stood at £326,000, turned out, like everyone else's, to be a work of fiction.

Vossen's business relationship with the Bakers served another important purpose. If Vossen was able to pay a retired couple such a comfortable and regular dividend then it established, beyond per adventure, that he was a man who could be trusted implicitly. It was one of the reasons that Steven Walters felt so comfortable introducing Vossen to other friends.

One of those friends was Peter Leinster, a creative director who had come to know Walters well through the Soho advertising world they both inhabited. Coincidentally, Leinster and his wife Jane has also come to know the Petersons by dint of their children attending the same school.

The Leinsters met Vossen in late 2007. In their case, one of the shared passions that Vossen homed in on was Peter's love of film. It was to become central to their long relationship. For good measure, he also identified with Peter's pre-occupation with health and would use that to further cement their friendship. Jane, his wife, says:

> Steven mentioned Felix as a long-standing friend who was a day trader in tech stocks. He said he had a close circle of friends, family and other individuals he invested for and was making good returns.
>
> Steven introduced Peter to him and they clicked. Felix came across as highly intelligent, funny, charming and emotionally sensitive. Peter strongly sensed they were going to be friends well beyond Felix being a professional investment manager. He was funny and well-read and interesting to talk to.
>
> He and Peter used to meet up at least once a week but if they didn't they'd be on the phone for at least an hour or so discussing films and whatever else came into their heads. Felix was also a hypochondriac and said he had health issues. He used that a lot. He was really clever at tapping into that, creating an empathetic bond. He did that with everyone in the group. He was highly intelligent and emotionally astute. He could read people and knew how to manipulate them.

Peter Leinster himself says: 'There was an instant compatibility that made me very open to doing business with Felix.'

Following a now common pattern, the Leinsters were invited to visit Vossen's offices in Jermyn Street to observe his set up. Vossen put on his by now well-rehearsed floor show, appearing to make $50,000 in the space of 40 minutes.

The Leinsters were oblivious to the fact that the trade was entirely fictitious. Cleverly, Vossen was careful not to force himself on would-be investors. Once the seed was planted, he preferred to let investors come to him, in keeping with the illusion that they were being admitted to membership of a very exclusive investment club.

Jane Leinster says: 'With us there was an eight or nine-month courtship or grooming if you like. He was in no rush to take the money from us. In the end, we almost had to force him to take our money. Initially we put a small amount in just to test the water because he was a one-man band.'

Once they had invested, the friendship went from strength to strength. Although the Leinsters never went on holiday with Vossen, he stayed with them on two occasions at their home in the country. Their son even did two days' work experience with him.

Prior to being introduced to Vossen, most of the Leinsters' money was being looked after by a private bank which had invested a big chunk of their portfolio in a major US company. When that company went bust and had to be rescued, the Leinsters lost significant sums. 'It was then that Felix got under our skin,' says Jane Leinster. 'He was on the phone a lot saying don't worry. He recommended, surprise, surprise that we get out of that investment, take the hit and put our money with him and he would make up our losses as quickly as he could. By then, Peter and he were close, Felix could do no wrong.'

Jane, however, just like Mandy Collins, Mavis Baker and Jon Peterson's wife, had misgivings about Vossen.

> He was one of the most charismatic people but there was also something about him. I was always worried because we were putting huge trust in him. We got quarterly statements from him of varying degrees of sophistication, but we often had to chase him because he wasn't great with the paperwork. Towards the end we were trying to take out regular dividends although it was always a battle to get the money.

As with other investors, the Leinsters were told that if ever there was a 'crystallising moment' in Vossen's life, his computer trading systems had been programmed to cope with such an eventuality and his accountant had been given instructions about how to disburse the funds in his accounts. Like others, the Leinsters asked for details of this arrangement but never actually received them.

The Leinsters made their first investments with Vossen in August 2008, transferring a little over $1.3 million into one of his UBS accounts in St Moritz in six separate transactions, according to the indictment prepared by Swiss prosecutors at the fraudster's eventual trial. They went on to become the third biggest investors in Vossen's funds, with further significant investments between 2009 and 2011, court documents show. In total, they entrusted him with £3.8 million of their money. They managed to get £1.98 million of that back before Vossen disappeared, according to financial details attached to the judgement at Vossen's eventual trial. The day that Vossen fled with his Ponzi exposed, the Leinsters thought their pot had grown in value to £8.6 million.

Peter Leinster says towards the end, the constant difficulties getting money out of Vossen had put a big strain on the relationship and taken the shine off their friendship. 'But having said that, I completely trusted him 100 per cent, up until March 2015.'

Encouraged by the returns the Leinsters were generating from their investments, Peter's brother Roy and his wife, Julie, who lived in Yorkshire, also decided to wager their money on what appeared to be an ultra-safe one-way bet. After meeting Vossen in 2009 at his apartment and viewing his set-up, they went on to invest £2.25 million between January the following year and November 2012, according to court documents. They had little direct contact with him, relying instead on the statements of account they would periodically receive. The last one they saw put the value of their pot at £3.7 million. ' Roy later recalls:

> Being based in the north I didn't have the very close relationship that quite clearly the majority of investors had. Therefore, I didn't experience the daft voices and that side of him. I did of course receive the full charm offensive from his gregarious personality, particularly during discussions regarding withdrawals and previous false promises he made. On one occasion I told him about a friend who had terminal cancer. He was incredibly sympathetic and sad for me. He went on to mention his sister's illness and told me about a family meal during Christmas where they had all held hands and thanked God they all had each other. In a later discussion he told me about his father's cancer and the fact that hair treatment drugs had inadvertently shielded detection of it. His voice was breaking up, interspersed with silences as if to hold back the tears. This led to a sympathetic discussion and I felt uneasy about pressing him too hard regarding outstanding transfers. It's a shame he didn't make acting his career.

Peter's sister, Margaret, also took the plunge, investing £1 million. However, she was one of the very few lucky ones to get all her money out before the Ponzi collapsed.

In the same year that Steven Walters introduced Vossen to the Leinsters he also effected an introduction to another long-standing friend and client for whom he had edited, Jake Sinclair, a BBC radio and television producer turned successful TV commercials director. 'Steven was constantly talking about this guy called Felix who amazingly was getting him returns of up to 20 per cent annually,' says Sinclair.

> Other members of his investor group were successful businessmen, and fellow members of the film industry and I came to the view that if it was good enough for them it was probably good enough for me. So, we eventually got to meet in his grand Jermyn Street apartment and he showed me his multi-screen trading station complete with a huge emergency generator in case there was a sudden loss of power during a trade. I instantly liked the man. He seemed to be highly intelligent, extraordinarily charming and above all risk-averse.
>
> I know next to nothing about trading and investments and it all seemed highly credible. I watched him trading and he explained how at the end of each day he got out of the market and safely parked his fund. Vossen presented it as a very exclusive club in which you were very lucky to be a member. I was told there was a minimum entry level of half a million pounds.

The bare statistics of Sinclair's relationship with Vossen are these: Investment $3.2 million. Withdrawals $845,000. Statemented value on 31 December 2014 $7.7 million. Loss $6.755 million.

Behind those raw figures lies a story of seduction, deception and invention that would keep a psychoanalyst entertained for a very long time. In the same way that Vossen had used his supposed love of gastronomy to inveigle his way into the affections of the Huntleys, he immediately homed in on Sinclair's passion for all things cultural. A self-confessed aesthete and avid consumer of culture, Sinclair would go out four times a week to enjoy the opera, ballet, cinema, classical music or theatre. All the more so following the death of his wife from cancer. He was also a lover of fine dining and art.

> These are some of the attributes that drew Vossen towards me. Many of the things I did, Vossen wanted to participate in too. He and I started dining together monthly in rather grand restaurants – the Ivy, Rules, J. Sheekey's, Green's. He liked these old-fashioned English places. We established a relationship based on a shared interest in film-making and, to a lesser extent, theatre. Before long he was coming to have dinner at my home. He was meeting my friends.

And yet for all his supposed interest in the aesthetic, Vossen never seemed bothered about cultivating his own connoisseurship. He was keen to learn but not to commit. And so, in the case of this friendship, it was always Sinclair who would suggest the next cultural outing and buy the tickets. It was much the same with respect to Vossen's claim to be an art lover.

> As an art collector, I remarked that it was strange he only had reproductions of Rothko paintings in his flat. Frankly they were rather embarrassing. I asked him on a number of occasions whether

> he would like me to take him to a few auctions to get him started but it never happened. Of course it never happened. Vossen never spent money on anything other than a restaurant tab and obligatory Christmas presents. With hindsight, it's amazing none of us stopped to wonder why a man running a multi-million pound fund had zero extravagance in his life. No art. No fancy cars. No holidays. Nothing except for a showcase rental flat in Jermyn Street.

But it was without doubt another bromance and it did cause Sinclair to wonder, as others had, about Vossen's sexuality. 'He always gave me a long and generous hug at the end of an evening out which invariably went on one beat too long. I wouldn't have been surprised to learn that he was bi-sexual,' he says.

Sinclair says there also appeared to be an interesting biographical overlap between him and his nemesis.

> If he was telling the truth he was estranged from his parents for a number of years and spent his later teenage years being brought up by his grandfather. I was estranged from my father for quite a few years in my twenties, so we had this thing in common. We'd exchange quite intimate family information in a relationship characterised by great mutual affection. We delighted in one another's company.

The reality was that Vossen's grandfather had died when he was aged just seven. But he maintained the pretence that the old man was still alive and even told friends that he was driving Burkhardt's ancient black Mini Cooper around London.

And so, Sinclair began investing. Initially he transferred £350,000 to Vossen in July, 2007 from the profits that he had made from a commercial property deal. Court records show that over the following seven years he went on to make periodic deposits, often running into six figures and mainly paid into one of Vossen's business accounts with UBS, whenever he had accumulated enough spare cash. His final investment was in May, 2014 when he lodged £375,000 in one of Vossen's Barclays accounts in London. He was undaunted by the fact that the initial investment contract he signed with Vossen was a photocopy and that he failed to receive any form of financial statement of account for 18 months.

'When I eventually got one it was a single page which stated the profit achieved and the current balance. He'd made over 20 per cent so I was extremely pleased and forgave him for the 18 months it had taken to get the statement and the amateurish way it has been supplied to me.'

A key element of Vossen's approach, he says, was to make the professional side of their relationship as unprofessional as possible, blurring the boundaries between friendship and financial advice as often and as comprehensively as possible. 'It was a trap into which we all fell, one after another, as our relationships became more intimate,' says Sinclair.

With the benefit of hindsight, Sinclair says he too missed many of the danger signs: for instance, Vossen's extreme sentimentality

> It's interesting how all the great brutes of history, Hitler, Mao and other dictators down the ages had deep sentimental streaks which disguised their complete lack of genuine empathy. Vossen I'm sure was a similar character – deep down a man devoid of any conscience. He also loved to wallow in victimhood. There were always things going on in his life, ill health or instances of

> personal misfortune, which were used as excuses for why he hadn't produced the latest quarterly report you'd asked for. We were forever hearing stories about how his brother had broken a leg, or a good friend died or his mother having cancer and then his father having cancer too.
>
> My wife died of cancer and when you have cancer surrounding you, the one thing you want to do is bury yourself in work. You don't want to sit endlessly around a sick bed. So, there were things that kind of didn't add up.

Sinclair was sufficiently concerned about Vossen that, prior to investing, he asked his long-standing financial adviser James Renton to do some due diligence and check him out. 'He met with Vossen – again in his Jermyn St apartment – and this time Vossen successfully pulled the wool over a proper industry professional. James told me that he was impressed, describing Vossen as "a complete trading nerd",' recalls Sinclair

All the while, Vossen lubricated the relationship with his famous acts of kindness which occasionally bordered on the ridiculously generous. Sinclair recalls one instance: with their friendship continuing to blossom and the high returns seemingly rolling in, he asked whether Vossen could take charge of the rest of his pension fund, at that time invested with Renton's fund. Sinclair says that Vossen promised to investigate the possibility but then proceeded to prevaricate for the best part of two years. As it turned out, Vossen's fund was never eligible to receive investments from a pension fund.

Finally, Vossen called Sinclair one day and said matter-of-factly that he could not and would not manage the remainder of his money. However, as a gesture of goodwill, he said he would compensate Sinclair for the lost investment opportunity by crediting his account with an additional $100,000.

Perhaps that was the same $100,000 that Vossen persuaded David Benziger, a 43-year-old Swiss national and architect cum property developer, to invest. Or perhaps it came from one of his other investors. Or perhaps it never existed in the first place.

Benziger comes from another small sub-group of linked investors. He met Vossen in early 2014 while on a trip through Europe with his then girlfriend, Indira Roberts, a New York-based financial trader. Roberts herself had met Vossen a year earlier when her daughter, who was in boarding school in England at the time, went to an orthodontist called Clare Obsorne for some dental treatment. Obsorne had known Vossen since 2008 and had latterly become his girlfriend, replacing the glamorous Sophia Rafaat. Unsurprisingly, a short time after meeting Obsorne, Vossen blossomed into a keen student of orthodontistry in order that he could engage in quite detailed conversations with his new friend about speech impediments, facial form, bite and many other aspects of orthodontic practice.

As Vossen's relationship with Obsorne blossomed, so did his generosity towards his new girlfriend. In 2011, they holidayed on the tiny and exclusive island of Mnemba, off the north-east coast of Zanzibar. It is a popular scuba-diving destination because of the 600 species of coral reef fish it boasts and the opportunity it affords to observe nesting green turtles, humpback whales, dolphins and whale sharks, the world's largest fish. But Mnemba is also an expensive experience. It is a private island and the cost of a one-night stay is a minimum $1,200 – the equivalent of six years' wages for the average Zanzibar worker. Resort staff patrol the shore in a flotilla of small boats, ready to repel anyone who snorkels within a 200-metre radius of the island.

Obsorne did not stop to ask how Vossen could afford such an extravagant vacation. She assumed, as did other investors, that it was all paid for by his fabulously successful stock market trading.

Nor did Indira Roberts stop to question Vossen's financial acumen. She was so impressed with his apparent track record that she invested $2 million with him on behalf of herself and her mother Darsha in the space of just nine months between April 2014 and January 2015, according to court records. All of the money was lodged in Vossen's VCP Investment Advisers account at Banque Cramer in Zurich. Although the bulk of the money had only been on deposit with Vossen for three months before he fled, he still told the Roberts's that he had already made a $300,000 profit for them.

Indira had no hesitation therefore in recommending that her boyfriend become an investor with Vossen too. Benziger, who had a background in real estate credit risk with several investment banks, had quit his job with Citibank and moved to Hong Kong to start up his own real estate business. He had bought and sold an apartment in China and had managed to triple his money, helped by the booming Chinese property market and the appreciation of the Chinese renminbi. He was looking for a home for his money.

'I went to see him in his flat on Jermyn Street and he took me out for sushi,' says Benziger. 'He was a very nice fellow. We talked about various things. I asked him about his work, mostly out of curiosity because I wasn't interested in investing at that time. He certainly wasn't pushy. Then we saw each other again in Zurich. He invited us to a very nice hotel. He was trying to show us he was very successful and therefore we should trust him with our money. He also paid for our hotel in Zurich. I then saw him once in New York. We were friends. We talked about his returns and his low-risk approach and his various clients. We always met him alone.'

With his by-now familiar technique, Vossen affected an interest in Benziger's particular passions: furniture design and modern art. 'He was like Selig in the Woody Allen movie,' says Benziger. 'A chameleon basically. He wasn't so much interested in architecture or property development but I have a great interest in furniture design and art, and in his house in London he said he had some reproduction Rothkos, and so we talked a lot about art and furniture design and he knew about some pieces I liked.'

And so, he invested $100,000 with Vossen. 'He had my money for nine months. I thought Indira trusts him so there is no reason for me not to.' In that nine months, Benziger's $100,000 grew in value by a phenomenal 94 per cent to $194,108 – according, at least, to the last statement of account he received from Vossen on 13 February 2015. Over the same period, the Nasdaq index in New York, the market on which Vossen was supposed to be trading, rose by 11.7 per cent. He appeared to be achieving the kind of returns that not only beat the passive index funds hands down but which even the most talented active fund managers and stock pickers could only dream about.

Benziger, like others, had to pursue Vossen and his fictitious employee Jennifer Keller for the paperwork related to his investment, but he wasn't unduly worried.

> I decided, well, the guy probably spends most of his time investing rather than drawing up fancy balance sheets which I figured was

> actually in my favour because I was more interested in the returns he said he was achieving. Thank God I didn't put all my money with Felix, just $100k, so in my case it wasn't a gamechanger.

For others, investing with Vossen was not just a game-changer but a life-changer. As well as being Vossen's girlfriend, Clare Obsorne also gave him very substantial sums of money, in the form of either loans or investments in his various funds. At first, Vossen told Obsorne he was investing her money in movie production. He then told her it was going into technology stocks. He then claimed he needed a loan to fund an investment in an off-plan property development.

Over a three-year period from 2012 to 2015, Obsorne gave Vossen £842,000. She got about half her money back (though still thought there was £670,000 in her pot the day Vossen disappeared). As for the other half, she was repaid with lie after lie by the man she was then living with. He lied to her about owning a boat moored on Lake Zurich; he lied about having suffered a brain tumour in 2010; he lied about his parents having both suffered cancer. 'When I pressed him on a lie, which of course I didn't know it was at the time, he would become either aggressive or say it did not want to talk about it,' Obsorne later said. 'For example, I would ask him about his brain tumour and he would refuse to talk about it because he did not have the correct information to hand to lie well about it.'

Obsorne also had to endure Vossen's violent mood swings. 'He had a bad temper and tried to control it but I could see he would lose it very easily,' she later recalls. 'I would say he was passive-aggressive. He lost his temper with me in a restaurant about nothing while we were on holiday so I got up and walked out on him and that made him really mad.'

As his girlfriend, Obsorne also witnessed at close quarters Vossen's obsessive-compulsive nature, the manipulative way in which he would identify a target and then find common ground with them and his perpetual need for approbation, praise and reassurance.

What made it all the more hurtful is that Obsorne genuinely believed she knew the real Felix Vossen, having shared his life and his bed. It was only later that she realised she did not know the man at all. At the time, she was as wrapped up in the myth and as carried away with Vossen as were his other victims.

For good measure, Vossen also used his romantic involvement with Obsorne to extract money from her sister, Jane, and brother Neil – cash which, again, they never saw back. Jane lent him £5,000 and Neil £30,000. Not huge sums in the scheme of things but with Vossen every little bit helped.

A large chunk of the £842,000 that Clare Obsorne entrusted to him had been destined to go into a new orthodontal practice that she was planning to set up in 2015 with her friend and business partner Maria Martinez. It was through the friendship with Obsorne that Martinez had met Vossen two years earlier. Martinez quickly became friends with Vossen. Together, the two women had £1m to invest in the business. Vossen suggested they park the money with him while they finalised their business plan, so he could earn a little extra for them. He said he would invest it in Apple shares. Martinez gave him her half of the money, £500,000, in April 2014. Within nine months it had grown in value by an impressive £70,000 to £570,000, Vossen told her. It was money that she had diligently saved over the previous ten years to help launch the next stage of her career.

If Vossen's courtship of Benziger and Roberts was lightning quick, then it was positively glacial in the case of two other victims: Stewart Gregory – another of the investors introduced to Vossen by Steven Walters – and Jurgen Maas, who met Vossen after his daughter Anna had invested with him in 2000. Gregory, a 54-year-old freelance commercial film director living in Islington, north London, had first met Vossen in 2004 but he did not finally invest with him until 2014. Maas did not invest until 2011 when he handed over EUR150,000. 'He was a slow burn con artist,' Gregory now says.

> He would light small fires with investors and then come back to them to see how they were burning. And if they'd taken light he would stoke the flames. I saw him probably once a year. He used to say 'Don't give me all of it, we are in no hurry, give me some now and if it looks it's a goer give me the rest in six months.' Little did I know that was all part of the play.

Until he invested with Vossen, Gregory had always put any money he'd saved with big, reputable investment firms such as St James's Place who are regulated, answerable, responsible and liable.

> I was very happy with SJP up until 2013. I'd been spread across five investment funds.
>
> I rather foolishly thought that Vossen, because he was operating in the markets, was regulated correctly and was above board. He was recommended to me by Steven Walters, poor Steven, who can't look at me in the eyes these days.
>
> Vossen would talk at length about what he does and how he trips the markets and has guarantees and could buy 'flags' in the

> market on the way up so he could buy his way back in this roster. He had all the jargon. It sounded to me that he knew what he was doing. He made me bring in my passport, said there were a whole load of documents I needed to sign. I asked for copies of everything.

Gregory had £260,000 in his St James's Place account and was debating whether to use the money to pay off his remaining mortgage or re-invest it elsewhere. Apple had just launched the iPhone 6 and Vossen said he was a big fan of the company and its products. So too was Gregory. An investment in Apple shares was surely, therefore, a one-way bet.

So he agreed to invest the entire amount with Vossen. Court documents show that it was paid into the Vossen's VCP Asset Management account in the Zurich branch of Banque Cramer in three instalments over a three-month period. The last tranche was transferred to Vossen just before Christmas, 2014. Gregory even remembers wishing one of Vossen's non-existent employees a happy Christmas when the email came through confirming receipt of his funds.

> He told me it was all invested in Apple shares, which I had stipulated, and Felix said he had done quite well with them in the past. He'd send me little graphs showing how well the shares had done on a given day. They were like little fishing lures spinning through the water and attracting you to invest more. I thought I was being invited into an opportunity that was precious and had value in itself. That's how I was made to feel. Felix was saying, 'I don't normally take investments of this small amount, but as it's you…'

On the day that Gregory transferred the last chunk of his £260,000 to Vossen, the two men had dinner at Fredericks, a local restaurant in Islington favoured by Cherie Blair. Unusually, Vossen made Gregory pay. 'The little cheapskate,' says Gregory.

Gregory was to be one of several investors who never received a penny back from Vossen. Maria Martinez, Indira Roberts and her mother and David Benziger, all late investors, also found themselves in the same boat for the simple reason that by this time there was no money to give back.

For most of the years that he was systematically defrauding his friends, Vossen lived with Sophia Rafaat, though it was a sometimes tumultuous relationship. She appeared to divide her time between co-habiting with Vossen and then, when their relationship was experiencing one of its not infrequent rocky patches, moving out to live with her widowed mother who owned a flat in High Street Kensington. Vossen would seemingly chide Rafaat for what he saw as her excessive drinking, smoking and lack of exercise, and tell her he could not live with her until she had sorted out her life. He talked incessantly to his other girlfriends about the need for Sophia to see a therapist, reasoning that he had taken control of his own life by giving up alcohol and smoking, and taking up exercise and healthy eating. She should do likewise. Yet, he was also cross that she had given up her television career – interpreting it for some reason as a personal insult to him – and took pride in the fact that she had modelled nude in various magazines, explaining that she had a beautiful body and therefore it deserved to be seen by everyone. It was almost as if she was a commodity to be bought and sold. Much like the stocks and shares in which he claimed to trade.

Vossen's relationship with Rafaat was undoubtedly complex. 'He was incredibly jealous of Sophia and would be physically aggressive to anyone whom he thought was coming on to her,' recalls Mickey de Fernandez-Paz, a close friend of both of them. 'She, in turn, was completely smitten by him. Sometimes he would cry to her and ask for her forgiveness. At other times he would buy her extravagant gifts, as if paying Sophia for her silence. As a couple, they cast themselves as two people against the world. Nothing could or would come between them.'

Rafaat told friends that she had frequently talked to Vossen about the two of them buying a house together and settling down. But he expressed no interest whatsoever and so Rafaat finally dropped the subject. Indeed, Rafaat told friends that even when she and Vossen were 'happily together' and travelling abroad, there was nowhere he seemed comfortable to call home, wanted to return to or expressed any real interest in. The last trip they took together was a visit to Hamburg to see Vossen's godfather, Michael Jahr, a few months before he disappeared. The visit was not unproductive. Afterwards, Jahr wrote his godson a cheque for EUR100,000. He never saw the money again.

But was she aware of the fraud that Vossen was committing? Vossen's investors are divided over whether Sophia was complicit in his activities or, like them, conned by a very plausible and charismatic fraudster. Asked to list her qualities by a *Guardian* interviewer in 2004 Sophia replied: 'Sincerity, enthusiasm, hard work and a refusal to take "No" for an answer.'

Mandy Collins would add duplicity to that list because she is convinced that Rafaat was aware of the fraud: 'Looking back, I think Sophia was on the lookout for rich people to introduce to Felix,' she says. 'I am almost sure that towards the end she fully understood what Felix was doing. I am convinced she knew what was going on.' So too is Stewart Gregory:

> I believe Sophia to be complicit in all this. If it were to be found that Vossen did indeed buy a flat for her in Notting Hill then that would presumably have been paid for by us. And there must have been pillow talk, she wasn't a stupid woman and she knew which side her bread was buttered on.

However, Elizabeth Shaw gives her the benefit of the doubt: 'I think it's the biggest case of sticking your head in the sand,' she says. 'Sophia allowed herself to be totally duped, she's been lying to herself for years and years. She knows a lot of things and will have seen so many things but she never asked any questions because he was her total saviour. She idolised him.'

Jon Peterson also believes Sophia was taken in by a man he describes now as a dysfunctional sociopath. 'I think she was naïve but deep down I don't think she knew about Felix's skulduggery. She enjoyed life with him and assumed he was exceptional at what he was doing. She was always hanging onto his shirt tails, a brassy girl, a glamour puss for want of a better phrase.'

Fernandez-Paz says this of Sophia's involvement:

> I think she knew that something dodgy was going on but he had such a powerful hold over her, she chose not to question it. Sophia was blind, oblivious to his double identity.
>
> Sophia knows a lot for sure but she was very loyal to this crook. She would get Gucci or Chanel gifts from Felix to keep her quiet.

> She knew exactly what was going on. He was supplying her with goodies and she was happy with that. You know he was promising her that she was going to be in one of his movies because she always wanted to be an actress. He would tell her 'don't worry darling, you are going to be a superstar'.

Whatever the truth of Sophia's involvement or otherwise, she undoubtedly benefited from Vossen's fraud. She has subsequently told friends that in the early years she received no financial support from Vossen beyond the gifts and holidays he would naturally provide as her boyfriend. In later years he did support her to a very generous extent, particularly after her mother died in 2013. Indeed, bank records show payments to her from various Vossen accounts of £402,723, $40,293 and 7,637 euros. She is also living in a very well-appointed Notting Hill flat, bought for her by Vossen – or perhaps by Vossen's investors.

After Vossen had gone missing, Matthew Allen met Sophia for coffee in Wholefoods on Kensington High Street, close to her London flat. The purpose of their meeting was to see whether Rafaat could assist the investor group on two fronts: first to help in their search for Vossen; and second to help track down any assets he might own. Allen concluded that there was very little to be gleaned from her. He came away from the meeting certain that Vossen had compartmentalised his relationship with Rafaat so that she was never privy to the activities of his fraudulent alter ego. 'She was very upset but she was mainly devastated about her own situation,' Allen recalls.

He also came away knowing that he had just spent time in the company of a woman who also felt utterly betrayed, although in a different way to Vossen's investors. Allen reported back the following to the investor group on Basecamp, their shared online chat room:

> On a personal level, she is utterly broken and lost. She has found out that she doesn't know/never knew the man she has loved for all her adult years.
>
> It turns out that they haven't been together as a couple for four years. And despite this and the fact that he has been pushing her away in some senses, she has never let go. She was always hoping that she might move back in with him – despite the fact that she says she had dinner with him no more than a handful of times in the last two years.
>
> He appears to have been the one constant in her life from the age of 20 and she just couldn't live without at least the shadow of him, whether that was because he was manipulating her to feel like that or whether he did still feel things for her/felt a moral obligation for her I don't know.
>
> Whether it might be hard for us to feel sympathy for her or not, it's a fact that she is simply heartbroken.

What Allen only subsequently discovered was that Rafaat had not been entirely truthful with him. She insisted, for instance, that she had not received any money from Vossen for four years. His bank records told a different story.

Apart from that one encounter with Matthew Allen, Rafaat has gone to ground since Vossen's disappearance and has remained incommunicado ever since. She has almost entirely erased her social media profile and although she has remained in touch with Vossen's family, she has had no further contact with any other investors despite promising to be available to help them with their initial search for her former boyfriend.

Mickey de Fernandez-Paz's apartment in Chelsea overlooks Brompton Cemetery, where Sophia's mother is buried. He would see her occasionally when she was visiting the graveyard to lay flowers for her mother. The last time he recalls meeting Sophia was in early 2015 when they bumped into one another in a club. 'She was very chatty and said we should get together, she even gave me her new phone number,' he recalls. She has not been in touch since.

As for Sophia herself, the last time she saw Vossen was Valentine's Day, 14 February 2015 when he called round to deliver some flowers. Three weeks later he disappeared from her life and everyone else's.

5

KEEPING IT IN THE FAMILY

One of the more remarkable aspects of the Felix Vossen story is the way in which he was content to deceive not just close personal friends and professional colleagues but even his own family. Most fraudsters draw the line at defrauding their own kith and kin on the grounds that, no matter how much bad blood may exist, it is, in the end, almost always thicker than water. There were, for instance, 4,800 victims of Bernie Madoff's securities fraud – but his family members were not amongst them. On the contrary, he enabled them to share in the proceeds of his crimes. Madoff's brother, Peter, was the chief compliance officer at Bernard L. Madoff Investment Securities – a role which was to earn him a 10-year jail sentence when the fraud was exposed. Both of his sons also worked for the family firm, as did his niece Shana. From the great Charles Ponzi himself and onwards down the years it is difficult to find a fraudster who felt that their mothers and fathers, brothers and sisters were fair game.

Not so Felix Vossen. He appears to have had no such qualms, no moral off-button. Indeed the closer the relationship with Vossen, the more dangerous he was to know. The two biggest victims of his Ponzi were his own parents, Norbert and Cornelia Vossen. Between them, they invested £5.4 million in his various non-existent investment schemes and lost virtually every penny.

It was an especially cruel way in which to repay the trust and faith his parents had placed in Vossen, repeatedly welcoming him back into the fold after earlier business ventures had turned sour and continuing to support their eldest son, even though he was determined not to grant his father's wish and take over the running of the family firm.

Of the four Vossen children, it seemed that Felix was always destined to be the one that was singled out for special, preferential treatment. Having sent him to one of Switzerland's most prestigious boarding schools, Lyceum Alpinum Zuoz, Norbert and Cornelia would then visit their son on a regular basis. There, they would stay in the five-star Carlton hotel, in nearby St Moritz, in one of the sumptuous lake-view suites that the establishment boasted. Felix became such a familiar face at the hotel that he was instantly recognised by the concierge.

His mother, Cornelia, was tall, beautiful and rather regal. Even though she was German, Felix's fellow pupils christened her the Italian aristocrat, partly because she spoke the language fluently and partly because of her 'sovereign' demeanour and her relaxed, radiant smile. His father Norbert, shorter and stubbier than his wife, cut less of a dash and consequently made less of an impression. Felix's friends saw in Norbert a rather proud and prickly man who felt he had something to prove to the world.

Sometimes, the parents would have their younger son, Norbert Junior, in tow. Occasionally, they were also accompanied by his sister Christina, who would go on to become a teacher. Friends said Christina was outgoing and approachable but Norbert Junior was quiet and diffident, quite unlike his elder brother.

In term time Felix's parents would entertain their eldest son in the Carlton and indulge his passion for skiing. When term ended, Felix's father would whisk him away from St Moritz on exotic vacations to Asia and America. One of Vossen's schoolfriends, Ralph Weber, remembers Felix returning from these trips at the start of the new academic year, dressed in Armani and laden down with the latest electronic gadgets – CD players, Sony Walkmans and the like.

Unfortunately, Felix's expensive education was an academic failure and a personal disappointment to his parents in two ways: first, he left without any qualifications; second, his time at Alpinum Zuoz convinced Vossen that he would not enter the family business because he was more interested in the movie world and consumer technology. Despite this, his parents continued to fund him – paying for Vossen to study for an International Baccalaureate in England, a business degree in Germany and a law apprenticeship in Madrid.

They also helped fund his first business venture, retailing Apple equipment in Spain. But when this business went bust, it appears to have been the last straw. What followed was a lengthy estrangement from his parents which only came to an end a decade later. By this time, Vossen was well-established in London and running, to all intents and purposes, a very successful fund management business.

Perhaps as a way of repaying his parents for having let them down so often in the past, Vossen encouraged them to invest with him. They did so, entrusting their son with EUR1 million in April, 2009 and a further EUR1 million ten months later.

Vossen told them that he was regulated and audited by the Swiss Financial Markets Supervisory Authority, he vouched that their money was safe and promised them returns of 20 per cent a year.

As proof of this, Vossen's fictional employees, Robert Gassner, Natalie Casanova and Jennifer Keller, would send regular performance reports detailing how well Norbert and Cornelia's investments were doing. The first such report showed that Norbert and Cornelia's initial EUR1 million investment had turned in the space of just three months into a pot worth almost $1.5 million thanks to their son's miraculous ability to pick stock market winners in the American technology sector. By October, 2011, their fund had increased in value to $3.25 million. But, of course, the account balances, unit prices and profit margins contained in these reports were all entirely fictitious.

Alas, they encouraged his parents to inject yet more of the family fortune. So, in the course of 2013, they invested a further EUR1.45 million into their son's personal account held at the St Moritz branch of Credit Suisse. Significantly, they also went on to invest a further EUR2.1 million and £500,000 into Vossen's film financing vehicle Exponential Media Ventures Limited between November 2013 and September 2014. Having initially been reluctant to encourage their son's love affair with the movie business, they were now confident enough to help bankroll it. Felix told them, untruthfully, that he needed help funding his latest film production, *I, Anna*, because someone to whom he had lent money had failed to make a loan repayment on time. At the same time, he was also lying to his film production partners because the money was not going into movie financing either. It was being used to pay dividends to other investors, keep assorted creditors at bay and fund Vossen's own lifestyle.

When Vossen fled his London apartment in March 2015 and vanished into thin air, the family's initial reaction was one of shock at his disappearance and concern for his welfare. But as the scale of his duplicity became clear, their compassion quickly turned to anger. Within a month, Vossen's parents had hired their own lawyers, filed criminal charges against their son and registered themselves as private criminal prosecutors for the purpose of joining the pursuit of their son and establishing their claim for damages and compensation.

Today, Norbert and Cornelia are owed £4.6 million. They have disowned their eldest son, declining to visit him in prison. They have also shut themselves off from the rest of the world in order to deal in private with the disgrace he has brought to the Vossen name.

It wasn't just Vossen's actual parents who fell prey to his deceit. Over a period of many years, he also defrauded one of his godparents, Michael Jahr.

Jahr was a very old friend of the Vossens. His family constituted one half of Gruner + Jahr, one of Europe's biggest magazine publishers with a stable of more 500 titles including the influential weekly Germany current affairs publication *Stern*. The firm was set up by Michael's father, John Jahr Senior, in Hamburg in 1965. His other son, John Jahr Junior, sat on the board for a period. Michael was not involved in the management of the firm but he did very well out of the mountains of cash the business threw off.

The links between the Vossen and Jahr families are many and varied. Like Felix, Michael Jahr was schooled at the

Alpinum Zuoz in Switzerland. Like the Vossen family business, Gruner + Jahr was a shining example of Germany's privately-owned small and medium-sized business community, the Mittelstand. Felix's father Norbert came to know the Jahrs as they inevitably bumped into one another on the business circuit and shared many of the same challenges and opportunities that confronted other members of the Mittelstand. Norbert and Michael went on to become close personal friends.

Gruner + Jahr was eventually acquired by the rival publisher Bertelsmann, which had been building up a shareholding in the business for many years. Bertelsmann, by coincidence, was also headquartered in the Vossens' home town of Gütersloh. In the year before the takeover, Gruner + Jahr was generating more than EUR2 billion in sales and making operating profits of nearly EUR200m. When Bertelsmann finally took control of the company, buying out John Jahr's remaining 25.1 per cent stake in 2014, the family netted an estimated EUR400 million.

Michael Jahr used the family fortune to do two things. First, he established his own investment company, also based in Hamburg. Second, he created the Michael Jahr Foundation, a charitable organisation dedicated to promoting sustainable forestry and supporting scientific research into nature conservation and landscape management. The foundation works closely with the Faculty of Advanced Sciences at Dresden University in Tharandt. Every two years it awards a doctoral scholarship to a Tharandt graduate to fund a research project into a given aspect of applied forestry and every year it runs an award scheme under which the best graduate from its masters degree course receives a EUR1,500 endowment.

How could Felix look such a gift horse in the mouth? How could he resist the temptation to part his godparent from some more of the family money? And so, he came up with a rather cunning scheme. It came to him not long after he first arrived in London at the turn of the millennium.

As we now know, Vossen's initial business foray in the capital was to open a sandwich bar in Bond Street Underground Station with another German expatriate called Alexander. Although the partnership was short-lived, it had at least given him the germ of an idea for another little money-spinning deceit that would help pay for his running costs and his drug habit.

Alexander had graduated from the European Business School in Regent's Park. Vossen, according to a friend at the time, Mickey de Fernandez-Paz, decided to enrol there too to study for its 12-month MBA in International Business Studies. Although not quite as prestigious as its near neighbour, the London Business School, the European Business School was nevertheless one of the most fashionable and academically-influential institutions at which to be tutored. Part of Regent's University, it is the UK's oldest private business school and attracts a high proportion of international students who are typically multi-lingual – 70 per cent of its graduates are fluent in at least four languages. So is Vossen. The school also boasts a strong pedigree in banking and finance, with around a third of its students pursuing a career in one of those two fields. In addition to the main campus in London, the school has sister facilities in Paris, Milan and Frankfurt together with partnerships with a string of other universities around the world. What better education could Felix Vossen have to round off his academic studies and hone his skills as an expert in business strategy and investment fund management?

There was only one problem: how would Vossen afford the £18,000-a-year tuition fees and fund his day-to-day expenses whilst living in one of the world's most expensive cities? Felix had the answer. He would persuade a generous benefactor to bankroll his studies. The benefactor he alighted upon was his godfather, Michael Jahr. There was only one slight wrinkle in Vossen's scheme: he never actually enrolled at the European Business School and therefore never attended a single lecture or seminar. What, then, was Vossen to do when his godparent said that he would like to come over to London to see Vossen graduate from his non-existent MBA?

According to Fernandez-Paz, Vossen simply staged a fake graduation party and persuaded an Italian acquaintance to forge his graduation certificate. Mr Jahr attended the celebration in good faith, unaware that it was not real and that Vossen's degree was bogus. Fernandez-Paz says:

> Felix needed to have a group of people to make it look like a genuine graduation party, so a friend of mine agreed to help him.
>
> He persuaded some girls he knew to act as guests and they brought some other guys along with them. My Italian friend put the whole event together. She provided the guests, the drinks, the gowns, the whole thing. She also helped Felix to forge his graduation certificate. He never went to university. He simply claimed the money from his godfather and spent it on drugs.

According to Fernandez-Paz, this unnamed Italian was also a good friend of Vossen's long-term girlfriend Sophia Rafaat. Sophia will not speak about her time with Vossen so we do not know whether she was party to this deception. But we do know that Sophia was with Vossen the last time he saw his godparent and benefactor. The two of them travelled together to Hamburg to see Michael Jahr in late 2014. It was around the time that the Jahr family received its windfall from the sale of their remaining shareholding to Bertelsmann. It was also a short time before Vossen's Ponzi came crashing down around his ears and he was desperately trying to stave off the inevitable by securing fresh funds. Vossen left Hamburg with EUR100,000 of Michael Jahr's money in his back pocket.

That Vossen had faked his own graduation party would have come as an unsettling and unpleasant surprise to those who would later invest their money with him, had they known about it. But it was par for the course: years later, he would carry out a strikingly similar deception, complete with bogus employees and borrowed offices, to dupe investors in his non-existent fund management business.

6

FELIX THE FILM MAKER

There is good serendipity and there is bad serendipity. The day that Barnaby Southcombe discovered Felix Vossen, after a chance encounter one afternoon, in the middle of Chelsea was undoubtedly a case of the latter. It was a spring day in 2000 and Vossen was strolling down the King's Road, not long after he had arrived in London, when he spotted Southcombe filming some street scenes with a Super8 camera. With his usual ebullience and brashness, Vossen approached the man holding the camera and said: 'Hey, I've always wanted to be in film.' It was friendship at first sight.

Southcombe, a budding young film director, was steeped in the movie business. His mother was the British actress Charlotte Rampling, icon of the Swinging Sixties, pioneer of the art house cinema scene and star of seminal films including Richard Lester's *The Knack* and *How to Get It*, *Gregory's Girl* and *Farewell My Lovely*, where she appeared alongside Robert Mitchum. His father was Bryan Southcombe, a New Zealand actor and later publicist best known for appearing in the 1972 movie *The Man With Two Heads*, a schlock-horror remake of *Dr Jekyll and Mr Hyde*.

Vossen had only just arrived in London and, as he told Southcombe that day, was desperate to get into the movie business. Together, they made a perfect match: Southcombe with his family lineage and film-maker's eye; Vossen with his charm, enthusiasm and the promise that he would one day have the resources to bankroll Southcombe's celluloiud dreams and turn his movie projects into reality.

Although they had never met each other before and did not possess any mutual acquaintances, the two men quickly became great friends. They were only two years apart in age – Vossen was then 26 and Southcombe 28 – and they shared similar values and interests. As the two men grew to become firm friends, Vossen confided in Southcombe. He told him how he had always wanted to become a film producer from an early age and how his parents had bought him a subscription to the bible of the movie world *Variety* magazine, when he was just 13. Vossen also told Southcombe how he had subsequently become estranged from his parents following his unsuccessful and financial ruinous foray into the retailing of Apple computers in Spain in the mid to late 1990s.

Vossen was keen to learn from his new friend and within a few months of them meeting, he asked Southcombe if they could make a short movie together. Vossen already had an idea in mind: he wanted to film an updated version of *Abwarts*, a 1984 psycho thriller by the German film director Carl Schenkel about three men and a woman trapped in a lift in a tower block. One of the men has just carried out a robbery elsewhere in the building and has the proceeds with him in a suitcase he is carrying.

Southcombe thought the project was far too ambitious, especially as Vossen had never produced a film before, and so the idea was abandoned. Instead, they made a short film together called *Weekend* but even that ended up wildly over budget.

But that did not matter. It had marked the start of Vossen's movie career. Vossen loved the artistic milieu in which he was able to mix, courtesy of his friendship with Southcombe, who also happened to have a half-brother in the magician David Jarre, the result of his mother's relationship with the French composer Jean-Michel Jarre.

If Vossen was at the start of his career as a stock market investor, then Southcombe too was just beginning to make his way in the world of film and television. Southcombe had studied French and History of Art at University College, London where he developed a taste for theatre. On graduation he went to Paris where he directed an adaptation of Harold Pinter's *Betrayal* at the Studio des Champs Elysees. After stints in New York and Auckland, where he wrote and directed his first short films, Southcombe moved back to London and began making music videos and TV commercials.

Southcombe's first big break in television came in 2001, not long after he had met Vossen, when the aspiring young film maker was chosen to direct *As If*, Channel 4's cult comedy-drama about a group of teenagers growing up in London in the new millennium. From that point, Southcombe's television career blossomed, as he graduated to direct episodes of *Night and Day*, a drama revolving around the lives of six London families, the MTV-produced 'dope opera' *Top Buzzer*; *Bad Girls*, *Teachers* and *Footballers' Wive$*, *Extra Time* over the next four years. By 2007 Southcombe was sufficiently well-established to be asked to direct the pilot episode of *Waterloo Road*, BBC1's award-winning peak-time drama. Directorial roles on two other medical dramas, *Holby Blue* and *Harley Street*, followed in 2007 and 2008.

As Southcombe's reputation in television burgeoned, so too did Vossen's apparent career as a day trader and investment guru. Whilst Southcombe was notching up directorial credits, Vossen was busily accumulating new clients. Over that same period of seven or so years, the supposed size of his investment fund grew impressively, as did the length of his client list. Bound together by their common interest in film, the two men spent much time in each other's company. They socialised at one another's homes and Southcombe invited Vossen to holiday with his family in the south of France.

Curiously, however, Vossen never seems to have made any serious attempt to convert Southcombe from friend into investor. Perhaps he realised that, whilst Southcombe might be a talented television director, he also had a large mortgage and family to support and therefore little in the way of spare cash.

In any event, Southcombe was valuable in other ways. He was Vossen's route into film production, even if it meant having to hand money over to this friend rather than taking it from him, as was Vossen's more usual modus operandi.

And so the two friends began to work on several potential film projects together. By 2009, Southcombe, with Vossen by his side, was ready to enter the world of big-screen movie making. Vossen's investment empire, built entirely on fraud, was doing fabulously, to all intents and appearances, and he promised Southcombe that he would help him build a movie empire to match by raising a £10m fund to finance the director's various film projects.

In 2009, another key player came into Vossen's life: a film producer called Chris Simon. Simon had worked that year with

Charlotte Rampling on *Boogie Woogie*, a comedy of manners set in the contemporary London art world, in which she had a cameo role alongside the film's main stars Gillian Anderson, Alan Cumming, Christopher Lee and Stellan Skarsgard. The movie was based on the book of the same name written by Danny Moynihan – the same Danny Moynihan who would later turn down Vossen's blandishments to invest with him on the grounds that he might be a mini-Bernie Madoff. That summer, Rampling introduced Simon to her son Barnaby at the Dinard film festival, an annual celebration of British film-making that has been hosted since 1989 by the French coastal town. Barnaby in turn introduced Simon to his film finance partner, Felix Vossen.

'Barnaby was a creative and he wanted a means to make his films. Felix was this successful, charming fund manager who came from a wealthy German textile family,' says Simon. 'He was generous, effervescent and an all-round honest and wonderful man. He was going to raise £10 million and we were going to make lots of movies.'

In return for access to funding, Southcombe and Simon gave Vossen an entree to their world of film producers, directors and financiers and, of course, film stars. 'Felix had a steep learning curve to get into the film industry and we were the way in,' says Simon.

Vossen quickly became a member of Bafta and used the connections he made to burnish his own image, embellish his life story and increase his appeal to existing and would-be investors. One investor, Jake Sinclair, vividly recalls an evening when he had been to the theatre with Vossen and was introduced later that night to the late Tim Piggott-Smith, whom Vossen greeted as though he were a long-lost brother.

Another investor, Jane Leinster, says: 'Felix's involvement in the film business gave him huge credibility. His face was in the movie press, he was going to film premieres and he was standing up on stage talking about his films.'

In 2010 the three men – Southcombe the film-maker, Simon the film-producer and Vossen the film-financier – formed Embargo Films. At the same time, Vossen set up his film-financing fund Exponential Media Group. In fact it was an umbrella entity for 11 other limited companies, some of them named after individual films, which Vossen used to shuffle money around.

Vossen coined a term for Southcombe, Simon and himself, describing the trio as the 'three-legged stool'. It meant that they were inter-dependent on one another and could only function properly when they worked together as one. If any one of the three was absent, then the stool would fall on its side. They were partners, they were brothers, they were family.

Curiously, however, only one of them – Barnaby – was actually a director of Embargo Films. Neither Simon nor Vossen got around to the formal business of joining the company's board. Vossen claimed that because his business was registered in Switzerland and he was classified for tax purposes as being non-domiciled, it would complicate matters if he were to become a director of Embargo Films. It also meant, of course, that he did not have any liability either, should the company ever run into trouble.

But it didn't matter that Felix was not technically a board member. His two friends trusted him implicitly with their livelihoods and with their money: so much so that Vossen was a co-signatory on the Embargo Films bank account and had the firm's corporate credit card in his wallet.

Embargo itself was a low-budget film-maker and prided itself on keeping overheads as low as possible to maximise the amount it could invest in film production. And it remains so today. 'We lived off very little and recycled our fees back into the business. All the money went onto the screen,' says Simon. In keeping with this policy of paring costs to the bone, Embargo based itself in tiny premises, located in a dingy alleyway off Wardour Street in the heart of Soho. Vossen did not even have his own office in the building. But he did, apparently, have the money.

In quick succession, Exponential provided the seed-corn for Embargo to develop three movies, all of which premiered within four months of one another at the end of 2012.

The first was a full-length re-make of *The Sweeney*, based on the 1970s cop series, starring Ray Winstone and Plan B as Regan and Carter and Damian Lewis as their long-suffering, play-it-by-the-book boss DCI Frank Haskins. The film topped the UK box office on its opening weekend in September 2012 and went on to gross a respectable $6.3 million worldwide.

The second was *The Pusher*, a crime thriller about Frank, a low-level London cocaine dealer who gets in over his head and finds himself on the wrong end of a Turkish drug lord's wrath after a deal goes wrong. At one point in the movie, in a scene which could have been lifted from the real life of Felix Vossen, Frank contemplates fleeing to Spain to escape mob justice.

The third and, in some respects the most important, was *I, Anna* – a noir-thriller written and directed by Southcombe and starring his mother. Based on the Elsa Lewin novel of the same name, Rampling played the role of Anna. It is the story of a murder in a London apartment told from the standpoint of the eponymous femme fatale who falls for the detective brought in to investigate the case, DCI Bernie Reid, played by Gabriel Byrne. Of the three films, it was the one that had been in gestation the longest and the one into which Southcombe, in particular, had invested most of his emotional energy.

I, Anna was also the most significant of the three films for Vossen because the year that Embargo began work on the project also coincided with the end of Vossen's long estrangement from his parents. His mother, Cornelia, subsequently visited the set of the movie and both parents attended a preview of the film at the 2012 Locarno Film Festival in Switzerland. Simon says he also met them at the official premiere of *I, Anna* in October that year at the Curzon Mayfair where it featured on the list of new films being shown as part of the BFI London Film Festival.

Unbeknown to Southcombe and Simon, by the time the three films were released Vossen's cocaine habit had progressed to a serious and expensive addiction, which he nevertheless managed to conceal from his friends and colleagues.

Simon recalls one strange and, with hindsight, significant episode during the filming of *The Pusher*. 'Felix used to sniff a lot which I thought strange, but I never questioned it. However, one day when we were making the film, he picked up the script, looked at it and said we'd got the street price of cocaine wrong. I asked him how he, of all people, who didn't smoke or drink, knew the price of cocaine. He made a joke of it and said, "Oh my dealer, my dealer, he knows everything".'

In all the years that Vossen was involved with Embargo, it was the only script edit he ever volunteered.

For all his charm and boyish enthusiasm for film, Vossen was never the most reliable of co-producers. He was, says Simon, more of an executive producer than a hands-on producer.

He could not always be counted on to attend meetings, often explaining his absence by claiming to be hob-knobbing on yachts in the Caribbean or South of France with other high net-worth individuals that he was busy making even wealthier. His secret life as a cocaine addict may also have had something to do with his lack of punctuality and poor time-management.

It is hard to know whether Vossen genuinely enjoyed the trappings of celebrity that his role as film producer brought with it. He would occasionally appear on-set but he always seemed to be happier away from the limelight. He preferred the company of producers and fellow financiers to the stars of the movies he was making. He was not an obvious fan of the film festival circuit and the hob-knobbing and networking that was part and parcel of connecting with the 'talent' and getting films made. There are some revealing images of him on stage with Charlotte Rampling and his fellow producers when *I, Anna* was screened at the 62nd Berlinale Interntional Film Festival in 2012. While the rest of the gang fool around, striking poses for the cameras, Vossen stands on the end looking faintly self-conscious.

There is no doubt, however, that at some level Vossen's vicarious connection to the real world of stage and screen was important to him. He may not have been an actor by profession, but he was remarkably adept at playing a variety of roles, as many of his friends and investors were to discover to their cost.

Notwithstanding his lack of reliability, Vossen was obsessed with Embargo's reputation and appearance, agonising over every detail of emails that went out from the company and micro-managing in a way that was sometimes productive but which, more often than not, resulted in procrastination and failure to take decisions.

Nor did he understand the creative process. 'With talent, he used to say, "why can't they do it like I tell them to do it?". That was one of the things we seemed to discuss quite often,' says Simon, 'and it was a source of constant frustration for him.'

Michael Eckelt, a Hamburg-based producer and another member of the team that brought *I, Anna* to the screen, also experienced Vossen's odd combination of enthusiasm and obsessiveness on the one hand and his terrible lack of dependability on the other. Eckelt told NDR Radio:

> He certainly wanted to be liked and he was, and probably still is, a sunny boy. He wasn't someone to force himself into becoming the centre of attention or someone who needed to satisfy his vanity by saying 'now everyone do as I say'. He wanted to spread enthusiasm and that's what he did.

Eckelt goes onto say that Vossen came across as a keen amateur rather than a professional film producer.

> But at least he was very enthusiastic. I'm more of a matter-of-fact kinda guy and he was getting in our way a little bit because of his enthusiasm. But he did everything to make the film a success... and was willing to pay for his enthusiasm with a lot of money. When you ask yourself today where he got the money from, the situation looks very different but back then it looked as if money wasn't an issue.

Indeed, even though *I, Anna* was a low-budget movie, Vossen, according to Eckelt, nevertheless hired no fewer than six London lawyers to write the legal agreement, who then contrived to produce 83 separate contracts between them. He also claimed that, contrary to Vossen's promises, the movie had failed to attract funding from the BFI or Film London and that when he chased Vossen about this because it was jeopardising parallel subsidies from Germany, he was either fobbed off or unable to reach his co-producer at all. 'For me, the issue was his complete unreliability and the fact that he disappeared for weeks or months at a time.'

The festering mistrust between the two men finally came to a head during a meeting in Hamburg. Vossen complained about Eckelt's scepticism towards the project and suggested he might want to terminate his involvement. Eckelt replied that, to date, the only funds they had succeeded in raising had come through his connections with the Hamburg film community. If Embargo wanted to proceed without him he was happy to leave and take the money with him. Vossen backed down and the film went ahead. But the working relationship between Eckelt and his fellow producers back at Embargo's London offices continued to be strained. The price for getting German funding was that part of the film had to be shot in Hamburg, which entailed building a separate studio set at considerable cost. Relations were not improved when Eckelt fell asleep in front of Southcombe, Simon and Vossen when they sat down to watch the first cut of the film.

Eckert, it is safe to say, never became a recipient of Vossen's legendary generosity or the small acts of kindness he was prone to shower on those around him. Instead, he reserved that for his fellow Embargo compadres. Simon recalls one episode which epitomised Vossen's customary kindness. It was Christmas 2011 and they were in pre-production with *I, Anna*. Simon's mother was taken seriously ill and he was called over at very short notice to Australia, where she lived. Simon booked himself an economy ticket to Sydney and flew out to the family home but while he was there his mother passed away.

> When the time came to fly back to the UK, Felix told me to rip up my return because he had bought me a seat in business class out of his own pocket. It was obviously a very emotional time for me and I just thought Felix was the most generous, kind, thoughtful human being. But he was like that. He was always buying presents for people, for our writers, things like iPads.

The Italian director Uberto Pasolini also encountered the empathetic, enthusiastic and, for once, organised side to Vossen's character. The nephew of one of Italy's greatest directors Luchino Visconti, Pasolini had enjoyed considerable commercial success as producer of the 1997 comedy *The Full Monty*, which grossed $260 million worldwide at the box office. He wanted to make a more intimate and quixotic film called *Still Life* about a council worker whose job it is to locate the next of kin of those who die alone. Starring Eddie Marsan and Joanne Froggatt, it was an exercise in creative and artistic expression, not a commercial blockbuster. Embargo agreed to back the movie, but it was largely Vossen's pet project; his two fellow partners having little to do with the film. While Pasolini wrote the script and directed, Vossen took charge of securing the finance. He did not put much of his own money into the production and what he did contribute he got back. But he succeeded in getting sufficient finance from other two sources, Redwave Films and Rai Cinema. 'It was all very smooth between the company and the other investors he brought in,' Pasolini told NDR Radio. 'He had committed to a certain share of the financing and the money arrived. The paperwork was completely on time as well. He was very supportive in my choices, particularly with the cast, he visited the set, shared ideas but was never pushy about it – he was an ideal producer in a way.'

The two men went on to become friends off-set. Vossen was successful in his own right and Pasolini was independently wealthy. And then one day, Vossen offered to invest Pasolini's money. He declined – not out of suspicion but simply because he did not want to mix their film activities with a personal financial relationship. In retrospect, had that always been Vossen's endgame? Had his professional relationship with Pasolini always been the prelude to a courtship designed to culminate in the Italian director handing over his wealth to his new best friend?

Back in London and buoyed by the moderate success of *I, Anna* and *The Sweeney*, Embargo set its sights on a bigger and more ambitious project. Simon had been developing a particular film concept for a number of years before he met either Southcombe or Vossen. It centred on two childhood friends whose relationship runs into trouble when one develops breast cancer and the other becomes pregnant for the first time. The film was to be called *Miss You Already*.

Having decided to produce it through Embargo, further work was done during the second half of 2013 to advance the project and develop a treatment for the movie. Simon then flew out to Los Angeles at the beginning of 2014 and signed up the American director Elizabeth Hardwicke to direct the film and Drew Barrymore and Toni Collette to star as the two women.

For his part, Vossen promised that he would raise the money to finance the film. He knew exactly where the bulk of the funding would come from. Having just made his peace with his parents after the long years of estrangement, he would tap back in to the bank of mum and dad. Over a 12-month period from September 2013 to September 2014, Norbert and Cornelia transferred 2.1 million euros and £500,000 into the account of Exponential Media Ventures Limited.

He also persuaded Jake Sinclair and his then girlfriend Lucy Carter to write cheques for £470,000 payable to Exponential while Angela Shaw provided a further £250,000.

In total, Vossen raised in the region of £3 million for Exponential. However, precious little of that money found its way to Embargo or the set of *Miss You Already*. Simon estimates that, at most, Vossen put £150,000 into the development of the film.

Neither Simon nor Southcombe were aware that Vossen had raised such a large amount. Quite the opposite in fact. 'Felix said that 2014 was proving a difficult year for him,' says Simon. 'He was depressed and erratic and not turning up for meetings. Nor did he come to the Cannes Film Festival in May that year. It became apparent to us that he was having trouble raising money.'

The two other partners in Embargo, therefore started talking to other film financiers as they did the rounds of drinks receptions and parties at Cannes. In the end, New Sparta Films, the production company that Simon now works for, came to the rescue and agreed to fully finance *Miss You Already*.

The erratic and volatile behaviour that Vossen was beginning to exhibit to his private investors, brought on by the extreme financial strain he was under, was replicated in his relationships with his two movie-making partners. He had never been the most diligent at turning up for meetings, but his attendance became even more sporadic and fitful. If his investors worried that he was spending too much time on his movie commitments and not enough on their affairs, then his two film partners thought the direct opposite.

Outwardly, he was still calm, confident and immensely charming. Inwardly, he had become a human pressure cooker building up a terrible head of steam. Simon says,

> His anger was irrational and would come seemingly out of the blue. Something would click and he would explode in the most hurtful and ugly way. He would get over it quite quickly and never seemed to bear a grudge or sulk, but his outbursts were quite shocking. I remember one incident where he was screaming at me under his breath in a restaurant while the person we were with went to the bathroom because, apparently, I wasn't representing the company in what he considered a perfect light. When she returned it was as if nothing had happened. His smile re-appeared and he was back to his old self.

It was the same flash of violent temper, the same ugly and sudden descent into aggression that had plagued Vossen for many, many years but which he had largely succeeded in keeping under control. Mickey de Fernandez-Paz, one of Vossen's earliest London acquaintances, recalls being on the receiving end of one such tirade a decade earlier after he had interrupted one of Vossen's 24-hour drug binges. 'He threatened to beat me up if I told Sophia about what he had been up to', Fernandez-Paz remembers. 'He grabbed me by the lapels, shoved me against a wall and punched me in the shoulder. In the end, I was a little afraid of approaching him.'

Vossen's apparent financial embarrassment was not limited to his inability to provide the finance for *Miss You Already*. It also extended to his other investment businesses. In June 2014, Vossen called Southcombe and Simon over to his offices in Jermyn Street. He told them he was in trouble because a few investors had let him down by failing to repay loans he had advanced to them personally. He then proceeded to tell them that he had taken a gamble on a £6 million property on the shores of Lake Geneva and needed to make a £300,000 repayment within a month or he would lose the entire property. He needed a loan. Could they provide him with one? It was a pack of lies from start to finish.

Vossen had often invited Southcombe and Simon to invest in his funds in the past but neither ever did for the simple reason that they did not have the money. But this was different. This was a friend in trouble who needed a helping hand in the short-term.

Neither Simon nor Southcombe were rich – they both had families to support and mortgages to pay and, as we know, they lived very frugally off the income generated from Embargo. Friendship notwithstanding, Southcombe told Vossen that, much as he would like to help, he did not have any spare money.

But Simon did agree to bail his friend out, re-mortgaging his house and maxing out his three credit cards. In total, he scraped £73,000 together and handed it over to Vossen.

'I said to Barnaby that even if Felix lost all the money I'd loaned him he would work until the day he dies to pay me back because we were brothers, it was family,' he says. 'I remember I was in Spain on the day I sent him the money because it was my birthday.'

Worse was to come. Unbeknown to the two other limbs of the three-legged stool, Vossen was preparing to steal even more of their money. By early autumn, *Miss You Already* was in pre-production and shooting was about to begin in London and on location in North Yorkshire. The £400,000 fee that Embargo was due from New Sparta for developing the project and bringing it in had just hit the firm's bank account.

Then, one day in mid-September, Southcombe rang Simon is a state of agitation. He had checked the Embargo bank balance that morning and had been shocked to discover that Vossen had transferred the £400,000 out of the company account and into one of his own personal accounts without notifying his two friends and partners. Southcombe and Simon immediately went over to Vossen's offices in Jermyn Street to confront him and insist that he reverse the transfer. 'We asked him what he thought he was doing because it was our money,' says Simon. 'He said "Look, guys, trust me. I am going to use this money to make money and then I will return it. This is what I do. Guys, just trust me".'

Reluctantly and for reasons they still cannot explain, Southcombe and Simon allowed the transfer to stand. In return, Vossen agreed there and then to become a director of Embargo at the insistence of Simon. He also signed a piece of paper pledging to return the money with interest to Embargo. It was the last they would ever see of it.

Nevertheless, the episode had left a sour taste in the mouths of Southcombe and Simon and their relationship with Vossen deteriorated from then on. Vossen was a famous hugger and patter on the back. But his pats had begun to turn into painful slaps, prompting his two friends to ask jokingly whether he was trying to kill them. The cooling of their friendship culminated in what Simon describes as a 'massive row' in January 2015. Simon had a cut of *Miss You Already* which he'd taken to Los Angeles. Vossen turned up at the viewing for four hours and then somewhat rudely walked out saying he could not stay any longer because he had to fly to New York to meet an important investor.

By now, Vossen had become even more erratic and emotional and Southcombe and Simon had actively begun to distrust him. Simon needed to get back the £73,000 that he had loaned Vossen to keep his bogus Geneva property deal alive. 'I was asking him weekly for my money back and he kept on saying it was coming but it never did,' says Simon.

In the year leading up to his disappearance Vossen was working on two other film projects. In one case he was wearing his Embargo Films hat. The other was more of a personal project. In both cases, however, he had chosen to involve close friends who were, naturally, also investors in his funds in the development of the two films. Why did he do this? Was it simply Felix being his famously inclusive self? Or was it one more example of his modus operandi in action: identify a common interest, blur the line between the professional and the personal and apply a generous dollop of flattery? After all, Felix had become a film producer of some repute. If he felt that someone else's talents could add value to a film or that their ideas were sufficiently exciting to merit his time and money, then what better testament – the Felix Vossen Good Housekeeping seal of approval.

The first project was *Plastic Fantastic*, a feel-good comedy about two women who win big on Bingo just before their fiftieth birthdays and decide to use the money to travel to Brazil for cosmetic surgery – a nose job in one case, a boob job in the other. Embargo hired the up-and-coming screen writer Lucy Moore to pen the movie and Simon travelled to Rio de Janeiro as part of a British Film Institute delegation to seek local Brazilian funding for the project.

Vossen persuaded his Embargo partners that another person they should bring on board was Elizabeth Shaw, one of the earliest investors in his Ponzi. Even though she had not worked in the film industry for a decade, Vossen was insistent that she join the project. 'He gave me a big spiel about how he only wanted to work with friends and how we would have so much fun together. I was very unsure about the subject matter, it was not my cup of tea, but he assured me it would not be crude or slapstick and more like *Calendar Girls*,' says Shaw. 'So, I agreed. I was flattered by his gushy desire to still want to work with me after all these years although I had no intention of going back into the film industry. I think it gave him a new hook into me.'

It is also one of the reasons why many of the investors believe that their money was secretly diverted into Embargo and used to help the company pay its way. Simon vigorously denies this, saying that Embargo was as much a victim of Vossen as his other investors. He agrees that Vossen put money into Embargo's film projects but that the funding always came from Exponential and any returns went back to Exponential. None of the money ever went directly into Embargo or helped its partners to live a life of Riley. 'We lived frugally in a tiny office on salaries of £2,500 a month. We had to re-mortgage our own houses and lend the money to the business.'

The second film was a project that had been developed by Peter Leinster, who had made a great many TV commercials in his time but, like others before him in the world of advertising, wanted to graduate to the making of full-length movies. By coincidence, the film also had a Latin American setting: it was about a British soldier who travels to Argentina to meet and make peace with the family of an Argentinian conscript he had killed during the Falklands War.

Vossen was hugely excited by the film initially and promised Leinster that it was exactly the kind of project that Embargo Films had been created for. The two friends met regularly to review progress on the script and discuss how the film would be taken forward. 'Then,' says Leinster's wife Jane, 'Felix phoned up one day and told us that the project would not be going ahead. It was as simple as that.'

It was around the same time that the Leinsters told Vossen of their decision to withdraw their original capital investment from his fund, leaving in only the 'profit' they believed he had made on their behalf.

7

THE PONZI BEGINS TO UNRAVEL

With the benefit of that most precious of gifts, hindsight, it is now clear that things had begun to go seriously wrong for Vossen as early as 2010. His moods were becoming more unpredictable and his temperament more irascible. It was proving increasingly difficult for some investors to get financial statements from him; others worried that the pre-occupation with his film producing career was proving too much of a distraction; and his personal behaviour was becoming more erratic and unsettling – especially his tendency to lapse into 'kiddy' voices and the disturbing transference that he manifested whenever he got among his stuffed toys.

His explanations for failing to show up for meetings or failing to make timely payments to investors were also becoming more outlandish and unlikely: he told his new girlfriend, Clare Obsorne, that he had suffered a brain tumour that year and then in 2011 he blamed his memory problems on the medication he was receiving for the aforementioned tumour – all of which was entirely fabricated.

Subsequent analysis of Vossen's bank records would also establish that what share trading activity he was undertaking had largely dried up by 2010. There was some evidence of small amounts of bond trading but little else that would make very much money. And there was nothing to support Vossen's oft-repeated boast that his fund had swollen in value to £350m. In reality, Vossen was struggling to make ends meet and keep his creditors at bay. He had begun sweeping his accounts regularly for tiny amounts of money to pay off outstanding bills. And there was clear evidence that when larger sums of money came in from one investor, they were quickly used to pay off other investors: in other words, the Ponzi was in full swing.

Although they did not recognise it as such at the time, the red flags were fluttering in the faces of investors. Angela Shaw says:

> Everything seemed fine until the end of 2009. Then things became erratic. I had to push him to get statements, to know what I was earning and very often he wasn't available. I think it was the film business that changed things. I got cross with him on several occasions because he was not available when he said he would be and didn't deliver statements when he said he would.
>
> Things hadn't been good but somehow or other I always managed to get money out of him. I thought it was because he had too many other pursuits and had got too involved with the film industry. Trading was how he made money, but film was his real dream. I believe he used our money to fund his films.
>
> I thought he had emotional hang-ups and difficulties in his relationships and I would have said even then that he was on the obsessive-compulsive end of the spectrum, but I would never have

> thought he was psychotic or psychopathic. It never crossed my mind that there was something going on with him. I couldn't see the side of him that was going wrong.

Jake Sinclair had also noticed a change in Vossen's demeanour and behaviour around the same time. He says:

> The scales very slowly lifted from my eyes. From 2010 there were signs that things were not as they should be. In my attempts to get regular financial feedback from him I started pushing harder to the point of being almost rude to him and saying the unmentionable. At one dinner with him and some other friends, I asked, 'How do we know you're not a complete crook?' We all laughed, of course. But it was also clear that I was uttering a truth that deep down we all dreaded.
>
> At this stage, I wasn't trying to get money out of him. My concern was that he wasn't providing me with regular financial information. Every time I wanted a statement, it became a campaign that would last for months so that by the time I got the information I would be exhausted.
>
> I remember calling him on one occasion and him picking up the phone with that familiar 'woe is me' tone and telling me about his father's alleged prostate cancer. I interrupted his story quite tersely and demanded an explanation for the lateness of his quarterly reports. Felix feigned outrage that I could be so brusque and callous given his personal circumstances. As ever, it was a brilliantly convincing Vossen performance.

Sinclair was so concerned about Vossen's health and general well-being that he volunteered the services of his own personal trainer and had a piece of Pilates equipment known as a 'Reformer' installed in his apartment.

> I thought 'this guy is looking after my money, I need him to stay well.'
>
> At the same time, I noticed a number of things going on in his life – ill-health or acts of personal misfortune which explained why he hadn't produced reports. I started to hear stories of his brother breaking a leg, his mother having cancer, his father having cancer or a very good friend dying.

As ever with Vossen, however, such occasional qualms about his reliability and probity were never allowed to harden into serious doubts, much less concerns about criminality. Part of that was down to his ability to banish doubts through the sheer power of his own personality; part of it was undoubtedly down to the willingness of investors to suspend their own disbelief – both over Vossen's personal behaviour and the extraordinary returns he appeared to be achieving. 'Throughout my relationship with him my judgement was overshadowed by self-interest and, if I'm really honest with myself, greed,' says Sinclair. 'With anyone else if you'd had that level of poor financial accounting you'd have called the police, but with Felix you didn't because Felix was Felix. He did things his own way and you made allowances for him.'

Charles Huntley says that with hindsight, the warning signs were also flashing for him and his wife. 'At numerous times, it was difficult for us to get money out of him,' he says. 'Felix would compare himself to a mad professor and say he was a genius at trading but was terrible at admin. Whenever you were doing your tax return you had to chase and chase him for statements. It was always a fight.'

But the danger signals were not recognised as such. 'Looking back, I'd have to say my attention to detail was not as good as it should have been,' Huntley concedes, 'but I was dealing with the deaths of both my brother and my mother.'

Matthew Allen also had nagging doubts. 'I had friends saying they weren't sure about this guy Vossen. A very good friend of mine who worked for a hedge fund said "why don't you just put half of your money in?" That was on my mind, but Felix said if you put this much in we can put you into this fund where you get a higher return.'

Allen, along with others, also recalls one of those pivotal moments when things could have turned out differently. He had been due to take his sceptical hedge fund friend to meet Vossen, but the meeting was postponed at the last minute because his friend was detained in the office. It was never rescheduled because Allen and his wife moved to Brazil a short time later.

On another occasion, Allen's mother, Christine, was meeting Vossen prior to making her investment and had been due to take along a good friend of hers who happened to be a very experienced investor himself. 'He was always asking my mum "How's this German of yours? He sounds far too good to be true." On the morning of the meeting, there was an emergency of some kind and he couldn't make it. I'm sure had he been there he would have stopped my mum or rowed her back.'

Despite the close relationship that had developed between her husband and Vossen, Jane Leinster also harboured doubts. 'He was one of the most charismatic people you could meet but there was something about him,' she now says.

> I was worried because we were putting huge trust in him. All the women partners had concerns. He was this totally controlled

> person who didn't drink and wasn't going on swanky holidays all the time. He could be a bit jittery at times, but we thought this was just because he was under huge pressure. It was only after his arrest that we found out he also had a cocaine habit.

The fact that Vossen was able to ride these occasional waves of investor disquiet is testament to the trust he ultimately engendered. Even his casual attitude towards administration and his lax approach to book-keeping were construed as positives. As David Benziger says:

> I had to pursue him and his fictitious employee Jennifer Keller for paperwork. Eventually he would send me something, but it was quite amateurish. My girlfriend Indira was more nervous than I was, but I decided, well, the guy probably spends most of his time investing rather than drawing up fancy balance sheets which I figured was actually to my advantage because I was more interested in the returns than the paperwork.

Vossen's hold over his investor friends also had something to do with the outward appearance of wealth and success he was able to project. How could he possibly be anything other than the genuine article when he was able to run his investment business from premises in London's West End and central Zurich with rent costs alone of CHF29,000 a month?

In fact, what little remained of Vossen's crumbling financial empire was slipping quickly into the sea. By 2012 he was struggling to keep his head above water and pay bills as they fell due. From this point onwards, he began to place less emphasis on his supposed investment strategy of day trading in technology stocks and started to market what he called 'short-term investment opportunities' to existing and new clients.

Vossen, so he said, had carried out extensive research on a small number of technology companies – his favourite being Apple. He would then wait for the financial results reporting season and put together a complex financial instrument enabling him to bet on what he believed would happen to the stocks in companies that he was following.

He claimed that he was primarily putting his family's own money into these short-term investment opportunities but generously offered to allow other private investors outside the family circle a slice of the action. For example, there was the half a million pounds that Jon Peterson had put into one such investment but got back after his wife became uneasy.

Mandy Collins and her mother Mavis had always been wary of Vossen, too. Mandy recalls one incident which should have rung alarm bells: her father had developed a new type of camera lens and had arranged a meeting with another, specialist engineering firm to discuss the possibility of them funding its development and ultimate production. Felix came along to the meeting. Mandy had grown used to Vossen's physicality – the very full body hug accompanied by a strange little noise that he would emit whenever they met. But on this occasion, he overstepped the mark. Half way through the meeting, he lent back in his chair, stretched his legs out and began playing footsie with Mandy under the table. 'It was odd and really unprofessional apart from anything else,' she says. 'There were quite a few things that put me off him.'

But for Mandy and her parents, the real Damascene moment came in May 2014. Bill's lifelong ambition had been to fly in a Zeppelin and so he booked a family trip to Friedrichshafen in southern Germany, the birthplace of the Zeppelin and now the location for tourist flights on board the iconic airship. For Bill in particular, it would be a weekend to remember. The only thing he had to decide was which particular flight to book from the three choices available. Should they choose to fly over the Baroque buildings of Ravensburg or would it make for a better experience to enjoy the aerial view of the 12th century castle at Salem? If neither of these made for the perfect trip then they could always select option three and enjoy a bird's eye view of the Bavarian island of Lindau, sitting as it does in the crystal-clear waters of Lake Constance.

He had one other decision to make: should Felix be there? Bill naturally insisted that his friend, mentor and financial guru absolutely must join their party. Mandy takes up the story:

> On the morning of the trip, Felix rang me on my mobile as we were driving to Heathrow. He spoke to me in a strange high-pitched voice and then switched back into his charming mode. He said he couldn't come because his sister had had a miscarriage. My mum looked at me and raised an eyebrow as if to say, 'I knew he wouldn't come'. The whole of the four days he was texting my Dad, saying I'm coming, book a table at dinner for me. But he never turned up. My dad was upset and at the end of the trip my mum said, 'He's just a liar'. I said, yes, there's something really weird about that bloke. That was the catalyst for me. It's those small things that you read into people, just before they lie, and he just couldn't disguise it.

The acute financial strain Vossen was under probably explains much of his odd behaviour. But outwardly, he continued to project an image of success, even as his financial empire was beginning to collapse. In the summer of 2013, he left number 107 Jermyn Street and moved across the street to an even bigger and more impressive apartment in number 15, a five-storey block adjacent to the upmarket leather goods retailer Osprey. It was the corporate equivalent of redecorating the company reception and renewing the chairman's limousine – sure signs, bankruptcy practitioners will tell you, of a business on the brink of collapse. The number of screens in his new office had shrunk from six to two. The huge 'back-up system' which took up so much room in Vossen's first Jermyn Street apartment had also disappeared. Instead, he seemed to spend even more time on the telephone. All of this struck some of his investors as strange. But Vossen re-assured them by saying his trading strategy was now so sophisticated and streamlined that he only needed a couple of terminals and a mobile to do what he needed to do.

And he could still fall back on his parents. Norbert and Cornelia had invested one million euros with their son in 2009 and again in 2010, in the belief that he was earning returns of 20 per cent and was properly registered with and regulated by the Swiss financial watchdog FINMA. In 2013 he tapped them for another three million euros and in 2014 they made two further investments of 600,000 euros and £500,000 – these final payments going into the account of the film financing venture Exponential Media Ventures. Why wouldn't his parents continue to invest? After all, their statement of account at the end of November 2014 showed them to be in credit to the tune of a shade under $5 million.

With the Ponzi in full-scale meltdown, a by-now desperate Vossen cast his net wherever he could, near and far, in search of more funds. During the course of 2014 he tricked Patrick Nugent and Niall Langley, both friends of Peter Leinster, out of £1 million and £150,000 respectively. He gathered in a further $40,000 from Robert Hales, a friend of Jon Peterson. He even tricked his godfather, Michael Jahr, out of EUR100,00.

Even that was not enough to meet the demands on the fund from other investors and so Vossen came up with another ruse over the summer months of 2014. He told his co-producers at Embargo, Barnaby Southcombe and Chris Simon, his girlfriend Clare Obsorne and a number of other friends, including Jake Sinclair, that he had been badly let down by an unnamed investor who had reneged on a very large loan Vossen had advanced to them. He told them that this temporary cash-flow crisis had put in jeopardy a £6 million investment he had made in a property on the shores of Lake Geneva. Unless he could raise £300,000 within a month, then he would lose the entire £6 million investment. As we know, Vossen used the same cover story to persuade his film partner Chris Simon to lend him £73,000 that he could not afford to give.

Another movie friend he approached for financial help was Uberto Pasolini, the Italian director with whom Vossen had co-produced the movie *Still Life*. Pasolini politely turned him down. But others were not so hesitant and the cash duly flowed in, including a substantial amount from a new victim – Jake Sinclair's then girlfriend Lucy Carter. With his usual methodical planning, Vossen had already seeded the ground with the couple. Six months earlier, Sinclair had casually mentioned to Vossen that Lucy had £100,000 sitting in the bank. Vossen suggested she deposit the money with him. 'He said he'd make sure Lucy made a £5,000 profit on her investment, says Sinclair.

> He rang up two months later to ask for her bank details so he could repay the money. Then, in a staggering act of duplicity, he rang back a few minutes later to say he'd made a mistake and that in fact he owed her £108,000 not £105,000 because he'd done this very successful trade in Apple shares. That small detail was absolute proof to us of his probity.

Lucy duly received her £108,000. So, when Vossen suggested six months later that she re-invest the money with him, there was no question of not handing most of it over. 'We thought, sure, why not,' says Sinclair. 'So Lucy made an investment of £95,000. She never got it back. He played us quite brilliantly.'

Another investor whom Vossen played brilliantly was Neil Osmond, a Guernsey-based businessman. Osmond had invested some £250,000 with Vossen over a six-year period, the last instalment being made in December 2014. A month before he made that final payment, Osmond visited Vossen in Switzerland in the company of one of his friends who also happened to be an accountant. They wanted to go direct to his office on the fourth floor of Bellevue Haus am See, overlooking Lake Zurich, but Vossen persuaded them to have something to eat first.

After a long lunch, he took them around the corner to the office. Osmond recounted the experience to the German newspaper *Welt am Sonntag*. He says that when they entered the office there was a bank of computers on display but no paperwork or files. Nor was there any of the usual detritus of office life – empty coffee cups, waste paper bins, post-it notes and the like. Two young women then appeared from nowhere dressed in coats and were introduced by Vossen as his assistants.

Osmond asked them whether Robert Gassner (the Vossen employee with whom he had been in regular email contact) was in that day. They both looked at him blankly until Vossen interjected and swiftly changed the topic of conversation.

Neither of the women had business cards and no one made or received any telephone calls during the hour they were there. When they left the office and entered the lift, Vossen had difficulty working out which button to press for the ground floor.

Osmond found it all a little odd at the time but thought no more of it. With the benefit of hindsight, however, it is far from obvious to him that he was ever in a functioning office with anyone employed by Vossen. He wasn't even certain it was a building that Vossen had ever been inside before.

By the time Christmas, 2014 arrived Vossen's Ponzi was on the very brink. Despite the cash injections from his parents and the money raised through the Lake Geneva property scam, Vossen was on the point of going bust. He had even resorted to bulk buying Lottery tickets in the vain hope that his numbers would come up and deliverance would be his.

Vossen, however, was still managing to conceal the enormous strains on his crumbling financial empire. Matthew Allen recalls a conversation he had with him.

> It was Christmas Eve. He was driving in the Swiss mountains and I was riding my bike down the Copacabana and life was good. I was trying to get in touch with his accountant over the dividend payment due on the short-term investment Felix had put our money into. He began chatting in his charming and funny way and asking about my mum and any anger that I felt disappeared. That was the last time I spoke to him.

In a last desperate burst of action, Vossen managed to secure some fresh investments from new and existing investors: he parted Angela Shaw from the remaining £250,000 she had left from her house sale; he scooped £240,000 from Stewart Gregory; the Roberts's gave him another $600,000 over Christmas and into January 2015, and a further £50,000 came from Neil Osmond who had previously invested $370,000 with Vossen.

Unfortunately for Vossen, history was repeating itself. Like other Ponzi fraudsters before him, the money coming in was not sufficient to meet the redemptions being sought by an increasing number of investors. Peter Leinster's sister Margaret had succeeded in getting Vossen to repay the entire £1 million she had invested with him in 2012 and 2013, making her the only investor not to suffer any loss.

And so, as 2015 began Vossen was encircled by increasingly nervous and suspicious investors either asking for their money back or demanding re-assurance that their money was safe. Naturally, individual investors kept their concerns to themselves for fear of provoking a run on the Bank of Vossen should other investors get wind that the redemptions were piling up. Little did they know that his Ponzi was teetering on the brink and a mere eight weeks away from collapse.

Jake Sinclair, for instance, had privately arranged to fly out on his own to Zurich to meet the new firm of accountants that Vossen had supposedly hired. The date for the visit was 13 March. Its purpose was to allow Sinclair to inspect the new state-of-the-art accounts system in which Vossen claimed to have invested. It would allow investors to track the performance of their fund online at any time of the night or day. Vossen even paid for Sinclair's airline ticket. He never got to use it because Vossen flew the coop 10 days before.

The Leinsters unwittingly struck the first blow. During their seven-year relationship with Vossen, they had invested £3.8 million and received back £1.98 million of this in lump sum payments and dividends. Two weeks into the new year, they phoned Vossen to tell him they had decided to take out the remainder of their original investment – some £2 million – leaving only their presumed 'profit' in the fund. It was money Vossen did not have.

Meanwhile, Angela Shaw was on the phone to Vossen almost daily because she now needed £250,000 back from her pot to purchase a house she had just found in Mexico, close to where her youngest daughter Grace was living. 'I was pulling my hair out and screaming at him because I was half way through the transaction and had already put down a £12,000 deposit,' she says. 'He promised he would send me the money and then made excuse after excuse, after excuse. It had been sent to the wrong account or his brokers in New York had lost it.'

Jon Peterson had also decided to take out the remaining £1.5 million that he thought he had left in Vossen's fund. It was, he says, partly a desire to do something else with the money and partly a sixth sense that it was time to move on. 'Some of his stories had become a little bit spicy and hard to believe. Towards the end we all began to get a gut feel that Felix was increasingly implausible,' he says. 'With Felix there was always a bit more sausage than there was sizzle.'

Despite the generalised feeling that something was not quite right, investors who were very good friends with one another were careful to keep quiet about their individual decisions to withdraw their money. 'Was it a selfish thing of wanting to get your money out before other people, or was it because people did not want to be seen questioning Felix or his business model?' Peterson wonders. In any event, his finance director was on the phone on a weekly basis to Vossen asking when the money would be transferred into Peterson's account. To no avail.

By now, it was February and the jitters were spreading to other investors. The Huntleys had been withdrawing money at the rate of $25,000 a quarter. But they now needed to make a much more substantial withdrawal. Charles was wrapping up his mother's estate following her death and needed to distribute the money she had invested with Vossen to the beneficiaries of her will. Vossen produced a bank transfer document which appeared to show that the funds were indeed being paid into their account. He would send a similarly forged document to Neil Osmond.

Mandy Collins had been emailing Vossen asking for her money back too. 'Steven and I had split up, it had never been my choice to invest with Felix and I didn't really like the guy and didn't have any contact with him. I wanted to start taking my money out in reasonably large chunks.'

Indira Roberts was also trying to repatriate her money. 'She called me and said that something fishy was going on and I should get my funds out,' says David Benziger. 'I brushed it off as female paranoia.' It would almost certainly have made no difference had Benziger heeded his girlfriend's warning because, by then, the game was almost up.

With the benefit of hindsight, it seems that Vossen himself was seeding the ground for his disappearance, tidying up his affairs and making his regretful farewells to those nearest and dearest to him. During the course of February he had lengthy telephone conversations with his on-off girlfriend Sophia Rafaat, apologising for the fact that he could never be what she wanted him to be, nor could he give her what she wanted from him – marriage and children.

A fortnight before he fled, Vossen went to stay with the Petersons for the weekend at their Oxfordshire home. Vossen knew that Jon Peterson was a great believer in value for money and generally liked to travel in the cheapest way possible, so he decided to rib him by taking a taxi from London all the way to their house. After a long country walk on the Saturday – with Vossen, as usual, wearing smart but entirely unsuitable shoes – the three friends enjoyed a quiet but convivial supper. It had been a long day and the Petersons were exhausted by Vossen's non-stop conversation. They therefore said they were retiring early. Because they had house guests, they had decided not to bother setting the burglar alarm. That night, shortly after everyone had headed off to bed, Peterson says he heard someone moving about downstairs in what sounded like the study or the kitchen. But he assumed Felix had just got up to fetch a glass of water or relieve himself and thought no more about it.

When Peterson discovered a short while later through the investor grapevine that Vossen had disappeared, he went straight to his study to retrieve the file containing records of all his investments. The file had disappeared. 'Felix took it, I have no doubt about it,' says Peterson.

A few days before his disappearance, Peterson tried unsuccessfully to contact Vossen to arrange a face-to-face meeting. After failing to reach him by phone, he called his old friend Roger Phillips to express his concern, only to be told not to worry. 'Felix often goes offline for weeks on end,' Phillips reassured his old friend.

In fact, Vossen was paying his very last house call to an investor. It was the afternoon of Sunday, March 1 and the person he was visiting was his girlfriend Clare Obsorne – described in the High Court as a 'cash cow' used by Vossen to provide him with the funds to pay off 'more assertive' investors. When he arrived at her parents' home in Essex, Vossen was in a clearly agitated state. He admitted to his girlfriend there and then that the bank transfer document he had shown to the Huntleys was, in fact, a forgery. He also begged her for more money and she obliged, transferring £40,000 to him a day later, Monday 2 March.

The day after that, Felix Burghardt Norbert Vossen disappeared off the face of the earth.

8

ON THE RUN

It was the second week of March 2015 and Stewart Gregory was preparing to make his way home from the House of Commons having enjoyed a convivial lunch with Julian Lewis, the Conservative MP for New Forest East. Gregory was interested in using his film directing skills to make a biopic about the World War One aviator Kink Kinkaid. Who better to speak to about the project than Lewis, who had long been fascinated by the airman and had written a well-received biography of him a few years earlier?

After thanking Lewis for lunch and his insights into Kinkaid, Gregory left the Palace of Westminster and strolled across the southern edge of Parliament Square and on into Whitehall, passing Downing Street and Horseguards as he headed east in the direction of Trafalgar Square. Spring was in the air and there was a spring in Gregory's step. He was making for Embankment Tube station where he had intended taking the Northern Line back to his Islington home. But as he neared the top of Whitehall, Gregory's destination changed. His pace quickened and instead of turning right for the Underground, he performed a sharp left and began to make his way round to Pall Mall and then across St James towards Jermyn Street. Towards 15 Jermyn Street to be precise.

Gregory had only been an investor with Vossen since the previous October, but he was already becoming worried about his £260,000 investment. 'I'd been getting very frustrated with Vossen,' he says. 'I hadn't received any of my paperwork and I was starting to feel quite concerned. I got a text from him saying everything was fine and in hand and that we'd meet up after Christmas. That didn't happen, and I began to feel quite sick, you'd phone up and get an answering machine all the time. Cracks were starting to show, and I was not entirely convinced he was who he said he was. He'd also told me that if you ever want all your money back you can have it.'

So, on the spur of the moment as he walked through London that day, Gregory resolved to see Vossen face-to-face, not necessarily to get his money back but to gain re-assurance that his money was safe. Gregory had been to 15 Jermyn Street before to see Vossen's trading set up. With his shock of jet black hair, piercing eyes and bohemian dress sense, it is fair to say that Gregory strikes a memorable cut. When he arrived at Vossen's building, he pressed the buzzer and was let in by the concierge. 'The guy on the desk recognised me immediately and said: "He's gone. Do you want to sit down?" He said Felix's brother Norbert has been in looking for him and the family are very concerned.'

At that moment Gregory knew his money was decidedly not safe. He was not alone. The same shocking realisation had also dawned on other investors in the previous few days as news began to spread of Vossen's sudden and unexplained disappearance.

This is what we know of the flight of Felix Vossen. On Tuesday, 3 March 2015 he wakes early and takes a taxi from Jermyn Street to London City airport. There, he buys a coffee using his credit card and then boards a plane to Zurich. Prior to his departure from Jermyn Street, Vossen has left instructions with a removals company to take his remaining personal possessions out of the apartment, empty a Yellow Box storage facility he had been using and shred all his financial and personal files. After landing in Zurich he goes to Waaggasse 4 and clears his office there of files and any other material that might incriminate him or provide clues as to his eventual destination.

Vossen has CHF500,000 (approximately £380,000) in cash with him. This is his getaway money, stashed away at his various addresses in London and Zurich, ready for the day when his Ponzi inevitably collapses and he is forced to flee. He will need it to survive during his year on the run.

At some point that same Tuesday he also spends £800 by credit card booking three other flights with Swiss International Airlines. In addition, he emails a bank remittance form, seemingly from the Zurich branch of Credit Suisse, to one of his investors, Neil Osmond, confirming that he has made a payment from his personal account to that of Osmond. It is another forgery.

His credit card is also used to pay CHF46 for fuel at a BP petrol station in Pratteln, close to Basel. It is unclear where he is heading, whether he is by himself and whether he is even in the car. In Basel, his Embargo Films credit card gets charged CHF500 by a local taxi company – a big enough fare to get him back to Zurich airport.

Vossen's final act that Tuesday is to contact his family and a small number of friends. He sends his family an email with three emoji red hearts and two kisses in the subject field but nothing in the body of the message. Chris Simon and Barnaby Southcombe, his business partners at Embargo Films, receive identical emails. At the time, they were putting the final touches to *Miss You Already* and were at a meeting in the Soho offices of the post-production company Molinaire. Roger Phillips, the second biggest victim of Vossen's fraud, receives a picture text message. It appears to be a cartoon of a cat running off with a bag.

The following day, Wednesday, 4 March, Vossen's credit card is used at a café in Zurich airport and he uses an ATM at the airport to withdraw a further 14,140 euros and CHF11,000 from the private banking account he holds with Credit Suisse in St Mortiz. It is unclear what he did with his previously purchased airline tickets and what mode of transport he uses to escape Switzerland. But we do know that at some point after leaving Switzerland, and before he arrives in Spain, he spends some time in France. Once in Spain, there is speculation that he spent time in the Sierra Nevada mountain range in the Andalucian region close to Granada – an area he knew well from the time that his family owned a holiday property there.

On Thursday 5 March, Osmond has what he describes as 'telephonic communication' with Vossen and is able to place him in Zurich on that day. After that, his phone goes dead. On the same day, Vossen's mother Cornelia contacts the Swiss police to express concern about her son's well-being and whereabouts.

The last financial trace of Vossen appears to be on Monday, 9 March when his Embargo credit card is used again to pay for a CHF400 taxi ride somewhere in Switzerland.

After that, he disappears from the radar.

Save for one final text message, apparently composed on a Playstation terminal, sent by Vossen ten days later on the evening of 19 March to his former girlfriend Sophia Rafaat and his current one, Clare Obsorne. By turns apologetic and self-pitying and punctuated with inappropriate exclamation marks, this is what he writes: 'I'm so very, very sorry! I never meant to hurt you or anyone and always thought I could make it right in the end but it just kept getting worse and worse. I am trying to figure out a way to make things better. I don't know how yet. I've let so many people down. You didn't deserve any of this. I really am so sorry!'

Not as sorry as Vossen's family, friends, investors and colleagues would be. The first they knew of his disappearance was the same day that his mother had reported him missing, Thursday, 5 March. That morning Barnaby Southcombe, disconcerted by the peculiar email he had received two days earlier, contacted the Leinsters to ask if they knew where Vossen was. Jane was outside working in one of the flower beds, dead-heading some roses. 'I came in from the garden and Peter was on the phone to Barnaby,' she recalls. 'Barnaby was asking him if he had heard from Felix because he had not showed up at the office. The moment I heard mention of his name I knew that something was wrong. The penny dropped that something was awry though our initial thought was that something had happened to him, that he was ill perhaps or had suffered a mental breakdown or maybe even dropped dead with a heart attack.'

With the benefit of hindsight, it would not have been a surprise if Vossen's drug addiction had claimed his life – deaths from cocaine have more than trebled in the UK over the past five years as purity levels rise, street prices fall and access to the unregulated internet makes cocaine easier to obtain. Cocaine can now be delivered in England and Wales faster than a pizza, according to one drug addiction specialist.

But Vossen's friends and investors were not aware of his drug dependency. Only that he was not where he was supposed to be. Uberto Pasolini, his Italian film producing friend, worried for example that Vossen might have had a relapse following an earlier operation he had supposedly undergone to remove a non-existent brain tumour.

With the speculation as to Vossen's possible whereabouts and fate going into overdrive, Southcombe decided to get in touch directly with the family. Vossen's younger brother Norbert came over immediately. He was ready to break into Felix's flat but there was no need to as the concierge held a spare key. Once inside, it became clear that Vossen had not fallen ill at all or disappeared temporarily on one of his by-now-familiar periods of unexplained absence. The apartment had been stripped bare of Vossen's personal possessions and the wardrobes and drawers were empty of clothes. He had flown the coup.

Over the subsequent weekend and into the following week, the bush telegraph buzzed red hot as, one by one, investors made contact with other investors to communicate the dire news about Vossen. Patrick Nugent, a late investor, called Chris Simon on the Monday to say that Vossen had missed a meeting with him. Simon had the painful task of telling him why Vossen had not shown up.

The shock waves were felt most forcibly 5,000 miles away on the north-east coast of Mexico, where Angela Shaw was in the middle of her house purchase in Puerto Morelos, a few miles south of Cancun. 'I went dead. I went into total shock. I was so traumatised,' she says. 'I could not believe that all my money had disappeared. I thought I had nearly £3m million in a fund by this time. I'd been with him 12 years. It was not only that which had gone but my house money. Everything had gone – my future, the roof over my head, everything. Also, the betrayal was so horrendous. I couldn't believe he had betrayed me like that, taking my last money knowing I was already 74 and couldn't just go back to work again and start my life again. He knew all that and knew how much I relied on that money for my retirement. How could he do that? Whatever emotional disorders he had, how could he be that cruel?'

Back in London, meanwhile, Steven Walters was in his London flat, one of two properties he owned, the other being a small house in Hertfordshire. A bundle of creative and nervous energy, Walters divided his time between the two homes during the rare periods when he was not obsessively working away in an editing suite. He remembers it as if it were yesterday: 'I'd just got the manual out to set the heating – four days in one place, three days in the other – and that's when I got the call from Peter to say that Felix had gone missing. The next thing I knew, Stewart Gregory rang me to ask if I knew about Felix and where he had gone.'

On the Wednesday of that week, 11 March, Neil Osmond broke off a holiday with friends in the Swiss Alps and took a train to Zurich in the faint hope that there might still be some trace of Vossen in the city. He visited the office of Vossen's trading companies in Waaggasse 4. On the outside, the building still bore the VCP brassplate. On the inside, however, Vossen's office was empty, save for an iPad and UK mobile phone which had been left on a table. Osmond contacted the City of London police to report Vossen missing and register a claim of suspected fraud. He also spoke to Severin Roelli, a partner in the Swiss law firm Pestalozzi Law who as well as being Vossen's attorney, had been a director of VCP Asset Management until the previous October. Roelli was one of the two advisers – the other being Michael Conrad – that Vossen had supposedly entrusted with disbursing his fund and returning the proceeds to investors should anything happen to its founder. Roelli expressed concern at Vossen's disappearance but said he had not seen him for a number of weeks. Client confidentiality, he added, prevented him from telling Vossen's investors much more than this.

Osmond then headed for Zurich's main police station to report that he may have been the victim of a fraud perpetrated by Vossen. Earlier that day, Norbert had also been in to see the Zurich police to provide them with personal details of his brother to assist with their search. Osmond was interviewed by two Swiss detectives – Alexander Wust and Christian Vuille – who quizzed him at length on his relationship with Vossen. The two officers told Osmond that they too were looking for Vossen. However, until the moment that Osmond walked into their station they had been unaware that Vossen might be guilty of any financial crimes. That evening, the police investigation changed from a missing persons enquiry into a manhunt.

Finally and for good measure, Osmond made one last call to Andrew Domaille, the head of financial crime investigation with the Guernsey police. Osmond knew that Vossen had offshore accounts in the Channel Isles and wanted to make sure he had covered all his bases. Domaille told him that he would notify the Guernsey Financial Services Commission of the information Osmond had passed to him.

The speed with which Vossen's victims were able to organise themselves into an action group was remarkable given that prior to his disappearance many of them were unknown to one another. On Thursday, 12 March – still only nine days after Vossen fled his London apartment – a core group of 13 investors held their first crisis meeting, gathered together for the first time in the cramped Soho offices of Embargo Films. Amongst those present at the meeting were Barnaby Southcombe and Chris Simon from Embargo, the Leinsters, Roger Phillips, Steven Walters and Mandy Collins. Indira Roberts had also flown in from New York. Other victims were invited to join on a telephone conference line.

Peter Leinster quickly agreed to take on the de facto role of group co-ordinator to marshal the huge amount of information that had begun to circulate among investors and prevent everyone drowning in a sea of emails and extraneous information. The group established a series of urgent workstreams and different members were given responsibility for each one: legal representation, liaison with police authorities, checking of assets, tracing of Vossen's movements, investigation of his registered Swiss and offshore companies.

Indira Roberts agreed to lead a team of investors researching Vossen's Guernsey connection. Clare Obsorne was trawling her records for any conversations she had had with Vossen about his Geneva property in the hope that this was a real asset as opposed to a fictional one that the group could lay claim to. Leinster himself recalled that Vossen had once confided to him that he had invested in an Old Master as a means of keeping some of his money safe and was investigating whether the work of art actually existed. Southcombe and Simon at Embargo, meanwhile, were tracking Vossen's use of the company credit card following his disappearance.

Finally, Roger Phillips agreed to head up discussions with two firms of private investigators, Haymarket and Rubus, that the group had contacted believing that this might be a quicker and more effective avenue to hunting down Vossen than waiting for the combined police forces of Switzerland, Britain and the Channel Isles to crank into cumbersome action.

The group also agreed to set up a fighting fund, with each member contributing in proportion to the amount invested with Vossen. The fund raised £118,000. By this time, the investors had already hired the law firm Russell-Cooke who in turn instructed James Ramsden QC as they prepared to go after Vossen. Ramsden stressed two things: first, that if the group were to have any hope of recovering their money then they needed to get a judge to issue a worldwide order freezing Vossen's assets as rapidly as possible; second, for that to succeed then they needed to be able to present the court with as much corroborating evidence as they could lay their hands on – signed investment contracts, records of investments made, statements of account, bank account details and the like.

After 36 hours of frantic evidence gathering, Mr Ramsden appeared in the High Court before Mr Justice Lewis on Friday, 13 March on behalf of Vossen's investors to apply for the asset freezing order.

Had the press been alert to it, the hearing before Mr Justice Lewis would have yielded an impressive crop of lurid headlines and some even juicier copy. Sat behind Mr Ramsden, QC were 19 of his clients. For some of them, it was the first time they had met their co-investors and, now, fellow victims. Then, the QC proceeded methodically to set out the prima facie evidence that would justify the granting of the freezing order by demonstrating how his clients had fallen victims to a Ponzi. There were, he told the judge, eight characteristics of a Ponzi scheme and each of them applied in the case of the fraud perpetrated by Vossen.

First, the arrangements made by Vossen with his investors were 'unconventional and erratic' in nature – consistent with his deliberate intention of keeping relationships sufficiently informal to make it easier for him to subject them to 'dishonest manipulation'. This social relationship with many of the claimants enabled Vossen to brush off requests for repayment or divert them with sob stories about the supposed illnesses of various family members.

Second, when repayments were made, they were often in 'small tantalising amounts' which were just big enough to prevent investors from reaching for their lawyers or becoming overtly aggressive with him but not so large as to make a serious dent in the size of Vossen's investment fund.

Third, the way Vossen reported back to investors on the performance of his investment funds was 'episodic and inconsistent'. When investors complained about the lack of reporting they would receive impressive-looking flow charts demonstrating an encouraging upward trend in returns or simple statements of account apparently showing the quarterly gain attributable to their particular portion of the fund.

Fourth, Vossen employed the same tactics of delay, prevarication and obfuscation when dealing with investors and each of them could cite numerous examples of this.

Fifth, the use of forged documents purporting to show that money had been transferred from one of Vossen's accounts to that of an investor – of which the Huntleys and Neil Osmond were just two examples.

Sixth, Vossen's urgent appeals for short-term loans, usually on the basis that he was temporarily illiquid, so that he could make limited repayments to those investors who had stamped their feet and insisted on getting money out of him.

Seventh, the use of 'especially cynical lies' to explain away Vossen's inability to make particular repayments at particular times – for instance, the wholly fictitious claim that his father was dying of prostate cancer.

And, the final piece of the Ponzi jigsaw, the close and personal relationships that Vossen developed with nearly all his victims. These made Vossen appear more of a best friend than a professional adviser.

As he digested all this information, the judge sat back and passed a kind of sentence in absentia upon Vossen, 'He is an incredibly shady figure.' Mr Justice Lewis concluded.

Not that the hearing was without its lighter moments – such as when the subject turned to Vossen's career with Embargo Films and the QC and judge segued into an exchange about the merits of the original ITV drama *The Sweeney* and the subsequent big-screen remake of it produced by Embargo Films. 'I may have heard of [*The Sweeney*]. I may even have seen it. I may not have followed it in detail,' said Mr Justice Lewis.

When Mr Ramsden pointed out that it had a high-profile cast including Damien Lewis and Ray Winstone, the judge commented dryly that he only recalled the original television version vaguely, and then 'only because the guy [Dennis Waterman] has gone into New Tricks'.

The serious point of referencing Embargo, as James Ramsden QC went on to explain, was that his clients feared some of their money had disappeared into the film business, as evidenced by Vossen repaying one loan to his girlfriend Clare Obsorne via Embargo Films.

By the end of the one-day hearing, Mr Justice Lewis was satisfied that the claims of 'deceit, fraudulent misrepresentation, knowing receipt of money and dishonest assistance' levelled at Vossen meant that the UK courts had the necessary jurisdiction. He had no hesitation, therefore, in granting the 'very serious and draconian' order freezing Felix Vossen's assets anywhere in the world.

Mr Ramsden told the judge that the plaintiffs thought Vossen was 'holed up somewhere in Europe' and ventured the hope, forlorn as it turned out, that court-appointed enquiry agents would be able to track him down and personally serve the order.

A week after the freezing order was granted, Russell-Cooke obtained what is known in legal circles as a Norwich Pharmacal order against Vossen's three banks – Barclays, UBS and Credit Suisse – compelling them to disclose their dealings with Vossen and whether they held any of his monies. The banks were asked for details of Vossen's bank statements going back three years. The investor group had, however, to pay the banks' costs of complying with the order.

The lawyers were reasonably hopeful that they would be able to get information out of Barclays. But they and the investors were less optimistic about Switzerland's famously secretive banks playing ball.

As the days ticked by, further victims came to light and their names were added to the group email chain. The latest addition was Ricardo Morales Garidele, another UK-based investor who had known Vossen for more than ten years and who was 'still in a state of shock but relieved to find out about our action group'.

Roger Phillips meanwhile was notified by the City of London police that they had formally logged Vossen's criminal actions under the crime reference number NFRC150300982868. But they cautioned that it would take a further 28 days to determine whether any investigation would be launched.

Concerned that time was of the essence, the group had now interviewed the two firms of private investigators and instructed one of them, Rubus, to see whether they could trace Vossen through his phone records. There was a discussion about employing Rubus to launch a full-scale hunt for Vossen at an estimated cost of £50,000. Jon Peterson was the most enthusiastic advocate of this course of action. He volunteered to put up £20,000 of his own money to fund this extra expenditure – 20 times his pro rata contribution – and urged other group members to scrape together the money even if it meant selling possessions, delving into spare savings or borrowing from family members. In the end, the group baulked at the extra costs involved, fearing it might be a case of throwing more good money after bad.

The group also debated the option of going to the media in the hope that the publicity might flush Vossen from his hiding place or lead to a sighting of him by an enterprising amateur photographer or citizen journalist. At the very least, it might encourage the various police agencies to prioritise the case or at least take a more pro-active approach.

The legal advice was that press coverage was unlikely to smoke Vossen out. Moreover, several investors dreaded the story appearing in the newspapers, fearing it would identify them in public and only bring them yet more pain and embarrassment.

After a month of frenetic, exhausting and emotionally-draining activity, Leinster emailed the group to say that he was stepping down as lead co-ordinator. He had, understandably, found the task of channelling so much anger, anxiety and frustration into a constructive and coherent plan of action an enormous burden of responsibility.

By this time, legal costs had already eaten up all but £18,000 of the group's £118,000 fighting fund. Leinster left whoever was going to take up the reins an extensive checklist of the many outstanding issues to address. And news of one further and final victim: Germany now had a representative in the shape of a gentleman called Jurgen Maas, another old acquaintance of Felix Vossen.

Despite the drama that had been played out two weeks earlier in the High Court, the outside world remained unaware for a further three months of Felix Vossen's vanishing act and the worldwide order freezing his assets. It was not until 10 June that the news of Vossen's strange disappearance broke on the online film industry website *Screen Daily*. Even then, the reason for his disappearance remained unknown to the media. Far from being exposed as a fraudster, the subsequent newspaper reports focussed on the mystery of where Felix Vossen had gone and concerns about the fate that might have befallen him, rather than why he had absconded. 'Fears grow over whereabouts of producer behind the film remake of the Sweeney' ran the headline in the Daily Mail.

Behind the scenes, however, criminal investigators and the investor action group had both been busy. Lawyers for the defrauded investors had already informed law enforcement agencies in the UK and Switzerland of Vossen's disappearance urging them to issue a European arrest warrant. In the UK, the Metropolitan Police's Operation Falcon team, part of the Serious Fraud Squad, opened an investigation as did the Swiss Prosecutor's Office in Zurich. The German police were also involved for some time as was the FBI, although it never launched a formal investigation on the grounds that only two US investors, Indira Roberts and her mother, had been defrauded by Vossen.

Right: Burkhardt Vossen, Felix's grandfather. He founded the Vossen textiles company after discovering how popular terry towelling had become whilst holidaying in England shortly after the end of the First World War. The first terry material was spun on his loom on 6 May 1925. Burkhardt was an old-style employer – patriarchal, paternalistic and omnipresent. He died in 1981 aged 87. (Courtsesy of Goldbecker, Stadarchiv, Gütersloh)

Below: The sprawling Vossen textiles production site on Neuenkirchener Strasse, Gütersloh. The business began life with just five staff but by the mid-1980s Vossen boasted a worldwide workforce of 3,500, making it the biggest textile manufacturer in Germany and the third biggest private sector employer in Gütersloh.

Above: Felix's parents, Norbert and Cornelia Vossen. Norbert became managing director of the family business in 1972 and steered it along the path of overseas expansion in an effort to beat off low-cost Asian and east European competition. He took full control in 1981 and ran the business until its collapse in 1996. Cornelia was responsible for product design amongst other things but she also ran a 'wife's club' for women married to the owners of Gütersloh's other big companies such as Miele and Bertelsmann.

Left: Norbert Vossen in 1991. He started work later than his father, preferring to have breakfast at home with his wife and four young children. But he often appeared in marketing and advertising material for the Vossen brand along with other members of the family. (Hans-Dieter Much, Courtesy of Stadarchiv, Gütersloh)

Cornelia Vossen with her four children at the entrance to the family home: Felix (top right), his sisters Isobel and Christina next to him and younger brother Norbert Junior. Neither sister went into the family business but Norbert Junior became manager of its Moeve subsidiary and still works for the company today.

The Vossen family villa in Gütersloh, a short walk away from the company's production site. The house was built by Felix's grandfather Burkhardt, who regularly entertained at home. The house was sold in the early 1990s when Norbert and Cornelia Vossen decided to relocate so they could live close to another of the family's production sites near Jennersdorf in the Austrian countryside.

Left: Horst Wormann, one of Vossen's longest-serving employees. He joined the business in 1943 as an apprentice weaver and rose to become manager of the Gütersloh site until his retirement in 1989. He still believes the company could have been saved had Norbert Vossen followed his father Burkhardt's motto: sparing in words, dynamic in actions, convincing in performance.

Below: The aftermath of a disastrous fire in 1963 which closed a large part of the Gütersloh site. The fire caused DM70 million worth of damage and stopped production for two months. Employees had to be temporarily housed in nearby hotels. When production resumed, Vossen went from strength to strength. (Courtesy of Stadarchiv, Gütersloh)

Above left: The only visible trace of the Vossen name that remains today in Gütersloh – a cul-de-sac next to the site of the former Vossen factory named after the family.

Above right: The modern glass-fronted edifice of what was once the Vossen textiles mill in Gütersloh. The bulldozers went in and razed the remainder of the site on 2 February 2001 – some five years after the business went bankrupt. Today the site is a mixed retail, commercial and residential park.

Felix in various guises. He was obsessed with his weight and appearance. Sometimes he would wear glasses, sometimes he would not. Shirts were often worn once, laundered and put back in their packaging. He was a prodigious meat eater but rarely touched vegetables, with the exception of potatoes.

Above left: Vossen's first Jermyn Street apartment, number 107, in the heart of London's clubland, St James's and a stone's throw from his favourite shop, Fortnum & Mason.

Above middle: As the business grew, he moved to the bigger and more opulent 15 Jermyn Street. Visitors remarked on how pristine and spotlessly clean it was.

Above right: Vossen's Zurich office-cum-apartment at 4 Waaggasse, nestling in the shadow of the city's famous Fraumunster Abbey.

Felix celebrating his 37th birthday. He loved cakes and once ate a whole one in a single sitting after receiving it as a Christmas present from a grateful investor.

Felix the film producer: with Charlotte Rampling and his fellow film producers from Embargo Films at the premiere of *I, Anna* at the Berlinale Film Festival in 2012. Vossen claimed he could raise a £10 million fund to help Embargo produce a series of movies. He never told investors that was where their money was going and Embargo itself only ever received a fraction of that amount.

Felix the sailor man: Vossen claimed to have a yacht moored on Lake Zurich but, like so much else in his life, it was an invention. He once invited a group of investors to join him on a Mediterranean cruise onboard an 80-foot yacht he had borrowed from friends but it turned out the yacht had been hired – using money from those self-same investors.

Left: Cash, false passports, laptops and mobiles seized by Spanish police from Vossen's apartment in Valencia after his chance arrest in February 2016. Vossen is still facing possible prosecution in Spain for identity fraud when he is released from prison in Zurich.

Bottom left: The final, lachrymose email sent by Vossen to his former and current girlfriend 16 days after he fled London in March 2015 owing £45 million to his investors. In it, he claims that he never meant to hurt anyone and is still working out how to 'make things better'.

Below: Poschwies Prison on the outskirts of Zurich, Felix Vossen's new home. He says he dreads the day when he gets out.

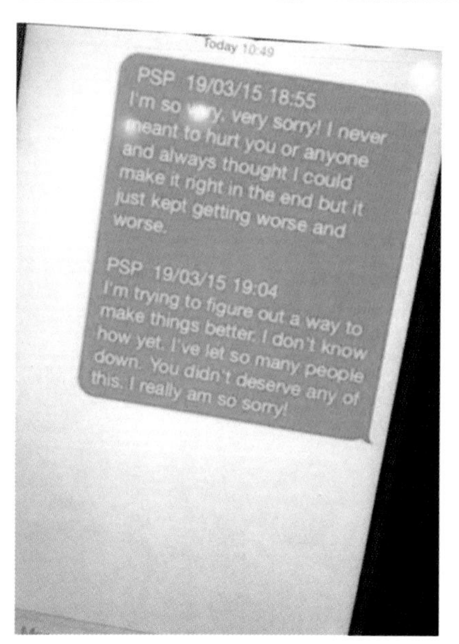

Today 10:49
PSP 19/03/15 18:55
I'm so very, very sorry! I never meant to hurt you or anyone and always thought I could make it right in the end but it just kept getting worse and worse.
PSP 19/03/15 19:04
I'm trying to figure out a way to make things better. I don't know how yet. I've let so many people down. You didn't deserve any of this. I really am so sorry!

Eventually a meeting of the Swiss and British police took place in the Hague – though not until September 2015, some six months after Vossen had fled London. At the meeting it was agreed that the Swiss would take the lead in hunting down and prosecuting the fugitive. Although the vast majority of his victims were British, the registered offices of the companies through which his fraud was perpetrated were all in Switzerland.

That same month, *Miss You Already* received its world premiere at the Toronto International Film Festival. It was premiered in London a week later. Vossen's credit as co-producer had been hastily taken off the film.

Meanwhile, the action group was busy too. They reported Vossen to FINMA, the Swiss financial markets watchdog, the UK's Financial Conduct Authority, the Financial Services Commission in the British Virgin Islands, and the US Securities and Exchange Commission. In addition to hiring lawyers, the victims considered employing Grant Thornton as forensic accountants to try to trace where their money had gone. They came increasingly to the view, however, that there was little point spending more money on this as there probably wasn't a huge pot of cash lying hidden anywhere. In addition, legal costs were piling up and rapidly eating through the fighting fund the group had raised from its members. There was little obvious appetite amongst investors to throw more money into the fund,

But Grant Thornton did put the group in touch with the Birmingham-based law firm Trowers & Hamlins which began working with a third-party broker, CVR Global, to see if they could raise the necessary funds to go after Vossen's three banks – in particular Barclays in the UK, to seek compensation.

Frustrated with the lack of police progress in the manhunt, the group finally went public with the truth behind Vossen's disappearance on 4 October 2015, launching a website, vossenmanhunt.com, and releasing a press statement and short video about their nemesis.

The press release contained case studies of seven of Vossen's victims: Steven Walters, Angela Shaw, Elizabeth Shaw, Stewart Gregory, Bill Baker and Indira Roberts. Many other victims were too traumatised by the experience, too ashamed at the way they had been hoodwinked by Vossen or too fearful of the consequences for their own reputations and livelihoods to go public. To this day, many of them will only talk about the fraud on condition they remain anonymous. Others will not speak at all.

The British, Swiss and German media duly committed much print space to the scandal. In contrast to the 'Where is he?' tone of the *Daily Mail*'s coverage four months earlier, its headline now ran: 'Movie tycoon at centre of international manhunt after being accused of £45m fraud'. The aim of the group's publicity blitz was to place the spotlight firmly back on Vossen and, hopefully, force him out from wherever he was hiding.

But where was that? Despite six months of investigation, the British, Swiss and American police forces had drawn a collective blank, unearthing few clues about Vossen's whereabouts and even fewer as to the location of the missing funds. There was speculation that Vossen had disguised himself with plastic surgery and assumed an entirely new identity. Ironically, cosmetic surgery had been the subject of a film project Vossen had been working on prior to his disappearance.

The Vossen video was the idea of Jake Sinclair – he both produced it and provided the voice-over. 'I wanted to bear witness to his crime and bring him into disgrace in Europe and America or wherever he was holed up. I also wanted to make it difficult for him to hide and help force him out,' he says. 'For me, it was a highly cathartic act. I could address him directly and he could hear my voice.' Interestingly, as Sinclair compiled the footage of Vossen that would form the basis of the film, he noticed something odd: 'Every time the camera was trained on Felix, he would try to conceal his face. It makes you wonder whether he already knew he was going to do a runner one day and didn't want the footage out there.'

It was not, however, until that chance arrest in Valencia some five months later, that investors would receive the answer to the question posed in their video: Where are you, Felix?

9

THE DOGS THAT DID NOT BARK

Felix Vossen chose his banks with the same care and attention that he selected his office locations and his wardrobe. He had relationships with half a dozen banks, conducting his financial affairs through as many as twenty different personal and company accounts in the UK, Switzerland and the United States.

His three principal lenders were Credit Suisse and UBS in Switzerland and Barclays in the UK. He could scarcely have chosen more prestigious symbols of the financial community. Between them, the three banks possess more than 600 years of history while their total collective assets exceed £2 trillion.

Alongside this trio of bulge bracket financial institutions, Vossen also banked with the cream of Switzerland's regional and private banks: Zurcher Kantonalbank, Switzerland's largest cantonal bank and the prime provider of financial services in the Greater Zurich area; and Banque Cramer – motto: Swiss Private Banking for the Connoisseur.

The £31 million of investors' money which Vossen deposited with these banks is small beer when set against their enormous balance sheets. Nevertheless, they had the same duty of care to look after every pound, euro and Swiss franc deposited with them, regardless of the customer, the origin of the money or the importance of the depositor.

Around two-thirds of the money investors handed over to Vossen was deposited in accounts at Credit Suisse and UBS, while Barclays accounted for around 10 per cent, according to an analysis carried out by Swiss prosecutors. Around 8 per cent went into accounts at Banque Cramer, a further 5 per cent went to Zurcher Kantonalbank and the remainder was deposited elsewhere.

Although Vossen selected his banks with an eye to convention, the manner in which he used them was anything but conventional. A complex banking transaction carried out by Vossen over the course of a single weekend in February 2015 – a month before he disappeared – serves to illustrate the lengths to which he was prepared to go to make his financial affairs as arcane, confusing and impenetrable as possible. It also highlights how easily Vossen was able to use and abuse the banking system without let or hindrance – or any apparent checks on his activities by the guardians of that same system.

This is what takes place: on Friday, February 20, 2015 Banque Cramer loans CHF150,000 (about £114,000) to VCP Investment Advisers, one of Vossen's front companies. The money is paid into an account held by VCP Investment Advisers at Banque Cramer's Zurich branch. However, it only stays there for a few short hours before Vossen transfers the money to his private client account at the St Moritz branch of Credit Suisse. It is then moved into another euro-denominated account held in the same name and at the same bank. Further funds are added and the total amount is transferred again, this time to a sterling account, again at the same bank, where it shows up as a £115,000 credit. There the money sits for the remainder of the weekend.

When the bank re-opens on Monday, 23 February, the money is quickly on the move again. Vossen transfers the £115,000 from Credit Suisse in St Moritz to an account he holds at Barclays Bank in London, again in the name of VCP Investment Advisers. From there, the money is switched again into an account in the name of Exponential Media Ventures 1 Limited, one of Vossen's film financing businesses. It does not stay there for long either. Later that same day it makes the journey all the way back to where it first began – Banque Cramer in Zurich. There, it is converted into euros and Swiss francs and transferred in two payments of EUR92,460 and CHF66,749 into separate Vossen accounts.

The final act in this bizarre paperchase across the European banking system sees CHF65,000 transferred back into the VCP Investment Advisers account at Banque Cramer, where it had first been deposited the previous Friday. The EUR92,460 are withdrawn in cash by Vossen.

Over the course of four days, then, Vossen has used eight different accounts at three separate banks in two countries to move money in a giant circle, ensuring that it ends up where it began. With Vossen taking a fat cut along the way.

Vossen's banking records are littered with examples of similarly convoluted transactions which appear to have been undertaken with no concern for the bank charges and foreign exchange losses he was incurring along the way – or regard for the rules and regulations which govern private banking.

Anyone who has ever attempted to move a large amount of money from one bank to another – for instance to lodge a deposit on a house purchase or transfer money to a pension pot – will be only too aware of the money-laundering hoops and hurdles they must negotiate first. In the UK, banks will very often require proof as to the provenance of the money. And the limit on the amount of money that can be transferred on any one banking day to an external account is typically set at £10,000 or £20,000, depending on the lender.

Vossen, however, seems to have been able to transfer hundreds of thousands of pounds at will, in single transactions, across borders and in varying currencies without any interference.

What was the purpose of these intricate games of financial tag? Was it to create the impression that Vossen's investment activities were actually generating a profit from genuine trading? Or was it an attempt by Vossen to hide his tracks by laying endless false trails?

Whatever the motive, Swiss state prosecutors decided they were proof of money-laundering on a pre-meditated and systematic scale.

Criminals have engaged in money-laundering since time immemorial either to disguise the illegal source of their wealth or to deploy money raised through legitimate means for illegitimate purposes. In some cases, criminals have been known to put crisp new banknotes, quite literally, through laundry cycles to age their appearance before re-cycling them through the banking system. Although no reliable figures really exist as to the scale of this particular strain of financial malpractice, the International Monetary Fund once estimated that between two and five per cent of global GDP consisted of laundered money.

What can be stated with a good degree of reliability, however, is that in the battle to stamp out the practice, regulators have invariably remained one step behind the launderers. This helps to explain why every fresh attempt to clamp down on money laundering has tended to be a belated response to an existential crisis that law enforcement authorities could no longer afford to ignore. Thus, the very first anti-money laundering laws were introduced by the US government in the Prohibition years of the 1920s to cut off the huge profits being made by the Mob from illegal alcohol sales. A further raft of money laundering initiatives was launched in the 1980s in an attempt to stem and preferably confiscate the profits being made by Mexican drug cartels from the worldwide narcotics trade. Likewise, the 9/11 attacks in 2001 heralded a fresh slew of laws to combat money laundering in a forlorn attempt to interrupt sources of funding for terrorism.

In particular, the world's richest nations, in the shape of the Group of Seven, used the newly-created Financial Action Task Force on Money Laundering to pressurise other governments around the world to step up their own efforts to prevent money laundering by increasing their surveillance and monitoring of financial transactions and imposing new and more onerous requirements on their banking institutions.

The long campaign waged mainly by Western governments against money laundering has resulted in some spectacular successes and claimed some extremely high-profile scalps. The Bank of Credit and Commerce International, which quickly became known as the Bank of Crooks and Criminals International, famously collapsed in 1991 owing £10 billion to creditors after being exposed for having facilitated the laundering of an estimated £17 billion on behalf of clients including Saddam

Hussein and the Panamanian dictator Manuel Noriega. But mullti-million pound fines have also being levied against some of the most prestigious names in international banking – Wachovia, HSBC and Standard Chartered for example – for money-laundering offences. The sums laundered through these august financial institutions were huge – £192 billion in the case of Standard Chartered, for instance.

Laundering generally involves taking 'dirty' money such as the proceeds of crime, drugs and prostitution and converting it into 'clean' money by re-investing it in genuine businesses which produce legitimate returns. But Felix Vossen was guilty of something known as reverse money-laundering. This is the process by which legitimate sources of funds are used for illegal purposes. The investor money which Vossen treated as his own – life savings, windfalls from house sales, inheritances and the proceeds of sheer hard graft – could scarcely have been cleaner.

In court, the chief prosecutor Maric Demont produced copious evidence of the way Vossen had persistently engaged in reverse money-laundering as he defrauded and forged his way through life.

Attached to the Swiss criminal indictment are pages of appendices setting out Vossen's money-laundering activities. Appendix B shows that Vossen made cash withdrawals totalling £522,000 from his private banking account with Credit Suisse in St Moritz in various denominations – sterling, euros and Swiss francs – over a five-year period from July 2010 to February 2015. The withdrawals were mainly made from banks in central Zurich and Zurich airport. On one occasion Vossen withdrew EUR100,350 in cash in a single transaction from the bank's branch on Paradeplatz in the middle of Zurich. Other cash withdrawals were for sums ranging from £5,000 to £60,000.

Appendix C shows that Vossen's company VCP Investment Advisers made cash withdrawals from various Swiss bank accounts totalling £220,000 in various denominations – sterling, euros and Swiss francs – over a 10-month period from April, 2014 to February, 2015.

Appendix D shows that Vossen transferred £519,522 from his private client account with Credit Suisse in St Moritz to two offshore companies in the Channel Isles – Virtus Trust and Alderham, both based in Guernsey – over a four year period from 2009 to 2013. Virtus Trust was the nominee for Vossen's shareholding in Embargo Films.

Finally, Appendix E shows that a total of £1.32 million was transferred over a 10-month period from April, 2014 to February 2015 from various Swiss bank accounts to Vossen companies in the UK. Some £600,000 was transferred from Vossen's Credit Suisse private banking account in St Moritz to VCP Investment Advisers in the UK. More than £700,000 was transferred from Banque Cramer accounts to VCP Investment Advisers in the UK.

These are only sample cases of Vossen's money-laundering. The prosecution could have cited many more instances going back further in time if it were not for the fact that Swiss law imposes a seven-year time limit. By withdrawing the money in Switzerland or transferring it from Switzerland to other jurisdictions, Vossen was attempting to conceal the proceeds of his crime and that amounted to money-laundering, says Demont. In total, prosecutors identified 40 separate episodes of money-laundering over an 11-year period involving £1.7 million, $224,000, EUR111,650 and CHF177,450.

The puzzle, therefore, is this: if the Swiss prosecutors were able to construct such a detailed picture of Vossen's money-laundering activities, how was he able to evade the money-laundering controls which his banks would have operated and why did those checks and safeguards not expose the money-laundering that was occurring in the first place?

'You would have to ask the banks that,' is Demont's dry response.

Vossen grew up in an era when *Wall Street's* Gordon Gecko was scarcely alone in believing that 'greed is good'. This might have been the mantra of a 1980s celluloid invention, but it was also the watchword of many young men and women entering the casino-like world of investment banking in London, New York and Zurich. They were happy to make a handsome living by gambling with other people's money and dealing in arcane, abstruse financial instruments which neither they nor their bosses truly understood themselves.

By the time Vossen began his life of criminality, such unabashed declarations of self-interest were no longer heard quite so often in polite company. For one thing, the developed world had been through a couple of bruising economic recessions which reminded everyone that one person's greed was another's penury. But what had not changed was the regulatory environment in which such sentiments were allowed, even encouraged, to thrive.

The global financial crisis which struck in 2008 had its origins in the US subprime mortgage market – where borrowers with poor credit histories or no credit history at all were encouraged to take out 100 per cent home loans at very low interest rates, only to default as soon as borrowing costs began to rise. The contagion was fuelled by fee-hungry investment banks packaging up these bad loans into financial instruments known as collateralised debt obligations, or CDOs, and selling them to other banks. It was then spread further by the practice of slicing up and repacking these CDOs, before selling them to yet more investors until the whole western financial system was infected.

But it was a lack of regulation, or at the very least lax regulation, which permitted these practices to flourish in the first place. It was the same lax regulatory system that allowed the LIBOR-rigging scandal to happen, that enabled every major British banking institution to market PPI insurance policies and allowed unscrupulous HBOS bankers to rip off or in some cases destroy small business customers.

And, perhaps, it was the same laissez faire attitude to investment and investor protection that enabled Felix Vossen to get away with his criminal behaviour for as long as he did. If the financial crisis taught us that that some bulge-bracket banks such as Bank of America, Citi Group and RBS were simply 'too big to fail', then maybe Vossen was allowed to prosper because he was too small to notice.

In any event, he sailed through the stock market collapse of 2008-09 untouched. Whilst the financial world's three leading stocks and shares indices - the FTSE100, the Dow Jones Industrial Average and the S&P500 – fell by almost a half between the autumn of 2007 and their low point in February, 2009, Felix Vossen demonstrated an extraordinary ability to buck the market. Over that same period, the value of his investment fund continued to rise and the investments continued to pour in to the tune of $2 million and £2.2 million.

In the aftermath of the financial crash the world's banks, among them Vossen's three principal lenders, faced their day of reckoning. As the price for supporting them and, in some cases, rescuing them from oblivion, governments demanded their own pound of flesh. Banking regulation was overhauled and strengthened and the banks were forced to put their own houses in order. If the crash had exposed one fatal flaw in the financial system, it was that the banks were far too thinly capitalised. They simply did not have sufficient reserves or a big enough financial buffer, to support the loans they were extending or to survive the level of defaults they were experiencing.

And so, their statutory capital requirements were increased significantly – forcing many of them to raise the necessary money from their shareholders. Along with these more stringent capital requirements came a whole plethora of new curbs: minimum loss-absorption requirements for banks whose financial failure would cause wider structural damage to the economies in which they were operating, labelled as Systemically Important Banks or SIBs; ring-fencing of retail banking operations from riskier investment banking activities; restrictions on banker bonuses and the proportion that could be paid immediately and in cash; stricter vetting or executive appointments. And still tougher rules to curb money laundering and require banks to better know their customers and better understand what level of risk they presented.

Today, Vossen's three principal banks – Credit Suisse, UBS and Barclays – all take money-laundering very seriously, and for good reason. Not only is it illegal and bad for a bank's financial health, it can also have catastrophic consequences for its reputation. All three banks are under investigation in connection with suspected money laundering in different jurisdictions around the world.

Credit Suisse is one of a number of banks caught up in the Fifa bribery scandal, where it is under investigation by US and Swiss authorities to establish whether it failed to observe anti-money laundering laws and regulations or permitted 'suspicious or otherwise improper transactions' to take place.

UBS has been charged by French authorities with participation in the laundering of the proceeds of tax fraud – a case which resulted in the bank having to post a corporate bail of EUR1.1 billion. It is also being investigated in Belgium for alleged money-laundering.

Barclays, finally, is under investigation in South Africa in connection with suspected money laundering related to foreign exchange transactions by its subsidiary Absa Bank Limited.

The three banks also belong to a body dedicated to the eradication of money-laundering known as the Wolfsberg Group, so named after the chateau in north east Switzerland where the 11 global financial institutions which make up the organisation first met in 2000 as guests of UBS.

On its website, Credit Suisse goes to great lengths to promote its anti-corruption and anti-money laundering credentials, highlighting its involvement in 'the development and implementation of industry standards to combat money laundering and corruption'. It goes on to state that 'employees must ensure that transactions that may impact on the reputation of Credit Suisse undergo our bank-wide standardized Reputational Risk Review Process'.

The bank's 2017 annual report, meanwhile, states: 'We take our obligations to prevent money laundering and terrorist financing in the US and globally very seriously, while appropriately respecting and protecting the confidentiality of clients. We have policies, procedures and training intended to ensure that our employees comply with "know your customer" regulations and understand when a client relationship or business should be evaluated as higher risk for us.'

UBS's 2017 annual report states that the bank has a mandatory training programme in place for all employees covering a range of compliance and risk-related topics 'including anti-money laundering and operational risk'.

Finally, Barclays' website proclaims that its anti-money laundering policy is designed to ensure that it complies with UK legislation, regulations, rules and industry guidance for the financial services sector 'including the need to have adequate systems and controls in place to mitigate the risk of the bank being used to facilitate financial crime'.

For good measure, Barclays also employs a Group Money Laundering Reporting Officer and local Money Laundering Reporting Officers. They are part of a group-wide effort to ensure that staff are trained to spot potential money-laundering activity, that the bank's 'know your customer' procedures are observed and that the accounts and activity of higher risk customers are properly monitored. Finally, they require the bank to report unusual and suspicious activity to the relevant law enforcement authorities.

As members of the Wolfsberg Group, the three banks also abide by the Wolfsberg Anti-Money Laundering Principles for Private Banking, first enunciated in 2000 and revised and updated in 2012. These specify that banks must pay particular attention to the receipt and withdrawal of large amounts of cash and have policies and procedures in place to monitor such transactions. They also require banks to have a written policy for identifying and monitoring unusual or suspicious activities and, where necessary, taking action.

Unusual or suspicious activity includes cash transactions above a certain amount and what are termed 'pass-through' or 'in-and-out transactions', such as those undertaken by Vossen that weekend in February 2015 when he sent £115,000 on his very own European money-go-round.

The Wolfsberg principles state that once a bank has identified suspicious activity for which there is no plausible explanation, it has three choices: increase monitoring of the account; cancel the business relationship; or report the client to the relevant authorities.

Central to the way banks do their business is a simple three-word dictum: Know Your Customer (or KYC to give it its banking acronym). It applies equally to private banking clients and giant multi-national corporations. All financial institutions set tremendous store on understanding what their clients do, where their income comes from and how they run their businesses. Without these fundamental pieces of knowledge, it is impossible to have a proper banking relationship or advance any credit. All banks therefore have detailed KYC policies and all their client facing staff are drilled and trained in putting them into practice.

But when it came to Felix Vossen did any of his banks truly Know Their Customer?

Banking experts say that it is all very well to have money-laundering policies in place. Executing them is another matter. Too often compliance departments, even in very large banks, are understaffed meaning that the job of monitoring customer accounts passes by default to relationship managers whose job is not to police the client, but support them. In these circumstances, the important task of ensuring a client is acting within the letter and spirit of a bank's anti-fraud and anti-money laundering protocols all too often becomes a box-ticking exercise.

At the same time as he was freewheeling across Europe's banking landscape, shifting funds as he saw fit, it is apparent that the amounts of money being deposited in Vossen's various bank accounts bore precious little relationship to the amount of share trading he was actually undertaking. An analysis of Vossen's annual trading activity undertaken by one of the investors, Charles Huntley, and subsequently shared with British police and Swiss prosecutors, reveals how quickly Vossen slipped from being genuine investor to fraudster. 'We developed a financial spreadsheet but we couldn't match Vossens's financial activity against what he said he was doing on behalf of clients,' says Huntley. To add to that, his accounts were chaotic, says Huntley. Bills in one currency would be paid from accounts denominated in a different currency and no single account seemed to have a set or dedicated purpose. Whether they were in the personal name of Vossen or the name of one of his companies, they were used interchangeably. Investor money was pooled and Vossen used that pool both to trade in stocks and fund his lavish lifestyle.

Although only small amounts of bank account data are available for the period from 2003 to 2007, due to a rule which only requires them to be kept for 10 years, the annual summary compiled by Huntley makes for interesting reading:

2005 – Money coming in from investors and out to trading companies as expected

2006 – Less trading activity but nothing obviously untoward

2007 – Some more inflow of investor money matched by signs of share trading

2008 – Inflows from and outflow to investors, sterling and US dollar bond activity but only low levels of share trading

2009 – Inflows from investors but no correlation with corresponding investments and only a small amount of trading

2010 – Small amount of share trading and some bond activity but confined to early months of the year

2011 – Ebb and flow of investor money but no sign of any trading or bond activity

2012 – No sign of trading, indications of shortage of funds, inflow of investor money towards the year end

2013 – Significantly more money coming in from investors but no sign of any funds being invested or any evidence of trading

2014 – Healthy inflow of money from investors but no sign of any trading or investment. Complex multiple transfers between accounts, other accounts consolidated and drained. Bank loans start to be taken out.

In summary, what genuine trading Vossen was undertaking had shrunk to a trickle by 2008 and by 2010 it had largely dried up altogether. However, no one seems to have been aware of this: not Vossen's banks, not his accountants, not his lawyers and nor any Swiss regulator. And not his investors. Indeed, as the indictment formally charging Vossen with various offences subsequently acknowledged, had any of his victims become suspicious of where there money had gone to, Swiss banking secrecy would have quickly brought them face to face with a brick wall.

This financial analysis accords with the case that Maric Demont was assembling. He was able to establish that the Ponzi had effectively begun in 2003 because from that point onwards, the amounts being invested by Vossen in share trading never matched the investments he was receiving. Demont concluded that most of the investors' money was being used to support Vossen's lifestyle and very little of it to generate the claimed 20 per cent returns.

Detailed examination of Vossen's various bank accounts bears this out. It shows that he never distinguished between what was his money and what belonged to investors. He pooled all the funds he received from investors and treated their cash as his, irrespective of whether it was deposited in one of Vossen's personal accounts or one of the many accounts he set up in the name of his various trading companies.

Over a 12-year period Vossen paid himself CHF3.5m, £700,000 and $90,000 from Credit Suisse accounts into which investor money had been deposited. His Swiss currency account with the bank was used to pay credit card bills totalling CHF3.11m, withdraw CHF203,000 in cash, settle medical bills of CHF40,000 and attorney fees of CHF85,000 and pay his monthly apartment/office rental costs of CHF29,000.

He used his sterling account at Credit Suisse to withdraw £290,000 in cash and give Sophia Rafaat £405,000.

From his US$ account at Credit Suisse he paid off credit card bills totalling $42,000 and gave Sophia Rafaat a further $40,300.

The account that Vossen opened with Zurcher Kantonalbank in the name of VCP Asset Management was used to meet credit card bills, phone bills, insurance charges, lawyers, landlords, clothes bills and the rental of his Bloomberg terminal. The total cost came to CHF870,000, again all funded from money deposited on behalf of investors.

Vossen used his UBS accounts to pay bills and withdraw cash to the sum of CHF75,000, £320,000, EUR310,000 and $103,000.

He used the Vossen Capital Partners account at UBS to withdraw CHF75,000 in cash and make payments to his parents and Sophia Rafaat. He used the UBS sterling account to withdraw £196,000 in cash between 2007 and 2013 and he took a further EUR200,000 in cash from the UBS euro account. He used the Vossen Capital Partners dollar account at UBS to withdraw $73,000 in cash and settle $30,000 worth of credit card bills.

He also used his Embargo Media Holdings account at UBS to settle credit card bills, pay his lawyer and settle tax bills.

Finally, Swiss prosecutors were able to establish that Vossen used £315,000 of investors' money deposited with Barclays for his personal needs, including £213,485 that was withdrawn from his Embargo Films account at the bank.

The banks took Vossen at his word that he was the beneficial owner of the funds he was withdrawing and he signed documentation to that effect with three of his banks.

As Vossen reached crisis point towards the end of 2014, it is clear that he was having to resort to borrowing money from his banks – with what collateral, we do not know. In the final months before his disappearance, Banque Cramer alone lent Vossen almost £300,000 and a further $220,000 in addition to the CHF115,000 referred to earlier.

It was not only Vossen's banks who failed to bark. He also successfully hoodwinked a succession of lawyers and accountants, who were as impressed with his apparent share trading prowess and financial acumen as were his grateful investors. Vossen's Zurich office at Waaggasse 4 was around the corner from the city's banking district in Paradeplatz. There, he would introduce existing and would-be investors to Swiss bankers and lawyers who effectively acted as references for Vossen's credentials and professional standing.

Roger Phillips, one of Vossen's earliest investors, recalls a trip he made to Switzerland in March, 2007 to meet a group of Vossen's advisers and acquaintances. The first meeting was in Zurich at the offices of his attorneys, Pestalozzi, one of Switzerland's largest and best-known law firms with a heritage stretching back more than a century. He met three lawyers from Pestalozzi, including Severin Roelli, who also sat on the board of one of Vossen's front companies, VCP Asset Management, for six years until October, 2014. 'We sat around a big table and it appeared that all these lawyers regarded Vossen with some deference,' recalls Phillips. 'The impression was that Vossen was highly respectable. This was a huge endorsement.'

The following day, he travelled to St Moritz to meet another trio of professional contacts: Michael Conrad of the accountancy firm Riedi Berni Theus; Mario Pfiffner, a partner in the law firm Schwarzenback & Piffner and also a signatory on two other Vossen front companies; and thirdly Erich Schlafi, a banker from UBS who was keen to nurture Vossen as a customer so he could advise him on tax optimisation. 'If you're a friend of Felix, you're a friend of mine,' Phillips was told. To him, it was further proof positive of Vossen's authenticity and probity.

When Vossen went on the run, Phillips contacted Conrad, who claimed not to have seen Vossen for at least seven years and was unable therefore to help him.

It proved a similar dead-end with Severin Roelli. Questioned by the German newspaper *Welt am Sonntag* about his relationship with Vossen and why he had ceased to be a director of VCP Asset Management just five months before Vossen disappeared, Roelli said that Vossen no longer co-operated with him 'in the way that would be desirable for such a mandate' although he added that he did not have any concerns about the over-indebtedness of the company.

Roelli said his firm only received payments from Vossen for 'advocacy and board activity'. He also told *Welt am Sonntag* that VCP Asset Management had 'no asset management activity'. This is an odd statement given that, according to the Swiss commercial register, the precise declared purpose of VCP Asset Management was 'the provision of services in the field of asset management and financial advice'. VCP Asset Management does not appear to have ever filed any proper audited accounts.

Some of Vossen's investors believe his advisers still have questions to answer. 'Severin Roelli and all these guys need to be reminded of their obligations,' Stewart Gregory told NDR Radio. 'They are accountable to an extent, particularly as Severin was authorised to sign at Vossen's company VCP. They can't hide forever.'

Just as he lied to his banks about the source of his funds, so he deceived his accountants at Mathis Treuhand. On two occasions he falsely told Karin Dohm-Acker, the Mathis Treuhand employee auditing his accounts, that credits appearing against his name related to property transactions he had carried out. Mr Dohm-Acker duly recorded 'house sales' on the relevant balance sheets.

Vossen's investment companies were all domiciled and registered in Switzerland, two of his three principal banks were

Swiss, his attorneys were Swiss and he was, supposedly, regulated by the Swiss financial watchdog, FINMA. Given all of this, the investor group approached FINMA to ask that the regulator investigate Vossen's activities and assist them in their attempts to force his banks and lawyers to disclose information that might help trace any assets that Vossen held.

The request appears to have fallen on deaf ears. Claud Butler of FINMA's General Secretariat responded to the group saying that VCP Asset Management had not been licensed by the regulator to engage in financial services activities, nor was it a member of any self-regulatory organisation. His email politely referred the group to the explanation of FINMA's remit on its website.

Even if FINMA were to launch an investigation, the group would have no right to any information, records or documents that might be unearthed through the disclosure process because they were technically members of the public and therefore could not become party to any proceedings the regulator might bring. 'We are thus unable to keep you informed about our investigations regarding VCP Asset Management,' he concluded.

It was a dead end. However, the group is now pursuing what they hope will be a more fruitful route to securing compensation from Vossen's banks. Advised by their UK law firm, Trowers & Hamlins, the group has hired CVR Global, a leading firm of forensic accountants and insolvency practitioners specialising amongst other things in the recovery of assets obtained by fraud.

In April 2018, two of CVR Global's partners, Craig Povey and Adrian Hyde, were appointed trustees of Vossen's bankruptcy in the UK High Court. In the official notice of the appointment published in the *London Gazette*, Vossen's occupation is listed as 'Film Producer'. As trustees, Povey and Hyde have the power to seize Vossen's effects or debts from any other party in possession of them. More importantly, however, it gives them access to a treasure trove of information held by the banks detailing their dealings with him and supervision of his accounts. Thus far, the trustees are in 'fact-finding' mode and are asking a lot of questions of Vossen and his banks. Vossen is co-operating and has already been visited in prison by the trustees on at least one occasion. The trustees' powers extend to the UK. In order to obtain information from jurisdictions outside the UK – such as Vossen's Swiss banks – then they may need his authority to make requests for disclosure. Beyond this, CVR is not prepared to comment whilst the case is 'live and ongoing'.

They are searching for the smoking gun, if one exists, that will demonstrate the banks were negligent in their oversight of Vossen – and therefore liable to pay compensation to his victims. If anyone has deep enough pockets to recompense his victims, then it is Credit Suisse, UBS and Barclays.

These are some of the key questions facing Vossen's banks:

What processes, procedures and checks did they carry out before allowing him to become a customer?

Did they test Vossen against their specific Know Your Customer guidelines and did he successfully pass those tests?

Did any of Vossen's banks communicate any concerns at any time to him or banking and financial regulators about they way in which he was operating his accounts?

Did any of his banks consider terminating their banking relationship with Vossen at any time?

And, lastly, do any of Vossen's banks believe they have any responsibility towards investors whose money was deposited with them?

Credit Suisse, UBS and Barclays have an additional question to answer: did they adhere fully to the Wolfsberg Anti-Money Laundering Principles in their dealings with Vossen?

Credit Suisse declined to comment on its banking relationship with Vossen but responded with a statement which reads as follows:

> Credit Suisse is committed to operating its business in strict compliance with all applicable laws, rules and regulations within the markets in which it operates. We have stringent control mechanisms in place to combat financial crime related activities. These controls are designed to prevent the exposure of Credit Suisse and its clients to the risks of specific and systematic money laundering. In the circumstances where we identify any relationships which could have been used for such purposes or other illicit activity, we take prompt and decisive action which will include liaison with applicable regulatory authorities and restrictions of activity up until and including termination in line with respective requirements.

Barclays likewise declined to comment on its dealings with Vossen, citing client confidentiality. The bank added: 'Barclays has the highest standards against financial crime, including compliance with Know Your Customer and Anti-Money Laundering rules, and we work constantly to enforce them.'

UBS also replied that laws and regulations prevented it from commenting on individual clients but said that it applied 'a robust money-laundering prevention framework across its business operations globally and employs a sophisticated set of IT-based monitoring tools to identify suspicious transactions'.

The bank said that it trains employees on a regular basis 'in all relevant aspects' of anti-money laundering and added:

> In cases of suspected money laundering, as well as suspected membership of or support for a criminal organization, UBS is required by the Swiss Money Laundering Act to advise the Federal Department of Justice and Police and to freeze the funds once the report has been handed over to the law enforcement authorities. On a global basis, we file a significant number of such reports every year.

Finally, UBS said that it applied the standards developed by the Wolfsberg Group. 'This demonstrates our commitment to best practices in this area.'

Cedric Anker, the chief executive of Banque Cramer, politely declined to answer any questions relating to its dealings with Vossen, saying that the bank 'does not provide information about banking relationships which are regulated by confidentiality obligations'.

Zürcher Kantonalbank responded in similar vein saying it 'does not comment on potential or existing customer relationships'.

How successful has the banking world been in containing, if not eradicating, money laundering? Perhaps it was a coincidence of timing, but just as Swiss prosecutors were putting the finishing touches to the order which would see Vossen extradited from Spain to face trial in Zurich, the biggest money laundering expose of them all broke. On Sunday, 3 April, 2016, the International Consortium of Investigative Journalists (ICIJ) and its partner media outlets around the globe released the results of their investigation into the Panama Papers.

The biggest leak of confidential inside information in history, the papers consist of 11.5 million secret files held by the hitherto little-known Panamanian law firm Mossack Fonseca. They detail the secret offshore links of the rich and famous on an unprecedented scale, encompassing 214,000 offshore companies in 21 tax havens connected to individuals in 200 countries. Among these individuals are 140 politicians in 50 countries, including 12 current or former world leaders. And not just politicians and other public servants but also celebrities, film stars and sports heroes. Among those alleged to have used or benefited from the use of Mossack Fonseca's services were Vladimir Putin and the perpetrators of what, at the time, was the biggest theft in history, the 1983 Brinks-Mat gold bullion robbery.

The ICIJ calculated that over a period of 40 years some $2 trillion passed through the hands of Mossack Fonseca and the 14,000 banks, law firms, company incorporators and other assorted middlemen with which it worked. According to the organisation's analysis, more of these intermediaries operated from the UK and Switzerland than any other location with the exception of Hong Kong. Among the top ten banks most active in registering offshore accounts for their clients, Credit Suisse ranked third and UBS sixth.

10

THE TRIAL

Zurich: 22 November 2017. Dawn is breaking on a crisp and clear autumnal morning in Switzerland's financial capital. A lone photographer from the Associated Press stands outside the city's District Court on Badenerstrasse, stamping his feet and checking his equipment in the hope of snatching a picture of Felix Vossen as he prepares finally to face judgement. Two years and 264 days after he absconded from his London apartment, leaving a trail of debt and disbelieving investors behind him, Vossen is about to go on trial for fraud, forgery and money-laundering.

His lawyers have attempted, without success, to get the proceedings postponed on the grounds that Vossen wishes to plead diminished responsibility owing to his drug addiction and is not fit to stand trial. Vossen has been examined by a prison psychiatrist and his defence attorney, Reto Steinmann, and has twice gone to court requesting a postponement – the most recent occasion being only a fortnight previously. Steinmann's requests have been dismissed and so Vossen must throw himself on the mercy of justice, Swiss-style. The facade of the court building sports a large stone carving of a man on horseback slaying a dragon-like beast: Staatsanwaltschaft des Kantons Zurich v Felix Burghardt Norbert Vossen. Will the defendant be dispatched with the same cold efficiency?

As court officers begin arriving at 7.15am prompt to commence their day's work, a janitor emerges from within to sweep the steps clean of what few leaves and other debris are in evidence. A metaphor perhaps for what is going to be a very Swiss affair – punctilious justice meted out in fastidious fashion. The trial is only scheduled to last one day.

By the time the court doors open half an hour later, a gaggle of reporters, mainly from Swiss and German news organisations, has gathered outside, animatedly discussing the case, comparing notes and swapping war stories as journalists are prone to do. Among them are Christiane Oelrich from the German Press Agency DPA and Christoph Heinzle, a highly experienced broadcaster with the German radio station NDR. Oelrich's reporting on the case will ensure that it receives mass coverage in newspapers right across Vossen's native Germany and also in Switzerland. For Heinzle, the trial will form the basis for the final programme in his much-heralded and admired eight-part radio series, *The Talented Mr Vossen*.

Sadly, for all his diligence and perseverance, the snapper from Associated Press is out of luck: Vossen has already been spirited inside, having entered the rear of the building earlier in a prison van, well away from the prying lenses of the waiting press pack.

Vossen has already pleaded guilty and the prosecution has requested a prison sentence of six years and ten months. The only real matter for the judges to determine, therefore, is the length of time he will spend behind bars taking into account the pleas of mitigation made on his behalf.

When the oak-panelled doors to Court 31 open at 8.15am precisely, the presiding judge, Vice-President Sebastian Aeppli, is already seated in position. He is dressed in dark suit, white shirt and paisley tie and flanked by two junior court judges who sit a few feet either side of him. The court stenographer sits a few feet back and beyond her on either side of the court sit prosecution and defence counsel. There are no wigs or gowns on display and nothing that could be described as pomp or ceremony. It all feels rather administrative and vaguely informal.

The public benches fill up with the waiting journalists, the odd member of the public and one or two earnest-looking young men and women armed with A4 notebooks as if preparing to take copious notes – law students on work experience, perhaps. But there is a complete absence of anyone who is indentifiably a friend, relative or supporter of Felix Vossen. He is well and truly on his own.

The man himself then enters court, escorted by two security staff, and takes a seat immediately in front of the public benches. He looks thinner than in his photographs and the pock marks on his face appear more pronounced. He is wearing a black roll-top sweater beneath a lightweight Barbour-style jacket, blue cotton drill jeans and a dark pair of slip-on fashion trainers.

Vossen is called forward by the judge and glances nervously to his left and right. Where he is standing is not really a witness box – merely a position mid-way between the two sets of lawyers. The judge begins proceedings by questioning Vossen, almost in a conversational manner.

The session lasts a little over an hour. Judge Aeppli has the demeanour, less of a stentorian High Court judge, and more of a kindly but firm headmaster asking an errant schoolboy where it had all gone wrong. Vossen, in contrast, appears agitated and distracted throughout the gentle interrogation. He stands on one leg for extended periods, he repeatedly scratches his head and neck and the small of his back. And his body constantly twitches as he clenches and unclenches his fists and tenses and then relaxes his cheek muscles.

Mid-way through Vossen's testimony, there is a small disturbance at the back of the court as a couple enter the room and squeeze themselves onto a bench towards the back of the public gallery. The man is Roger Phillips, the biggest single investor with Vossen after his parents and the only victim to have made the trip to Zurich to witness justice being done. His partner has made the journey with him. Other victims had been advised in advance not to attend on the grounds that the trial would take place entirely in German with no facility for simultaneous translation and no opportunity for them to take part in the proceedings in any shape or form. This last piece of advice turns out not to have been entirely accurate. A small, dapper and self-assured figure in suit and tie, Phillips cuts a marked contrast to his nemesis. Vossen only realises that Phillips has been witnessing proceedings when he turns back to resume his seat. He acknowledges him with a brief, sheepish glance.

Vossen is no stranger to sobbing – he broke down in tears on seven occasions whilst being interrogated by the Public Prosecutor Maric Dement as he built his case against the fraudster. And this witness session follows a similar pattern. Vossen is reduced to tears on three occasions during questioning; first when Judge

Aeppli refers to the plight of Angela Shaw, the grandmother left destitute and homeless by Vossen; then a second time when the judge notices the ring on his left hand and asks him whether he is married. Vossen replies that he is not married and that the ring belonged to his grandfather. The third tearful outburst is prompted by the judge observing that the prosecution is demanding a prison sentence of almost seven years.

In between these lachrymose interruptions, the judge covers plenty of ground. He begins by asking Vossen about his family upbringing in Gütersloh with his brother and two sisters. Vossen talks warmly about his childhood and says that all three siblings visited him on remand, unlike his parents. He then delves into Vossen's education and his early ambition to become a lawyer. Vossen talks about his schooling in Switzerland, the international baccalaureat he studied for in England, the degree in business studies he planned to take and the law apprenticeship he began in Madrid with a firm of solicitors that acted for numerous German clients. The judge then pauses and asks Vossen about his relationship with drugs. Vossen admits to having been addicted to cocaine and prescription drugs for 12 years from 2003 to 2015 as well as suffering from depression, for which he is receiving treatment.

The defendant speaks in short sentences, delivered in a low, monotone voice which is sometimes difficult to detect. The judge's questioning moves on to the launch of his 'career' as an investment fund manager and his interest in film production. Vossen describes his investment activities not as a job but a 'hobby' and says his real passion was the movie business. He insists that the two activities were kept entirely separate.

According to his testimony, Vossen began day trading in the mid-1990s when he was aged 19 or 20, partly to finance his studies and partly because he did not want to end up working in a bank. He claims to have worked 14-hour days and says that his investment strategy was producing healthy profits until the dotcom bubble burst in 2000, after which the judge concludes that he was suffering losses on whatever share trading he was engaged in.

Vossen admits that he never had proper and full oversight over his business affairs, that he never distinguished between his money and that of his investors and that he did not keep proper books. He did everything 'Pi mal Daumen' – by rule of thumb, as the colloquial German has it. But Vossen strenuously denies that he set out with the intention of harming investors. He maintains that his investment strategy 'always looked very realistic to me' and says he believed it would be possible to make returns of 20 per cent for them. It was only much later that he realised he had over-estimated his own abilities. Even at that point, he thought it would be feasible to pay back the money he had been given. 'He had a plan to fulfil his obligations until the very end,' the judge noted, but finally accepted this was not going to be possible.

At the same time as insisting that he had never set out with the intention of defrauding his investors, Vossen tells the judge that he is sorry for his actions and the impact they have had on his victims. 'I regret all of that,' Vossen says. He then explains to the court how he had an obligation to make good to those family members and friends who had lost so much money, adding that, while in prison awaiting trial, he had written to a number of those he had defrauded making a similar promise.

Vossen's testimony is often confused and contradictory and occasionally self-pitying. It is also laced with the remorse that he has since expressed many times to his victims and which many of them believe to be ersatz.

Finally, the judge asks Vossen how he is pleading. 'Guilty', he whispers in reply.

There is then a short interval before Maric Demont, the state prosecutor, stands to confirm the charges Vossen is facing and the sentence that the prosecution is asking the court to impose.

After a 20-minute recess, the trial reconvenes and Roger Phillips is invited by the judge to make a victim statement. He throws a quick backward glance in Vossen's direction as he is called forward to address the court. His words are translated into German as he speaks. He does not speak for very long but what he does say sums up Vossen's long fraudulent career with devastating effect. It is all the more powerful for its brevity. This is what he tells the judge: 'I apologise for being late arriving in court but my partner was taken ill on the way here. As with many of his victims, the impact of this has been quite traumatic. I hope nobody here is fooled by the crocodile tears of Felix Vossen. For 14 years he lied and cheated and stole the life savings of good people. He stole money from loved and trusted friends and even his own family. He is cunning and manipulative, all wrapped in a believable bundle. Many people have been left utterly ruined and destitute by his actions.'

Phillips finishes his short, dignified statement with a broadside against the 'weak regulatory and banking systems' that he says enabled Vossen to perpetrate his fraud in the first place and the gullible lawyers and accountants who were taken advantage of by their client.

After Phillips has sat down, the prosecutor Maric Demont spells out to the court why it should not be taken in by those 'crocodile tears'. He explains in detail how Vossen's investment empire was built on a mountain of false documentation, fake emails from non-existent employees, fraudulent claims about the performance of his fund and regular money transfers out of Switzerland into overseas bank accounts and beneficiaries.

Mr Steinmann, counsel for the defendant, then addresses the court in a plea of mitigation. Steinmann says Vossen wishes to take responsibility for his actions and has become emotional and depressed by the way he had defrauded investors. He says that Vossen began investing, initially in Apple shares, as a means of funding his studies. He is aware that he defrauded both friends and family but this was never his intention. Rather, Vossen had found himself 'living in an illusory world'. When that world collapsed in 2015, he fled in panic, not as part of a pre-planned scheme to evade justice.

When both sets of lawyers are done, Vossen stands to make his own plea of mitigation. He is armed with a thick green folder full of notes and a prepared statement. In the end, however, he only speaks for a few short minutes, again in that low, mumbling monotone voice. He repeats how sorry he is for his actions, how he understands that this is of little or no consolation to his victims and how he still wishes to make amends. 'I totally over-estimated my abilities,' he confesses.

Maric Demont disagrees. Far from being a reluctant victim of his own exaggerated capabilities, he describes Vossen as 'hard boiled and hard-bitten'. Vossen's actions and his modus operandi were, he says, 'abgebruht' – a German word meaning premediated and cold-blooded. 'The high life was more important to him than protecting his friends from getting into deeper trouble', says Demont.

The trial concludes just before noon and Judge Aeppli and his two fellow judges retire to consider their verdict, which is expected around mid-afternoon. Vossen is removed from the courtroom, placed in handcuffs and escorted to a cell in the court precincts to await the verdict. When the time reaches 4pm, Judge Aeppli sends word that it will be at least another two hours before sentencing is announced. Finally, the court reconvenes at 6.30pm. Vossen is not asked to make any statement, nor does he move to say anything. In contrast to his demeanour earlier in the day – all hand-wringing, fist-clenching and cheek-sucking – he appears calm. It is almost as if the fraudster is relieved that the long wait is at an end. In a strange way, it appears he is looking forward to being sentenced.

In deciding the length of his sentence, the court has to balance a number of considerations. Several aggravating factors count against Vossen. First, the fraud was conducted over a very long period of time and was perpetuated by the deliberate use of fictional employees, fake emails and forged documents – nearly 100 bogus statements of account were sent to investors. Second, only a very small amount of investors' money was ever actually used for its intended purpose. Third, and most damagingly, Vossen fostered very close personal relationships with his victims in order to carry out the fraud.

On the other hand and in his favour, Vossen has pleaded guilty and he has also shown remorse for his crimes. Prolonged cocaine use had also lowered his 'inhibition threshold,' encouraging him to take on more clients and inflating his sense of self-believe that he could eventually repay the money he had stolen.

Judge Aeppli's 100-page written verdict examines the personal nature of the fraud in some detail and it is clear this bears heavily on the sentence. The judge notes that for many of his investors, the relationship went well beyond mere friendship:

Roger Phillips had described Vossen as 'an ex-boyfriend' whilst Jake Sinclair said of him: 'It's not just the loss of the millions, it's also losing a relationship with a man I loved.' Steven Walters had simply told prosecutors that Vossen was treated as though he were a brother 'and if it's someone who is almost family, then you trust him'.

For his part, Vossen had said of Sinclair: 'He was one of my best friends and I miss him terribly', while Angela Shaw was a woman he 'really liked' and for whom he had 'great respect'. Other victims, Vossen confessed, were 'just nice people and good friends. We did lots of things together and the relationship was very close'.

Weighing all these factors in the balance, Judge Aeppli concluded: 'The fact that, despite these deep personal relationships, the accused did not shy away from enriching himself at their expense and obviously exploiting their trust to gain access to their assets, is evidence of considerable criminal energy.'

Just how much Vossen enriched himself is laid out in detail in the judgement: over a 12-year period, Vossen spent £6 million of investors' money on his own personal needs. Vossen conceded in court that he had not exactly lived 'like a church mouse' while he was working out how to repay the money he had stolen from his victims. Judge Aeppli put it this way: 'If he had really only been concerned with correcting his wrongdoing, a more modest lifestyle would have been expected.'

Taken together, the three charges of fraud, forgery and money laundering on which Vossen was convicted, merited a tariff of eight years. However, his guilty plea and demonstration of remorse act in mitigation.

Judge Aeppli instructs Vossen to stand. He passes a sentence of six years imprisonment and says: 'I hope this is a lesson for you... I hope you will be able to rebuild your life when you get out.'

There is one other element to the verdict. Vossen has no money or other assets that anyone has been able to locate but he is still liable to pay his victims £14.5 million in compensation, plus interest of 5 per cent in some cases, according to a complicated formula calculated by the court. He also owes defence counsel CHF41,594.

Vossen turns to shake the hand of his lawyer and is escorted from court to begin his sentence. With good behaviour and taking into account time already served on remand, he can expect to be out in the spring of 2020.

11

IN PRISON

Prisoner TN950 NV1 is already pacing the visitor room of Justizvollzugsanstalt Poschwies, the Swiss penal institute on the outskirts of Zurich that has been his home for the past year, waiting for the afternoon influx of mothers, brothers, wives and assorted friends to begin. He receives few visits and therefore places a premium on being punctual, so much so that he has arrived early for this visit and is the only person, inmate or otherwise, in the room.

He accepts the offer of a coffee and a bottle of still water from the automated vending machine and gestures nervously, sheepishly almost, to a corner table by the window. He draws up one of the hard plastic chairs, sits down and leans forward with his elbows on the table and his chin cupped in one hand. From here at least he can feel the sun on his face and enjoy a view of the sky and the grassed area beyond the reinforced glass, albeit a vista that ends in a 12-foot high fence and, beyond that, another grass moat and more fencing topped off with razor wire.

Felix Vossen cuts a very different figure from the svelte, self-confident financier with the flowing auburn locks who graced the bars, restaurants and film studios of London. Vossen's expensive wardrobe and handmade Italian shoes have been replaced by a prison-issue uniform of baby blue T-shirt, brown cotton drill trousers and trainers and his wrist sports a cheap black plastic watch in place of the Rolex he once wore. He has grown simultaneously thinner in the face and fatter in the girth – the result, you presume, of a combination of prison food and the strain of incarceration. Since his arrest in Spain in February 2016, Vossen has been in detention for more than two years and the toll is beginning to tell.

His face is drawn and pock-marked and his pale arms are covered in ugly red lesions as though he has taken to repeatedly gouging or scratching himself. His T-shirt is soiled and as the afternoon wears on the sweat permeates further through its fabric. He is, by turns, manic, morose and histrionic. There are precious few glimpses of the Felix Vossen of old, save for one humorous interlude when he jokes about providing financial advice to his fellow inmates. He doodles incessantly on the blank sheets of A4 paper the prison guards had given him as he entered the visitor room. At the end of the visit he will have to hand them back in.

It is May 2018 and Vossen is six months into his six-year sentence. Taking into account the months he had already spent on remand prior to his prosecution and sentencing and provided he earns the maximum amount of remission, Poschwies will be Vossen's home for a minimum of two more years. His new accommodation is a far cry from the sumptuous central London apartment that he lived in not so very long ago. Where once house guests entered his Jermyn Street abode through a portico to be greeted by deep pile carpets and a uniformed concierge, anyone visiting Vossen now must ring the bell at Roosstrasse 49 and negotiate a security chamber with twin inter-locking steel doors before being interrogated by a distinctly surly prison guard, frisked and deprived of pen, paper and any means of electronic communication. Where once Vossen could look out and enjoy the eclectic mix of Palladian architecture and Georgian stucco facades that make up the streets of St James's, he is surrounded now by high walls, more high walls and beyond that dour, utilitarian residential blocks that house the prison staff. Poschwies, set in the suburb of Regensdorf, a 20-minute taxi ride from the centre of Zurich, is anything but the three-star hotel some might imagine a Swiss prison to be.

It is the country's largest prison, its linear, low-rise, concrete edifice housing a total of 426 inmates. Had Vossen been tried and sentenced in the UK, where most of his victims are to be found, then he might have been sent to a Category C jail with other non-violent and largely white-collar criminals, perhaps looking forward even to serving the last few months of his stretch in an open prison. As it is, Vossen has no choice but to do his time in the company of killers, paedophiles and armed robbers; something that he clearly finds unsettling and intimidating. Poschwies caters for a mixed bag of male adult prisoners serving sentences of a year or more, though some of its inmates are incarcerated there indefinitely. The one small consolation for Vossen is that he has been moved into a single cell from the shared one he was placed in on his arrival.

'I'm not in a good place', he says repeatedly over the course of the three-hour visit. Whether he is referring to his immediate surroundings or his state of mind is never entirely clear. As the room slowly fills with other prisoners and their visitors, many of whom have small children in tow, Vossen becomes more distracted and his voice louder. His delivery is rambling, he responds to many questions by asking a question straight back and his performance is punctuated by frequent, lachrymose breakdowns. What is obvious, however, is that Felix Vossen remains obsessed with Felix Vossen. If he has tears for his crimes and the victims of those crimes, they appear to be of the crocodile variety.

This is the only interview Vossen has given since he was jailed and it is the only interview he intends to give. We know this because Vossen has telephoned the Swiss prosecutor Maric Demont from Poschwies to tell him that he will not be responding to any of the great many media requests to talk about his crimes and his time in prison. What follows, then, is Vossen's own patchy account of his actions from 2000 onwards. You may choose to believe it – or you may conclude it is a masterclass in narcissism, self-pity and self-delusion. One thing is plain: to this day, Vossen has a great deal of difficulty acknowledging and owning his crimes.

Vossen says he has spent his early months in confinement writing two accounts of what he did. One is 'factual but dull'; the other spiced up and entertaining. He believes that if he could only publish a version of this, then those who read it will be sufficiently moved to crowd-fund a compensation scheme for his victims. The idea is as fanciful and fictional as the non-existent investment opportunities he dangled before his friends for so many years.

Where did it all begin, Felix? 'I had an interest in investing for as long as I can remember,' he says. 'I was 12 when I began trading and bought my first shares. They were in Sony and I had to get my parents' permission. I could not continue trading shares when I went to the Alpinum Zuoz because the school would not permit it.'

Vossen says that when he left school, he quickly began dabbling once more in the stock market. 'I had a budget of £180 a week for food and general expenses but I soon discovered that I could make $40,000 in a single trade,' he claims. That may or may not be true but it is certainly what he told his early investors. It is also what he appeared to be able to demonstrate when would-be investors came to witness his trading operation.

Blessed with such a Midas touch, it was only fair that he should begin to share the fruits of his stock market success with others. 'I was trading on my own account until the dot.com crash of 1999,' he says. 'After that I began investing other people's money. The internet had made it so much easier to deal. It started with me making more money that I had intended and then being super-generous by giving a lot of it away. I gave people money all the time in the early days. I wanted to take care of people and they wanted to take care of me.'

So, when did it all begin to go wrong? 'At first I was making lots of very successful trades,' Vossen claims. 'But later the trading became more risk-based depending on which button you pressed. I just found myself getting deeper and deeper into a hole.'

Vossen admits he began to incur actual losses on his share trading while continuing to report spectacular but fictional gains to his investors. 'I had two options: either stop trading and suck it up or try to fix it knowing it would probably be five years before I had made up the losses and my real accounts were back in balance,' he says.

Vossen admits he was always 'a terrible book keeper' with what he describes as 'a tenuous grasp of administration'. But how could any of this justify his creation of three entirely fictitious employees who then proceeded to communicate regularly with investors? In most people's minds, this would be the clearest evidence possible that Vossen was engaged in fraudulent activity on a grand scale. But he has a different and ingenious explanation: 'I had a rich friend who invented employees to make his business seem more extensive and impressive than it really was. Later, when he was genuinely successful, he would tell people what he had done. He made a joke of it. I decided that if he could do it then so could I, so I copied him.'

The many close friends who became investors failed to see the funny side of it. What would Vossen say today if he was sat opposite Angela Shaw, for example, who is subsisting in Mexico on a widow's pension and the generosity of her younger daughter? The question provokes another howl from deep inside his diaphragm followed by a flood of tears and a terrible shaking of Vossen's body. And something approaching penitence.

'I've abandoned and betrayed everyone who ever meant anything to me until the point that it became too much,' he says. 'I've cheated and defrauded people, there's no doubt about that. I've done some bad things.'

But barely has the confession left his lips than he is on the attack. 'There are people in the group [of investors] who didn't lose any money but are claiming that they have so they can make a profit,' he alleges. For good measure, Vossen adds that he wants to have a say in how any money is distributed should the investor group succeed in extracting compensation from the banks he traded through. Why so? In order that he can discriminate between 'deserving and undeserving' cases.

There are many things Vossen's investors would like to know from him. Not least what finally triggered his decision to flee London and go into hiding in Spain, rather than stay and face up to his criminality. Vossen will not say whether there was a catalyst. What he does say is this: 'When it all began to get too much I had three options: I could hide, I could run or I could play dead. I decided to run and pretend that it wasn't happening. I thought I would go crazy if I didn't disappear. I had to get away, the pressure was all too much.

'It was terrible to have to pull the rug from under everyone's feet. People are always looking for certainty and that is what I tried to offer them because I never had room in my own life for doubt. People want to smoke but they never think they will get cancer. They don't think about death.'

As Vossen recounts the moment when he elected to flee rather than face the music, he drifts again into self-pitying mode. 'I couldn't communicate with anyone because it was too dangerous. I had no access to social media. I went from receiving 300 emails a day to getting none. I was on beta-blockers when I disappeared and I had to double the dose. It felt surreal. Being on the run is very difficult.'

Beyond these few sketchy references to his initial trading strategy and his disappearance, Vossen is prepared to discuss little else: not his relationship with his siblings and parents; not the effect on him of the failure of the family business; not the tipping point at which he went from being a not very astute share trader to an outright fraudster; and, most importantly, what impelled him to do what he did, why he chose to betray his best friends in such a cruel and unusual way and what his conscience was telling him as he set methodically about the business of fraud.

He is, however, expansive on one of his favourite themes – the trials and tribulations of confinement. It took nine months in remand, he says, to be weaned off an addiction to prescription drugs. 'You can't imagine how horrible it all was'. At one point he complains about how he was locked up in the same cell as a dozen Nigerians for 'weeks on end', as if this is meant to convey something and illicit sympathy. On his arrival at Poschwies, his first encounters, he says, were with one prisoner who had killed several family members and another who was a serial paedophile. 'I don't know how I survived it.'

But survive he must until his earliest likely release date of February 2020. Prisoners at Poschwies are required to work and so Vossen has had several menial jobs. Initially he was put to work weaving baskets. He then moved to laundry and cooking duties and has now graduated to a job assembling electrical components. Poschwies also offers all inmates the opportunity to learn a new skill and so Vossen has been taught how to solder.

Poschwies offers yoga classes to its inmates but Vossen has not signed up, even though he was a huge fan of the discipline when he lived in London. He finds his days in prison 'quite pointless' and worries about the effect it is having on his mental as well as his physical well-being. He also laments, without any apparent hint of irony, how difficult it is to believe anything anybody tells you. 'Everyone in prison lies, it is impossible to take what other inmates tell you at face value.' Then again, Vossen is also struck by how much lawyers lie too, and how careless and incompetent financial regulators can be. 'All you have to do is tick the right boxes and you can do what you want.'

To this day, he also still believes in the investment strategy that he purportedly began with two decades ago. 'If someone else had approached me with that investment proposition, I would have done it, I would have believed in it,' he says. 'My trading strategy was sound at the beginning and people are still using similar strategies today, investing in Apple and the like. Think of the profit you'd be sitting on today if you'd invested $100 in Apple shares ten years ago and still held those same shares today.'

For the record, Felix, the answer is $737. Think, however, of the profit your investors would be sitting on today had they never entrusted you with their money in the first place.

It was a performance that would have been very familiar to those former friends and investors who made the painful journey to visit Vossen in prison in search of answers and information, or travelled to the Public Prosecutor's office in Zurich to give evidence against Vossen. They invariably left frustrated and empty-handed.

Jake Sinclair travelled to Switzerland twice following Vossen's arrest – the first time to cross-examine Vossen in the presence of the state prosecutor Maric Demont and then later to see Vossen on remand. He remembers the first encounter thus:

> I was outside the prosecutor's office waiting to go in when I saw Vossen walking past hand-cuffed to a policeman. Although he was wearing smart trainers and casual clothes, he looked an absolute wreck. He was white as a sheet and had lost weight. This was the first time I'd seen my nemesis since his capture and arrest and he was six feet away from me. I felt physically sick. This was the man who had betrayed me and betrayal is an extraordinary experience. It had never happened to me before. It fills you with shame and disgrace to think what an idiot you had been by falling for his claptrap. It is very easy to get into a downward spiral of shame and self-loathing.

I made it my business to be as professional a witness as possible, but I was constantly interrupted by Vossen breaking down in the most theatrical and histrionic way as if there had been some misunderstanding and he was being misrepresented. At the end of my cross-examination the prosecutor had built in time in the schedule for a more informal conversation between me and Vossen. I looked at the man in horror and decided I wasn't going to give him the pleasure. His crocodile tears were by now enraging me. He just wanted to weep publicly and somehow making out that HE was the victim.

He said he would write to me to set the record straight. It was a theatrical way of intimating there was a story we had not understood and if we only heard and knew his side of things his crime would feel less heinous. Of course, he never did write. After he'd left the room I broke down completely. It was difficult but in some respects it was also therapeutic.

Of the second meeting, he says:

I'd gone to visit Vossen to persuade him to furnish us with information to show that certain Swiss banks were infringing the rules. He sat down opposite us and the crocodile tears started. He was now a complete stranger. He lied with the same ease that most of us draw breath. He kept stating that he was trying to make everything good and make back everything that had been lost. I asked what particular deal he was going to do to magic up the money. It was quite clear that he simply hadn't taken responsibility for his actions, that he hadn't owned his crime. I was by now so furious that I determined to get a clear, unambiguous confession from the man. I said to him, 'Repeat after me: "I lied to you about my trading. I lied to you in every single financial statement".'

With agonizing reluctance Vossen slowly repeated Sinclair's words.

Very few of Vossen's victims and former friends want anything more to do with him. But he still feels the need to connect with them and has spoken on several occasions to both Jane Leinster and his former film producing partner Barnaby Southcombe. Is he seeking absolution or forgiveness? If so, he is yet to show genuine penitence.

Although he resents the loss of freedom, the monotony of jail, and the brain-rotting effects of confinement, Vossen conversely relishes the safety and solitude of his single cell. It is his security blanket in a closed and sometimes violent little world. What will Vossen do when he is released from prison? 'I've got to do something but what can I do? he says. ' I don't think they gave me a long enough sentence. I was expecting to still be in prison when I was 60.'

Just as he was first to arrive in the visitor room, Vossen is the last to leave and, after the place has emptied out, he says his goodbyes. He has a farewell message for those who have been put through so much misery and anguish by his actions. 'My hope and dream every night before I go to sleep is that I can find some way of making things better for all those people who have been put through such massive changes in their lives because of me,' he says. 'I'm so angry with myself that I can hardly get out of bed any longer.'

12

THE BENT TREE

What was it that turned Vossen from outwardly confident but inwardly insecure obsessive into the manipulative and premeditated fraudster that he was to become? Was it something in his childhood – sibling rivalry, perhaps, or his difficult relationship with his parents and closeness to his paternal grandfather? Was it the humiliating collapse of the family business and its resurrection under different ownership? Or was it being closeted in the Swiss Alps with a self-selecting group of other high-performers during his boarding school years, a suffocating experience which Vossen later described to friends as a terribly unhappy period in his life? If it was none of these then perhaps it was the result of some chemical change in the brain during his childhood followed by his descent into drug addiction in his late teenage years? Or maybe deception was already hard-wired into his psyche and engrained in his very genetic make-up when Felix Burghardt Norbert Vossen first came into this world.

In other words, was Vossen born a fraudster and possessed of an innate predisposition to deceive people? Or was it something that was fashioned by his upbringing and conditioned by the environment in which he found himself? Did he inherit his badness or did he achieve it? What shaped Vossen's personality and what twisted it out of shape?

We know that Vossen underwent psychiatric assessment prior to his prosecution. It formed part of the case his defence lawyer used unsuccessfully to argue for a postponement of trial proceedings. Vossen has also been assessed subsequently by prison psychotherapists. We do not know what the outcome of any of those assessments was because they remain confidential. But from all we know of the man it is reasonable to postulate that he probably suffers from some form of personality disorder.

A great deal more is known today about this condition than was the case half a century ago when Felix Vossen was born. Over the past 50 years personality disorders have become a more widely researched, well-documented, better understood and respected branch of medicine.

There is a school of thought which says that all conmen such as Vossen are by definition psychopaths in that they lack basic empathy for other human beings and it is this which enables them to carry out their crimes with the nonchalance, lack of guilt and absence of remorse that they typically display. Robert D. Hare, the respected Canadian psychologist, developed what became known as the Psychopathy Checklist in the 1970s and it is still used to this day. It is a 20-strong inventory of characteristics or attributes ranging from grandiosity, promiscuity, superficial charm and cunning to remorsefulness, responsibility, impulsiveness and manipulativeness. The test is carried out in the form of a lengthy, structured interview, carried out by a qualified clinician in scientifically-controlled conditions. If an individual scores highly enough, then they qualify as a psychopath. Vossen would likely produce a very respectable score, but then so might any number of FTSE100 or Fortune 500 chief executives and politicians, including a good few world leaders. Hare estimates that about 1 per cent of the adult male population are psychopaths.

Then there is Machiavellianism, named after the Italian Renaissance diplomat and writer Niccolo Machiavelli and shorthand today for an ability to deceive and manipulate born out of duplicitousness and amorality. Machiavelliansim is one of the 'dark triad' of personality defects, along with psychopathy and narcissism.

In the late 1960s, two psychologists from Columbia University, Richard Christie and Florence Geis, developed what became known as the Machiavellianism test – a means of measuring a person's capacity for deception and manipulation based on their response to a set of twenty statements. Those defined as 'High Machs' endorsed statements such as 'Never tell anyone the real reason you did something unless it is useful to do so' while' Low Machs' identified with statements such as 'There is no excuse for lying to someone else'. They went on to carry out a number of controlled studies in which subjects were presented with particular, stressful scenarios. The 'High Machs' almost always performed better because they were able to separate emotions from their thought processes, enabling them to bluff, bargain and cheat more effectively. These findings were presented in a 1970 book *Studies in Machiavellianism* and their test went on to become part of the standard tool kit used in the psychometric assessment of job applicants.

Call them what you will: are these personality defects inherited in the genes, learnt behaviour or can it they be physiologically-induced? And are psychopaths predisposed to become fraudsters and conmen or is it akin to the theory of smoking and cancer once pedalled by the tobacco lobby: that smoking does not cause cancer, rather those who develop cancer are also predisposed to smoke? Clinical studies have certainly shown that psychopaths give different physical responses – as measured by bodily functions such as pulse, heart and perspiration rates – when presented with stressful situations where moral or ethical considerations play a part in an individual's decision-making. There is also medical evidence to suggest that people who suffer lesions in their polar and ventromedial cortex in their early childhood years are prone to developing psychopathic tendencies.

The American neuroscientist James H. Fallon, professor of psychiatry and human behaviour at the University of California, subscribes to the view that psychopathy is largely determined genetically. He reached this conclusion whilst conducting a routine study into Alzheimer's, part of which involved brain imaging scans being taken of him and his family to form a 'control' group. What he discovered to his initial surprise was that one of the unlabelled brain scans bore a striking resemblance to the many brain scans he had seen of serial killers and psychopaths. His mother then confided to him that he was distantly related to a number of famous psychopaths in history including Lizzie Borden (she of the ghoulish nursery rhyme) who was suspected but acquitted of murdering her parents with an axe in 1892.

Fallon's discovery was reported in the *Wall Street Journal* and subsequently documented in a book, *The Psychopath Inside*, in which he describes himself as a psychopath, though one of the 'pro-social' variety. He does, however, concede that traumatic early childhood experiences and events can turbo-charge that genetic disposition to psychopathy by baking it in chemically before parenting and upbringing can teach the child a moral code. These individuals are what is known as 'primary psychopaths' whereas 'secondary psychopaths', or sociopaths to give them the better-known description, are individuals who suffer trauma in later childhood, by which time they have a basic grasp of what a moral code looks like but do not care. Fallon, like Hare, estimates that 1 per cent of the male population are full-blown psychopaths but as many as 5 per cent may be borderline.

The nature versus nurture debate rages on, but the burden of current thinking amongst psychotherapists is that psychopathy or personality disorder results from a combination of factors. Psychoanalysts like to compare the individual with such a condition to a 'bent tree'. The tree may become bent because it has been grown from a bad seed or because it has been planted in poor soil or because it is sited in a location exposed to strong prevailing winds. Likewise, a personality may become bent because of something an individual inherits from their parents, because of the domestic circumstances in which they grow up or because of difficulty in dealing with the external environment to which they are exposed.

In technical jargon this is what is known as 'biopsychosocial' causation and it is a theory of personality disorder to which many mental health professionals subscribe. In essence, the theory states that such disorders are not attributable to a single factor but are likely to be the complex and intertwined result of a combination of three different sets of factors: first, biological and genetic factors; second, psychological factors such as an individual's personality and temperament as shaped their environment and the skills they learn in order to cope with stress; and thirdly social factors – such as how an individual reacts with family, friends and other children in their early years.

The word 'psychopath' is a lurid, catch-all piece of terminology which disguises many more subtle and differentiated forms of personality disorder. The bible of psychoanalysts is *The Diagnostic and Statistical Manual of Mental Disorders (DSM)*, published by the American Psychiatric Association and now in its fifth edition. The authors of *DSM5*, to give it its shorthand title, describe personality disorder in the following dessicated, matter-of-fact language: 'An enduring pattern of inner experience and behavior that deviates markedly from the expectations of the individual's culture, is pervasive and inflexible, has an onset in adolescence or early adulthood, is stable over time, and leads to distress or impairment.'

According to *DSM5*, personality disorders may be exacerbated by the loss of or separation from a 'significant supporting person' such as a spouse or parent or loss of a 'stabilising social situation' – for instance, a regular job. Felix Vossen's childhood, adolescence and progression into early adulthood were punctuated by long periods of separation from his parents – first when they sent him to boarding school in the Swiss Alps and then when he entered his long and self-imposed estrangement from his mother and father. Some personality disorders – such as anti-social and borderline personality disorder – tend to become less acute the older an individual becomes. Others, such as obsessive-compulsive and schizotypal personality disorders, tend not to recede with age. Some are more prevalent among men than women and vice-versa.

The American Psychiatric Association classifies a dozen different types of personality disorder – from paranoid personality disorder to dependent personality disorder – and one catch-all category known as unspecified personality disorder where some but not all traits of several different personality disorders are present in one individual and that individual's personality pattern meets the threshold at which it would be classed as being disordered.

Then there are a whole subset of substance-related and addictive disorders relating to ten separate classes of drugs from alcohol, caffeine and cannabis to hallucinogens, opioids and stimulants such as cocaine, the drug to which Vossen was addicted. Personality disorders exist independently and are not caused by the physiological effects of substance abuse, but substance disorder can undoubtedly exacerbate the symptoms of personality disorder.

Most people with such disorders will not resort to criminality of any kind. However, it is also sobering to note that such disorders are more common amongst the population than perhaps generally thought. According to *DSM5*, the prevalence of borderline personality disorder amongst the general population is estimated to be 1.6 per cent but it may be as high as 5.9 per cent. For narcissistic personality disorder, the range is 0–6.2 per cent and for obsessive-compulsive personality disorder it is 2.1 per cent to 7.9 per cent.

Based on the markers which distinguish different types of disorder and judging by the testimony of those closest to him as he defrauded his way through life, Vossen would appear to be the product of a complex cocktail of several different personality disorders, mixed together and given an added twist and shake by his prodigious appetite for Colombian marching powder.

The three conditions which appear to align most closely with what we know of Vossen's character, behaviour and actions are borderline personality disorder, narcissistic personality disorder and obsessive-compulsive personality disorder.

Borderline personality disorder is defined in *DSM5* as 'a pattern of instability in interpersonal relationships, self-image and affects and marked impulsivity'. Those who suffer from this condition also make frantic efforts to avoid real or imagined abandonment. 'The perception of impending separation or rejection or loss of external structure can lead to profound changes in self-image, affect, cognition and behaviour,' according to *DSM5*. Onset typically begins in early adulthood and is characterised by nine distinct types of behaviour. The disorder is deemed to exist if an individual ticks five or more of the nine boxes.

One box is a tendency to be impulsive in ways that can potentially cause self-harm – for example by binge-eating, having unprotected or promiscuous sex, driving recklessly, abusing drugs excessively or spending extravagantly. Another is being prone to temper tantrums and inappropriate, intense or constant anger, and having difficulty controlling that anger. A third is engaging in unstable and intense interpersonal relationships which alternate between idolising and demonising the other person in that relationship. A fourth is suffering from chronic feelings of emptiness. A fifth is making frantic efforts to avoid a real or imagined fear of abandonment.

Felix Vossen displayed many of these behaviours. His cocaine dependency and abuse is well-documented by friends who knew him in his early years in London, such as Mickey de Fernandez-Paz. It was also acknowledged by Vossen himself in court.

His sexual proclivities were also witnessed and hinted at. Fernandez-Paz remembers Vossen's contact with prostitutes, male and female, and one of his investors, Charles Huntley, recalls an odd incident one evening in Soho.

> It would have been sometime in 2015. We went into a restaurant in China Town called Plum Valley and bumped into Felix. He was having dinner with a dubious looking Chinese guy. We thought it odd that we weren't introduced to this man but Vossen later came over to our table for a chat and made out it was all so embarrassing, as we had seen him smoking outside when he was supposed to have given up. From that point on we always suspected he was gay.

Another investor recalls Vossen, apparently in jest, suggesting that they call a couple of prostitutes to liven up an evening out. When the idea was met with an awkward and embarrassed silence, the subject was quickly dropped.

His chronic feelings of emptiness were also noted by a number of former friends and investors. Angela Shaw remembers Vossen thus:

> The length of his hugs was indeed intense and I just always felt he needed those hugs so much. I felt that deep down, he was so lonely and so unsure. He desperately wanted reassurance. Setting himself up in the film industry really gave Felix a great identity for a while, but then that started to challenge him too, leaving him feeling empty as well. I don't think he has any real emotional savvy, it was all a game for him because he was so damaged and empty inside.

Individuals with borderline personality disorder are prone to sudden, unpredictable and shocking outbursts of intense anger, sometimes accompanied by extreme sarcasm. These are often followed by shame, guilt and contrition as if the fault lies not with the object of the individual's anger but with the sufferer, who may regard the outburst as one more example of their evil nature. Vossen's unpredictable outbursts of anger are well-documented by friends and professional colleagues alike. Chris Simon, his co-producer at Embargo Films, recounted how Vossen's anger 'was irrational and would come seemingly out of the blue. Something would click and he would explode in the most hurtful and ugly way. He would get over it quite quickly and never seemed to bear a grudge or sulk, but his outbursts were quite shocking,' Simon recalls. 'I remember one incident where he was screaming at me under his breath in a restaurant while the person we were with went to the bathroom because, apparently, I wasn't representing the company in what he considered a perfect light. When she returned it was as if nothing had happened. His smile re-appeared and he was back to his old self.'

Then there is the time Vossen physically assaulted Mickey de Fernandez-Paz and threatened to kill him if he ever told his girlfriend Sophia Rafaat about Vossen's drug-taking habits and sexual peccadillos.

Vossen also had one of those intense, interpersonal relationships with Rafaat that characterise borderline personality syndrome, where the sufferer 'may quickly switch from idealizing other people to devaluing them, feeling that the other person does not care enough, does not give enough or is not "there" enough'. With Rafaat, Vossen veered erratically between lauding her beauty and showering her with expensive gifts to castigating her for excessive drinking and smoking and lack of exercise, to the extent that he warned her at one point that he could no longer live with her until she had sorted out her life.

There are two other traits of borderline personality disorder that are instructive in attempting to assess Felix Vossen. According to *DSM5*, individuals with this condition 'may have a pattern of undermining themselves at the moment a goal is about to be realised, for example, dropping out of school just before graduation.' Individuals with this disorder may also 'feel more secure with transitional objects (a pet or inanimate possession) than in interpersonal relationships'.

Vossen exhibited both of these characteristics. He flunked almost every educational milestone – quitting his expensive Swiss boarding school without taking his Swiss Matura or German Arbitur, failing to graduate from his business studies degree and becoming bored with his law apprenticeship (boredom being another classic sign of borderline disorder). As for a fascination with inanimate possessions, we know about Vossen's obsession with his stuffed toys, his penchant for taking them everywhere with him and the lurid games he would enact with them.

Borderline personality disorder is about five times more common amongst those whose parents or siblings also suffer from the same condition. It is also more prevalent in women than men – by a ratio of three to one. It occurs often alongside depressive or bipolar disorder.

Nacissistic personality disorder, the second condition which Vossen shows clear traits of, is defined as 'a pervasive pattern of grandiosity (in fantasy or behaviour), need for admiration and lack of empathy'. Vossen did display empathy of a certain kind in the way that he appeared to identify with the neuroses and pre-occupations of his victims. But it was empathy of the ersatz variety. It was carefully contrived but entirely fake. Narcissistic personality disorder is usually established once an individual reaches early adulthood. It is characterised by an exaggerated sense of self-importance, a pre-occupation with fantasies of success, power, brilliance, beauty or ideal love, an arrogant belief on the part of the sufferer that they are 'special' and can only be understood by those of a similar elevated status, a need for excessive admiration and a sense of entitlement. Sufferers are ruthlessly exploitative of others but they may also be envious of them. Between a half and three-quarters of individuals diagnosed with this condition are men. Cocaine users are especially prone to suffer from narcissistic personality disorder.

If Felix Vossen does not tick all these boxes, then he ticks most of them. Because of their overweening sense of self-importance, narcissistic personalities routinely over-estimate their abilities and inflate their achievements in an especially boastful fashion. By his own admission in court, Vossen massively over-estimated his abilities as a stock trader and how capable he was of making good the huge losses that his investors, unbeknown to them, were experiencing. At the same time, the braggadocio with which he flaunted the supposed size of his investment empire and the amount of money he had under management – which ranged from $250 million to $350 million – was quite breathtaking.

Propelled along by fantasies of his own power, brilliance and success, Vossen sought and demanded adulation from those around him. As *DSM5* notes: 'Individuals with this disorder generally require excessive admiration. They may be pre-occupied with how well they are doing and how favourably they are regarded by others. They may expect their arrival to be greeted with great fanfare and are astonished if others do not covet their possessions.' When Vossen did not receive the requisite adoration, or when he felt that those closest to him were not re-inforcing his perfect self-image of someone who associated with other high-status perfectionists, he became angry.

Although outwardly arrogant and self-important, sufferers of narcissistic personality disorder almost invariably suffer from low self-esteem. This can be witnessed in Vossen's desperate need for re-assurance from those around him and constant fishing for compliments, his preoccupation with how well others thought he was doing, his doubts about whether he really was cut out for a career in film-making and his confessions of loneliness and insecurity. Typically, he also sought to bolster his own self-esteem by ensuring it was mirrored by those with whom he associated. Sufferers are likely to insist on being looked after by the 'top' person or being affiliated and connected with the best institutions. For Vossen, this was reflected in his choice of Saville Row tailors, Fortnum & Mason as his grocery store and his selection of Barclays, UBS and Credit Suisse as his bankers.

Another trait of the narcissistic personality is an unreasonable expectation of favourable treatment and an intense dislike of being expected to wait in line – one reason, perhaps, Vossen eschewed public transport and took cabs everywhere. A further characteristic is the dedication and commitment they expect from others, the high standards they expect them to perform to and their disappointment, indeed puzzlement and occasional fury, when this is not forthcoming. There are many instances of this in Vossen's relationship with his fellow film partners at Embargo and elsewhere. Remember his furious encounter in Hamburg with Michael Eckelt, one of the German producers of *I, Anna,* when Vossen complained angrily about Eckelt's attitude towards the project and demanded he withdrew from it – only to backtrack when told that he needed a German producer in order to qualify for German arts funding.

Vossen was prone to discussing his own concerns and pre-occupations for many hours – whether it be the illnesses that had befallen him, his parents and siblings, the ups and downs of his romantic relationships or his frustrations with life and career – without necessarily reciprocating or recognising the feelings and needs of others. Again, a marker of the narcissistic personality.

As for his exploitative nature and willingness to take advantage of others to achieve his own ends, this virtually defined his 12-year-long Ponzi, while his lack of empathy was amply demonstrated by the attitude he displayed on trial and in prison. Given the opportunity to repent, Vossen offered only crocodile tears and faux contrition rather than genuine remorse for his actions and willingness to help his victims borne out of an understanding of their plight.

According to *DSM5*, narcissistic personality disorder does not necessarily predispose an individual to being deceitful and those with the condition 'usually lack a history of conduct disorder in childhood or criminal behaviour in adulthood'. This, however, begs the question of whether Vossen deluded himself to the point where he did not regard his own actions as criminal but rather the result of someone struggling to please everyone and keep too many plates spinning at once. As he himself said: 'It was terrible to have to pull the rug from under everyone's feet. People are always looking for certainty and that is what I tried to offer them because I never had room in my own life for doubt.'

The third condition which Vossen exhibited clear signs of is obsessive-compulsive personality disorder. What struck many of those who came to know and trust Vossen was his obsessive-compulsive tendencies, in particular his anally-retentive fixation with cleanliness, order and perfection: the pristine condition of his apartment which looked for all the world like a show home that nobody lived in; the immaculate patent leather Italian shoes he would wear on country walks; his habit of cleaning up around guests as they ate. Psychoanalysts diagnose this condition as 'a pervasive pattern of pre-occupation with orderliness, perfectionism and mental interpersonal control at the expense of flexibility, openness and efficiency'. Indeed, so obsessed is the sufferer with process – observing details, lists, organisation, schedule – that the end purpose of any activity becomes secondary to the manner in which it is achieved.

Obsessive-compulsive personality disorder occurs twice as often in men as in women and there are eight classic indicators of the condition. Vossen's behaviour corresponds to a number of them, but not by any means all. Obsessive-compulsives will allow their perfectionism to interfere with the completion of the task in hand. They also have a tendency to stubbornness and unreasonableness, insisting that there is only one correct way of doing something, issuing detailed instructions for the most menial of everyday tasks such as washing the dishes or mowing the lawn. In Vossen's case, an example might be the 83 separate legal contracts he had drawn up to ensure everyone working on the production of the movie *I, Anna* performed as they were expected to and did as they were told.

Obsessive-compulsives are workaholics, often subordinating leisure activities to their work schedule: we do know that Vossen put in 12–14 hour days, and was not good at taking holidays. They will typically also obsess about household chores and domestic cleanliness: Vossen had a daily cleaner and, when the cleaner was not there, he had his mini-Dyson to collect the crumbs that fell from the dinner table.

Individuals with obsessive-compulsive personality disorder are also prone to expressing affection in a highly-controlled or stilted fashion – which, again, chimes with Vossen's elaborate greeting of friends, his over-long hugs, his inability to end a conversation without saying goodbye and expressing his love of the other person over and over again.

But then there are traits of the condition that do not bring Vossen to mind. Obsessive-compulsives are characteristically scrupulous in matters of morality and ethics. Vossen did not have many moral scruples or ethical standards, he led a dissolute early life in London and he took a laissez-faire attitude towards the publication of nude photographs of his long-time girlfriend Sophia Rafaat. Obsessive-compulsives are unable to discard worn-out or worthless objects even when they have no sentimental value. This is not the Felix Vossen that his friends knew. He was a man who was capable of shedding his skin many times and moving on. His was a possession-lite existence. He may have carried an immense amount of psychological baggage through life, but he did not carry much of the physical variety. When he went on the run, many of his possessions turned out to be rented.

Obsessive-compulsives are hoarders and they are misers. They hate to spend money on either themselves or others. This hardly paints a picture of Felix Vossen, who loved to dress in expensive clothes and shower those around him with gifts, large and small. Whatever else one might say about Vossen, it would be impossible to describe him as being anything other than the epitome of generosity, even if it was with other people's money.

There is one other physical manifestation of obsessive-compulsive disorder to which Vossen appears to have become prone: skin-picking. He picked his skin in court and he picked his skin in prison. Psychoanalysts describe it as the compulsive response to the obsession: a repetitive act that an individual feels driven to perform in order to suppress or drive away a forbidden or taboo thought, often of a religious, sexual or violent nature.

Other examples of compulsive activity designed to keep obsessions at bay are repetitive cleaning, washing or counting. About a third of individuals with obsessive-compulsive disorders suffer these physical tics and they are most commonly found in males who develop the condition in childhood. In the United States, the mean age at which obsessive-compulsive disorder begins is nineteen and a half. A quarter of cases start by the age of 14 but onset is rare after the age of 35.

Overlaying these psychological disorders are the substance-related and addictive disorders to which Vossen was undoubtedly prey. There is also evidence that individuals such as Vossen with low levels of self-control – possibly as a result of impairments to inhibitory mechanisms within the brain – are predisposed to developing substance-use disorder.

We know from the testimony of work colleagues, friends and investors alike that Vossen would simply disappear and go 'off radar' for periods of time. Was this partly related to the serious substance abuse to which he admitted? In acute cases, substance misuse can result in an individual's daily life being consumed entirely by the task of accessing or using the substance in question to the point where they fail to fufill work, school or home obligations, withdraw from family commitments and drop out of important social activities. Many of Vossen's investors can testify to his non-appearance at events where he was to have been the special guest. The Bakers, for one, vividly remember Vossen's failure to make the trip to Friedrichshaven to join them on board their Zeppelin flight of a lifetime.

Cocaine, Vossen's drug of choice, is associated with obsessive-compulsive disorder. It is also linked with the insomnia and sleep disturbance from which Vossen suffered. His difficulty sleeping was so acute that his sometime girlfriend Clare Obsorne had to resort to ear plugs and Night Nurse to get a good night's rest – or else sleep in a separate room altogether.

There appears to be little proven causal link between personality disorder and substance-related disorders. But there are indications, according to *DSM5*, that substance abuse intensifies pre-existing personality disorders and that intoxication through the use of stimulants such as cocaine can exacerbate some of the behaviours associated with mental conditions such as narcissistic personality disorder.

As James Fallon demonstrated, it is possible to be a functioning psychopath without also being a lying, manipulative, deceitful fraudster. But is it possible to be a fraudster such as Felix Vossen without possessing some form of psychopathic or personality disorder? In her entertaining and informative book *The Confidence Game*, Maria Konnikova makes the point that few people set out with a determination, built-in or otherwise, to become a fraudster. Few people chose to become fraudsters in a vacuum and whether they do turn to fraud will very often depend on predisposition meeting opportunity.

In one study she quotes of 600 cases of company fraud in 78 different countries between 2011 and 2013, a fifth said they had committed the fraud because the opportunity had presented itself, 40 per cent said they had done so out of simple greed but the biggest proportion – almost half – said they had been encouraged by their own narcissistic sense of superiority.

Many fraudsters, Vossen amongst them, will also seek to post-rationalise their behaviour as an example of a good intention gone wrong – an attempt to please people and make them happy by earning them money. Typically, this is then overtaken by events and becomes an exercise in doubling down in a desperate attempt to make amends and recover ground.

However, there is, she says, a common denominator amongst fraudsters: once the con begins, it is too late to brake and get off the sled. There are also set phases of the con to which nearly all frauds conform, including that perpetrated by Vossen. In order, these are:

Stage One: The Put-up. This involves identifying the victim or victims. Vossen found his victims through personal introduction and by word of mouth. Sometimes they were friends of his girlfriend and sometimes he took the simple but direct route of approaching his 'marks' on the street.

Stage Two: The Play. This is the art of developing an empathy and rapport with the victim in order to gain their trust. Vossen's technique was to exhaustively research the passions, interests, occupations and sometimes obsessions of his victims and then, chameleon-like, use the knowledge he had gained to inhabit their world and share their lives.

Stage Three: The Rope. Now the fraudster must use logic and persuasion to reel the victim in. An important element of this is to be a 'patient listener not a fast talker'. Vossen rarely pressurised his victims to invest with him. Rather, he played the long game and let them come to him. Much of the time, his victims had to virtually beg Vossen to take their money off them.

Stage Four: The Tale. It is human nature to want to believe in stories. The best fraudsters give their victims a story and a narrative that they can invest in, not just financially but emotionally. Vossen created the illusion that his investors were part of a select and privileged group. He invested their money in fast-growing and seemingly fool-proof assets such as Apple shares and then, for copper-bottomed protection, would overnight convert their winnings back into the safest of havens – US government bonds. It was the perfect combination of conservative caution laced with a splash of adventure. Nothing short of a nuclear war could blow Vossen's investment strategy out of the water.

Stage Five: The Convincer. Theory is all very well but investors need proof of how much money they could, are or will be making. Vossen achieved this by inviting would-be investors into his little lair and allowing them to witness a seemingly incredible but simulated share trade. Once hooked, investors were kept sweet, either with handsome real dividends paid for by other investors or with impressive but wholly fictitious statements of account.

Stage Six: The Breakdown. Otherwise known as the 'spider and fly'. Vossen's victims were sometimes minded to break free. But the more they struggled, the harder they found it to extricate themselves and they would even put money back into their fund that they had previously take out.

Stage Seven: The Send. In any con, there comes a point when the fraud is about to unravel and the perpetrator needs to persuade his victims to double down and increase their exposure. Vossen did this by inventing new high-performing, high-earning investments and telling investors that the more they were able to invest, the bigger the payout would be.

Stage Eight: The Touch. This is the final act in the scam, the moment when the victim is fleeced of every last penny. Several of Vossen's victims were persuaded to put their entire wealth, often from the sale of family homes, into his stock market investments funds rather than leaving the money on deposit in low-interest bank accounts.

Stage Nine: The Blow Off. In the aftermath of a fraud, it is not unusual for the perpetrator to get away with their crimes because their victims prefer to remain silent through fear of exposure, shame or sheer embarrassment at their naivety. This is the only phase that the Vossen fraud did not enter. Within ten days of his disappearance, Vossen's victims had alerted police forces in four countries to his fraud and frozen his worldwide assets through the courts, even though they did not expose the fraud in public for a further six months.

Fraudsters are known as 'the aristocrats of crime' for a good reason. Their weapons are not guns, knives and explosives. They are not even grappling hooks and glass cutters. Rather, they employ trust, sympathy and persuasion. Their crimes rely not on the use of fear and brute force, but the deployment of refined and practised psychological skills. Felix Vossen could just as easily have been an actor, a barrister or a preacher as a fraudster. He proselytised and his people followed.

Fraudsters succeed because their victims want to believe and, as Konnikova says, the story of belief is the oldest story told, as Chaucer, Voltaire, Mark Twain and Carl Sagan have all observed. 'We've done most of the work for them: we want to believe in what they are telling us,' she adds. 'Their genius lies in figuring out what, precisely, it is we want and how they can present themselves as the perfect vehicle for delivering on that desire.'

There is an old saw which runs: if something looks too good to be true, then it probably is too good to be true. The truth, however, is that when a fraudster such as Felix Vossen comes along, dangling temptation before everyone's eyes, most people can be persuaded to focus merely on the word 'probably'. And the roll-call of victims could have been much longer, had others not escaped Vossen's clutches because they were lucky enough to be elsewhere that day, to miss his telephone call or fail to make a meeting.

Whether it is religion, politics, magic, mysticism or astrology, it is human nature to want to believe in something. Credulity, not incredulity is the order of the day. Why do we believe in magic tricks, even though we know them not to be real? Why do we buy the promises of politicians, even though we know party manifestos are little more than wish lists? Why do we believe our football team will win the league, when reason and experience tell us that the chairman has not invested in the necessary playing squad?

Everyone is a potential victim, whether they are seasoned stock market investors and astute businessmen or retired pensioners and financial ingenues. Konnika quotes a 2011 study by Karla Park and Doug Shadel of 700 victims of fraud which found that those who fell prey to investment scams such as Ponzi schemes were more likely to be well-educated older men with income of more than $50,000 a year. Another study carried out by The American Association of Retired Persons found that 37 per cent of people above the age of 55 admitted to having fallen for a con.

Whether someone is defrauded will have little to do with their intelligence and gullibility and a lot to do with their personal circumstances. Some of Vossen's victims succumbed at a time when they were under acute emotional stress, had suffered earlier financial losses or were seeking to extricate themselves from onerous financial commitments.

We are all, or very nearly all, only a heartbeat away from being conned. This is why the Felix Vossens of this world exist and how they are able to ply their trade.

13

SURVIVING VOSSEN

Whilst Felix Vossen languishes in Poschwies prison, a guest of the Swiss state in a cell paid for out of the public purse, his victims are left to serve out their own sentences in private. Rarely a day goes by when they are not haunted by an uncomfortable but ineluctable thought: how could I have been such a fool? Why did I place such unquestioning trust in someone and how could I have been taken in by his bogus claims and false promises? What made me believe that Vossen could defy gravity and continue to make super-profits during periods when the world's stock markets were in freefall and even the best professional stock pickers were finding it virtually impossible to spot winners?

In short, why did Felix Vossen's victims suspend their disbelief and choose to ignore that most basic rule of investment: that if something looks too good to be true, then it probably is.

In their own minds, some of Vossen's investors have come to regard themselves as victims, not of a fraudster, but of their own greed and naivety. Complicit in their own downfall. Brought low by their own avarice.

Such mental self-flagellation is understandable. But it is also unworthy. None of those involved in the pursuit, apprehension and punishment of Vossen – from High Court judges and QCs to arresting police and public prosecutors – have ever experienced a fraud quite like the one he perpetrated or encountered a fraudster with his degree of guile, cunning and believability. If one acknowledges nothing else, then it is necessary to admire Felix Vossen's sheer technique. He was in the Premier League of fraud. Remember, too, that he was convincing enough to fool not only his best friends and closest professional colleagues but also his own parents.

Maric Demont, the Swiss State Prosecutor, has investigated many crimes and put many criminals behind bars but Felix Vossen broke new ground even for him. 'I've never experienced a case quite like this before,' he says.' The mix of friends and family as victims, then the escape and the hiding for a year. It was a very unusual crime.'

The extent to which Vossen's victims have survived and been able to move on inevitably varies. Some have emerged from their exposure to him bruised but broadly intact. Others are still picking up the pieces of their worlds and rebuilding their lives. A small few have been broken, perhaps beyond repair.

Of all his 33 victims, Angela Shaw's story is the most heart-rending. Angela went from 'believing' that she had enough for a comfortable old age to 'knowing' only that she had enough to live on for a year.

She thought she had a pension pot worth £2.7 million, comfortably enough to enjoy the company of her two daughters and three grandchildren and provide them with a substantial inheritance. Instead, she had to focus on putting a roof over her own head in Mexico whilst getting by on a UK state pension of £5,000 a year.

She has built a house in Mexico where labour is, thankfully, still relatively cheap. But initially she had to sleep on the floor because she had no furniture. Along with her other belongings, the furniture went into store when she sold her home in West Sussex. When her new house in Mexico was nearly finished, her daughter Grace, who had been resident in Mexico for two and a half years, offered to ship the furniture from England. The Mexican Embassy in London gave her an import certificate, overlooking the fact that such certificates can only be granted in the first six months of residency. Nobody noticed this until a container with all Angela's wordly goods was sitting on the dock in Vera Cruz.

In the end, Angela was obliged to ship everything back to England and sell it off as quickly as she could. There, her possessions, including her precious collection of Meissen pottery birds, were auctioned off. The proceeds, together with some financial support from Angela's sisters, went into the fitting out of the house in Mexico.

On the rare occasions when she returns to England to visit her sister on the south coast, she stays in a specially-built log cabin because her asthma means she can no longer live in a house with dogs. But she still cherishes her visits home and she loves her cabin.

'I am a victim, yes, but I am also a survivor because I did not give him everything I had,' says Angela. 'I still think that some money will come back to me one day, but I am not waiting around for that to happen. I am living for the day and counting my blessings.'

It's been the worst two years of my life,' says Angela with heroic understatement.

> I am effectively an itinerant. I have £100 a week to live on which is hardly enough, even here in Mexico and I don't have enough wealth to get permanent residency. The house is not finished and I have lost all my furniture. I've got nothing of my life left. Vossen was responsible for taking everything away. I really have no idea of how I'm going to survive from here on in. I have no social life and can't afford to go out anywhere. It's heart breaking really.
>
> The word I would use is harrowing. I feel like I don't have any skin left on my body. It's gone right down to the bone. I can empathise with people who have lost everything in fires or hurricanes because I know now what it's like to lose all that you've been working for. It is also very disturbing to know you have been caught up in someone else's illusory world.

Christine Allen, mother to Matthew Allen and mother-in-law to Elizabeth Shaw, is another pensioner facing a very uncertain future. She is living in a rented house in Norfolk and has had to resort to selling some of her possessions, including her collection of paintings, to make ends meet. 'She is a great survivor but at some point she is going to completely run out of money,' says Matthew. 'She had a Hockney that she sold recently that pulled her back from the brink but we are worried about the bailiffs arriving and we are desperate for her to move. It's the devastation for my mum and Elizabeth's mum that is really tough. Both of them have had tough times anyway for the past decade and both of them are now in real trouble.'

Elizabeth and Matthew also have grown used to living hand to mouth since being forced to move back to the UK from Brazil. Elizabeth, too, has had to sell some precious possessions in order to help with cashflow – in her case an engagement ring – and borrow money from friends to pay the bills. But at least they are young enough to rebuild their lives. They have moved to an estate house with beautiful views in East Lothian within commuting distance of Edinburgh and have just had a second child. Elizabeth is building up her yoga practice and Matthew has formed a media and communications agency with a network of contributors around the world supplying content mainly to various Olympic sporting associations. Matthew says:

> All our friends in Rio and back home are amazed that we aren't more angry and that it's not eating us up. But it didn't feel like money I'd ever had in a bank account. It was in a property and then it went straight to Vossen. It did affect our lives in Brazil in that we suddenly didn't have that financial cushion to do some of the things we may have wanted to do. It was only when we came back to the UK that it suddenly hit home that this guy had come along and run off with everything.

Elizabeth says: 'I don't think I would be where I am now had it not been for my yoga training. It's been a real therapy for me. It helps me process my emotions without being overwhelmed by them. I'm not going to let what happened define me, much less destroy me.

'A friend said to me the other day, "Elizabeth, stop acting as if this is your entire life, it's just a phase". We've learnt so much and grown up so much and are making our own way so much more. We are rebuilding and that's good.'

The Leinsters are rebuilding, too. Peter has embarked on a new career in property. His in-tray is overflowing with work and he has made it his goal to earn back every last penny Vossen stole from him.

Living in reduced circumstances and on reduced means is something that many of Vossen's victims have had to adjust to, but there are degrees of adjustment. Jake Sinclair has had to let out most of his sumptuous four-storey house on the edge of London's Primrose Hill and is now confined to living in its garden flat.

Stewart Gregory is still working hard in the film business to pay the mortgage while trying to rebuild his pension pot through some property rentals he owns in Liverpool. But he no longer has the option of stepping off the treadmill or gifting a house deposit to his daughter. 'I have Felix to thank for that. I'm in my mid-fifties and you don't need this kind of thing when some of your best earning years are behind you,' he says.

When Steven Walters told his bank he had been defrauded out of £2.4 million, it responded by offering him a £200 overdraft. So, instead of a bank loan, he had to sell his treasured Porsche 911 – 'exactly like the one Tom Cruise drove in *Mission Impossible*'. The car sale raised £30,000 which kept him afloat. He was also forced to give up his London flat and now lives in Hertfordshire with 'a whacking great big' interest-only mortgage. 'I have no savings and no pension and I'll have to give the house back in ten years so I'm pretty screwed,' he says.

But what he does have is a powerful sense of self-belief, a love of what he does and a tremendous work ethic. 'I've never seen work as a chore because film editing is a lot of fun and now I'm building up a company of freelance editors.'

Like the Shaws, Walters too has listened to the sound advice of other, truly close friends. 'A week after it happened, I was talking to a friend and I had this knot in my stomach. She gave me some good advice, she said, "That was your life then, this is your life now, you have got to close the door and get on with it. You can be really miserable and tear yourself apart every day or you can just get on with it."'

That is precisely what Walters has done. 'I get up at 5.30am and work seven days a week. It's a bit hand-to-mouth and there is no one I can fall back on but there is no point in being down about it,' he says.

His former partner, Mandy Collins, is getting on with it too. The £450,000 she thought was sitting in her account with Vossen was going to finance a big change in Mandy's work-life balance. It would allow her to pay off the rest of the mortgage and provide her son with a deposit to get on the housing ladder while she gave up her full-time job to study for a PhD in business psychology. Vossen destroyed all those dreams.

'It was going to be my pension. All my plans for the future were pretty much up the swanee,' she says. 'It was largely my fault. I was angry for a long time but you've just got to let it go.' She now lives in a small flat in Shepherd's Bush with her husband and has returned to a full-time job in the world of advertising.

David Benziger says he has written off the $100,000 he lost and moved on. 'While it hurt, it did not slaughter me.' Roger Phillips on the other hand, is determined not to let Vossen become past tense because of the length of the deception and the amount of money stolen from him. Phillips has led the charge against him, appearing on both radio and television in Germany where there is huge public appetite among Vossen's fellow countrymen to know more about the man and the crimes he committed. Phillips seems motivated by a burning desire for justice which the successful prosecution of Vossen only partly delivered. And also a determination to get his money back. 'Let's just say my pension pot has been severely depleted,' he says. 'It's changed my life and I'm living on much, much less money and we do worry every day if it's going to be sufficient.'

The Huntleys have also found it difficult adjusting to life post-Vossen. 'We are having to recalibrate our lives,' says Charles Huntley. 'We were thinking we were comfortably off and our lives were heading in a particular direction. Instead we've wasted two years of our lives trying to restore our finances at the same time as dealing with two bereavements. We worked extremely hard to earn our money and Vossen robbed us of our dreams and our future.'

Trust in others and confidence in themselves and their judgement is another issue for many of Vossen's victims. 'I'd blame Felix Vossen but we've also got to blame ourselves,' says Jon Peterson. 'We were all overly naïve and trusting. It's not made me more distrustful of people in general but it has made me a bit less trusting of individuals with my money. Of course it's gruesome and an appalling betrayal but if you were to use the experience negatively you'd become quite miserable,' he adds.

Stewart Gregory admits he still feels 'extraordinarily foolish' for having trusted Vossen and says it has affected his relationships with family members, especially his daughter who never believed it a good idea to invest with Vossen in the first place. 'I told her

"Daddy knows best". Well, does he now? A lot of my legal friends have since told me they could have run a test on this guy and found him out in a quarter of an hour. I've lost a lot of face, though not professionally, thank God.'

For others, becoming entangled with Vossen has led to more than just loss of face. One victim, who prefers to remain anonymous, recounts how a multi-million pound business venture fell apart after a would-be investor discovered that he had been defrauded by Vossen and withdrew funding for the project.

Before meeting Vossen, Mandy Collins had always been quite careful with money and regrets that she allowed Steven to take so much control over what they did with their cash. 'I've gone back to the way I was before and I'm using my better judgement, she says. 'OK, I've lost a shed load of money and have got to work a lot more. But I'm healthy and so are my parents and I'm married to a lovely man with a lovely child. When something like this happens, it teaches you a lot about yourself and other people.'

Charles Huntley says this: 'It has changed my whole outlook on life. It knocks your confidence completely and makes you question your judgement. Nowadays, I constantly worry about money whereas I never used to.'

David Benziger admits to having become more circumspect about his finances since his encounter with Vossen. 'It's made me more cautious and maybe I'm not as naïve as I was. But I'm a relatively optimistic person and I continue to trust people – until proven otherwise,' he adds.

Steven Walters has adopted a simple maxim which he says he has borrowed from Joanna Lumley: 'Trust everyone until they screw you over and then never forgive them.'

Vossen's erstwhile film partners, Chris Simon and Barnaby Southcombe, have sought to come to terms with their betrayal in different ways. Simon is now CEO of New Sparta Films and has no desire to maintain any form of contact with Vossen, much less help burnish the man's notoriety. He does not want to see Felix glorified in celluloid like some latter day Frank Abagnale, the fraudster turned impersonator who inspired the film *Catch Me If You Can*, where he was played by Leonardo di Caprio. Abagnale was such an expert forger of cheques that he was hired by the FBI to help apprehend other criminals involved in the same type of fraud.

Although Simon wants nothing more to do with Vossen, the fraudster has not finished with him. The vapour trail left behind by Vossen's activities continues to lead back to his former film producing friend. As CEO of New Sparta, Simon travels regularly to Hollywood and New York to meet screen talent and studio chiefs. On numerous occasions throughout 2018 he found himself being stopped by US immigration officials at Los Angeles LAX and JFK airport and quizzed about Felix Vossen, how he knew about the man and what he knew about him. Finally, Simon was advised to apply for a new US visa. When he arrived at the new US Embassy in London's Nine Elms to collect the visa, he was subject to a further 30-minute grilling by an embassy official, again demanding to know everything Simon could tell him about Felix Vossen and the nature of their relationship. Simon thought it odd, since by this time Vossen had already been tried and convicted in a Zurich court and had begun serving time in a Swiss prison.

He decided, however, that it would be advisable to contact Maric Demont, the Swiss prosecutor who brought the criminal case against Vossen, and ask him to write to the US authorities making it crystal clear that Simon was one of Vossen's victims, not an accomplice of some kind in his crimes. It is not known what the precise nature is of the US government's interest in Vossen. Although two of his victims were US citizens, the FBI decided at an early stage to leave the pursuit and prosecution of Vossen to their European counterparts.

Unlike Simon, his fellow partner in Embargo Films, Barnaby Southcombe, is in contact with Vossen and has spoken to him several times in prison, perhaps as part of his catharsis. His most recent film, *Scarborough*, is a study of illicit relationships – one between a male teacher and female pupil, the other involving a female teacher and male pupil. Interviewed about the movie by the *Observer* in January, 2017, Southcombe said: 'I'm interested in films about human frailty and how people can continue to do things they clearly know are wrong.' Where could his inspiration have come from?

Southcombe is not the only victim that Vossen has spoken to since his incarceration. He has telephoned Jane Leinster on a number of occasions and Steven Walters at least once. It appears to be his means of seeking redemption. Walters gave him short shrift.

> He phoned me from prison saying he's very sorry and he spends every minute thinking about what he did. He asked me how much I'd need to get me back on the straight and narrow. I said 'All of it.' If it hadn't been for him I'd still be in my gorgeous converted bible factory in Bermondsey. He told me he was happy to take money off the rich but when he took that first small amount off me he didn't think I would invest more. He's put me back right where I was 14 years ago.

Walters adds that it's really the likes of Angela Shaw that Vossen should be apologising to. 'That's when you realise what a terrible, terrible human being he is.'

Others have neither spoken to Vossen, nor visited him. Jon Peterson, who is owed £400,000 by Vossen, says he has taken a conscious decision not to have anything to do with his nemesis. 'I wanted to cleanse myself. When we discovered that we'd been violated we felt bereft and that loss turned to anger. I think that anger would boil up again if I saw him so I have chosen not to. I'd rather use my time in a more productive way.'

Elizabeth Shaw does not wish to see Vossen, but nor does she believe Vossen genuinely wants to see any of his former friends. 'He will find it easy to start all over again and he will not miss us,' she predicts.

All of which brings us to the £45 million question: is there anything left of the money that Vossen fleeced from his victims? Vossen had an expensive cocaine habit and his running costs were considerable – the rent alone on his various office premises was CHF29,000 a month. He also had a penchant for designer clothes and rarely travelled anywhere by public transport. But he did not possess any other accoutrements of ostentatious wealth. There were no high-performance cars, no luxury yachts, no private jets. And, as his investors discovered when he fled, even his furniture did not belong to him. But £45 million, plus the money he will have earned from his film producing activities, is a lot to burn through in 12 years. Has some of it been secreted away, out of sight of those who entrusted him with their hard-earned savings and beyond the reach of prosecutors who have searched in vain for a hidden cache?

Bill Baker continues to believe that there may be 'pots of gold' concealed in offshore tax havens, just waiting to be accessed by

Vossen when he leaves prison. Stewart Gregory also suspects there may still be some vestiges of money left tied up in property and other assets.

Vossen himself is not saying and investigators have failed to find any evidence of concealed cash. State Prosecutor Demont says: 'It's difficult to say but I don't think there are millions waiting for Felix Vossen. It doesn't look like it from the way he was living in Spain.'

The investor action group considered hiring forensic accountants to trace any assets that Vossen might still possess but decided it would prove a dead-end.

Charles Huntley also doubts that Vossen has squirreled anything away. 'He had apartments in London and Zurich, an office in Zurich and he travelled extensively and not in economy,' he says. 'So, his running costs were substantial and it had been going on for years. The film business was his hobby and it's likely that some money disappeared into movies. He withdrew massive amounts in cash which I assume he spent on drugs. There is also the potential that he did actually lose some of our money with his share trading.'

Roger Phillips doubts there is any hidden money to be found, believing a more effective course of action is to pursue the financial institutions that Vossen banked with. It is one of the reasons that he chose to surrender his claim to the state, meaning that he is unable to benefit from any civil action investors might bring against Vossen to recover their money. Jurgen Maas did likewise. In return, the two men are entitled to share the CHF85,372 that Vossen had left when he was arrested by Spanish police.

Because he lost substantially more than Maas, Phillips is entitled to the lion's share of that money – some 96 per cent in fact. Vossen was also ordered to pay Phillips's legal costs of CHF13,182. Altogether that still amounts to less than CHF100,000 (£78,000). Not much of a return on the £4 million he invested and the £10.6 million he thought was sitting in his investment pot.

And what of the man who caused all this misery? Although he is eligible for release in spring, 2020, the criminal justice system is not done with Felix Vossen yet. He may have escaped drugs charges in Spain, but he still faces prosecution by the Spanish for identity fraud. The case is yet to be heard.

Vossen professes to be frightened at the prospect of his own freedom. 'You lose your mind in prison,' he says. 'You don't think so but you do. I dread the day I get out.'

The truth, finally, or one more fabrication?

14

THE PONZI: A BRIEF HISTORY

Ponzi [pon-zee] *n.* fraudulent investment scheme in which funds paid in by later investors are used to pay artificially high returns to original investors

There is a long and dishonourable tradition of investors being fleeced through Ponzi schemes. Felix Vossen is merely the latest practitioner.

They derive their name from the most famous exponent of all, Charles Ponzi, who defrauded thousands of US investors out of millions of dollars a century ago. Ponzi devised a bogus scheme to generate super returns by supposedly trading in international postal reply coupons. He operated the fraud from his offices in Boston, Massachusetts for eight months between January and August 1920 until he was arrested, tried and imprisoned.

But, in fact, the Ponzi scheme had been in existence long before its eponymous practitioner sailed from Italy to America on board the S.S. *Vancouver* in November 1903, to begin his life of fraud.

Charles Dickens wrote about what were effectively Ponzi schemes in two of his novels. In *Martin Chuzzlewit*, published in 1844, the fraudster Montague Tigg uses The Anglo-Bengalee Disinterested Loan and Life Assurance Company to settle the claims of initial policyholders with the premiums paid by later policyholders. In *Little Dorrit*, which appeared in 1857, the financier Mr Merdles also operates a Ponzi scheme, committing suicide when his crime is uncovered. Dickens based the character of Merdles on a real-life fraudster John Sadlier, an MP and Junior Lord of the Treasury, whose nefarious activities led to the crash of Tipperary Bank in Ireland a year before *Little Dorrit* was written. Sadlier, too, took his own life.

In 1879 a fortune-teller and fraudster by the name of Clare Howe, by coincidence also based in Boston, marketed a savings scheme called the Ladies' Deposit, available solely to unmarried female clientele and supposedly offering a monthly interest rate of 8 per cent. The bank attracted $500,000 in deposits from more than 1,000 women until it collapsed a year later. Howe was convicted and imprisoned for three years but that did not deter her from going on to set up other fraudulent schemes, including the Woman's Bank and Ladies Provident Aid.

A similar scheme operated in 1899 by a Brooklyn bookkeeper, William F. Miller, defrauded investors out of $1 million. Miller's Franklin Syndicate promised investors an interest rate of 10 per cent a week, earning him the title of Mr 520 per cent. He was subsequently sentenced to ten years in jail for grand larceny.

A decade later, Charles De Ville Wells, operating under the alias Lucien Rivier, opened a phantom bank in Paris which suckered in 6,000 investors by offering them interest rates of 365 per cent a year – 1 per cent for every day their money was on deposit.

Wells had earlier become famous as The Man Who Broke the Bank at Monte Carlo after twice visiting the casino in Monte Carlo in 1891 with a stake of 40,000 francs and winning 600,000 francs – comfortably exceeding the 100,000 francs float that every gaming table began the day with. When this happened, the practice was to lay a black cloth across the table – indicating that the bank had been broken – until such time as the float was replenished.

Wells' fake Parisian bank took in two million francs within weeks of opening in 1910. When his fraud was uncovered, Wells fled to Britain where he was arrested two years later and sentenced to five years in prison by a Paris court.

Had investors known about Charles Ponzi's chequered past they might not have been quite so keen to partake in the scheme that gained him his notoriety. Born Carlo Pietro Giovanni Tebaldo Ponzi in Lugano, Italy in 1882, he arrived in Boston aged 21 with, by his own account, '$2.50 in cash and $1 million in hopes'. He worked for a few years in various East Coast restaurants, perfecting his English, until he was eventually fired for theft. He then moved north to Montreal and got himself a job as a teller at the newly-opened Banco Zarossi, which was offering twice the usual rate of interest on deposits. Ponzi rose to become manager but the bank went bust when property loans it had advanced went sour and it emerged that Zarossi was using newly-deposited funds to pay interest on existing deposits. The owner fled to Mexico while a penniless Ponzi was eventually jailed for three years after being found guilty of writing a cheque to himself using a chequebook belonging to a former Zarossi customer.

After his release, he returned to the United States where he was jailed for a further two years in Atlanta for smuggling illegal Italian immigrants across the border. By the time he arrived back in Boston, therefore, Ponzi had a long criminal track-record behind him. What distinguished Ponzi's fraud and gained him such notoriety was the sheer scale, ambition and apparent simplicity of it. And the chutzpah with which he executed it. Ponzi dreamed up the fraud in the summer of 1919 when he received a letter from Spain requesting a copy of an advertising catalogue he was promoting. Inside the envelope was an International Reply Coupon (IRC) – essentially a postage stamp which Ponzi could use to despatch the catalogue.

The coupon was priced at the cost of postage in Spain, the country of purchase, but it could be exchanged for US stamps of a higher value. Ponzi reasoned that if he could buy IRCs cheaply in inflation-plagued Italy rather than Spain, he could exchange them for higher-value US stamps, then sell those stamps and pocket the profit. In order to raise the capital he would need, Ponzi started his own publicly-quoted enterprise, the Securities Exchange Company, in January 1920, offering investors returns of 100 per cent on their money in 90 days. In the first month, he attracted $1,800 from 18 Bostonian investors. By March, that amount had risen to $25,000 and by June 1920 Ponzi had banked $2.5 million of investors' cash as word spread about his remarkable returns and agents were hired on fat commissions to seek out new investors further afield.

The only problem was that Ponzi had not worked out a reliable way to convert the IRCs into cash. Even if he were able to, there were not enough IRCs in circulation to earn the profits needed to repay investors. Clarence Barron, a financial journalist hired by the *Boston Post* to analyse Ponzi's scheme, calculated that it would require 160 million IRCs to generate the returns he was promising investors. There were only 27,000 in circulation in the entire world. The only way, therefore, for Ponzi to meet his commitment to early investors was to use the money pouring in from newer investors to pay them their 100 per cent interest.

Through the month of July, the *Post* ran a series of highly critical and damaging articles questioning the authenticity of Ponzi's scheme, including one written by his former PR agent claiming the Securities Exchange Company was insolvent. The stories alerted the state banking commissioners and they moved in, concerned about a run on the banks that Ponzi was depositing his money with. The trickle of redemptions turned into a flood as anxious investors scrambled to get their money out. With rumours about his imminent arrest swirling, Ponzi handed himself in voluntarily to the federal authorities. The collapse of his company cost investors $20m and brought down six banks. Ponzi was charged with 86 counts of mail fraud, sentenced to five years in jail and released after three and a half. He was re-arrested almost immediately, indicted on charges of larceny by the Massachusetts state and sentenced to a further seven to nine years in jail.

He broke bail whilst appealing against the conviction, fled to Florida and launched another fraud based around the bogus sale of tiny parcels of land. He was sentenced to a year in Florida state prison but was released after posting a $1,500 bond. He attempted to flee the US on a merchant ship bound for Italy but was apprehended in New Orleans and sent back to Massachusetts to serve out his earlier prison sentence. Ponzi was finally released from jail in 1934 and deported back to Italy. He suffered ill health for the remainder of his life and died in poverty in a Rio de Janeiro charity hospital in 1949, aged 68. In one of his last newspaper interviews, he told an American reporter that his investors shouldn't really have complained – it had been worth it just to watch him carry out his audacious scam. It had been, he said, the best show in town 'since the landing of the Pilgrims'.

***

In today's money, Ponzi's postal coupon fraud would have cost investors $220 million. That pales by comparison with the biggest Ponzi in history – the $65 billion fraud perpetrated by the US financier Bernie Madoff.

Born Bernard Lawrence Madoff in Queens, New York on April 29, 1938, he founded Bernard L Madoff Investment Securities in 1960 and served as its chairman until December 11, 2008 when he was arrested after his two sons, Andrew and Mark, both of whom worked for the firm, tipped off the authorities that the company was a giant Ponzi. The previous day, Madoff had confessed to his two sons that the asset management arm of the business was 'one big lie'.

In June 2009, Madoff was sentenced to 150 years in prison for what the judge at his trial described as an 'extraordinarily evil, unprecedented and staggering fraud'. The actual estimated loss suffered by his 4,800 investors was a not quite so impressive but still eye-watering $18 billion. Even so, it was still comfortably off the charts: federal sentencing guidelines for fraud only went up to $400 million of losses.

His brother Peter, who was senior MD and chief compliance officer of Bernard L Madoff Investment Securities, was also sentenced to ten years in gaol. In addition to his two sons, Madoff's niece Shana also worked for the family firm as its rules and compliance officer and attorney.

Madoff had been investigated on numerous previous occasions by the Securities and Exchange Commission but no fraud was ever uncovered. He was later to tell investigators that he could have been exposed as a fraud as long ago as 2003 but incompetent officials had behaved 'like Lt Colombo' by failing to spot the evidence and ask him the correct questions.

He was also shunned by the major investment banks and derivatives firms on Wall Street because they did not believe his numbers were real. Confidence in his business was scarcely helped by the fact that Madoff's books were audited by a tiny three-person firm with only one active accountant.

Madoff claimed that the fraud had begun in the 1990s, but federal investigators believe it may have dated back as far as the 1970s. In 1999, the SEC was approached by a financial analyst Harry Markopolos who told the regulator that he believed it was legally and mathematically impossible for Madoff to achieve the gains he was claiming. Markopolos, who went on to write a book about the case, said it had taken him five minutes to work this out – four to conclude that Madoff's numbers did not add up and another one minute to conclude they were almost certainly fraudulent. Markopolos examined, for instance, Madoff's trading of share options (a financial instrument that allows an investor to buy or sell a security at a pre-agreed price). He established that, for Madoff to be generating the returns he claimed to be achieving, he would have to had bought more options on the Chicago Board Options Exchange than actually existed.

The mechanics of Madoff's Ponzi were quite simple. When Madoff needed to calculate the 'return' one of his customers had earned on their investment, he would instruct two back office workers on the 17th floor of the Lipstick Building where he was based to create a report with false opening and closing dates and trading data. This trading data would be gathered together by a separate team of employees who would look back at the closing prices of the S&P100 Index between the two dates, select the best-performing shares and then put them into fictitious stock baskets in order to produce the 'profit' required to match the return earned by the investor. On occasions, they accidentally recorded share trades as having taken place over the weekend or on public holidays when the markets were not open but, again, no one, including the regulators picked up on these inconsistencies.

In reality, Madoff was simply pooling investors' money, depositing it in his business account at JPMorgan Chase and then withdrawing it when investors requested redemptions. The Ponzi finally collapsed when he could no longer meet the level of redemptions being requested. By the first week of December 2008, Madoff's fund was facing redemptions totalling $7 billion. He only had $234 million left in his Chase account to meet those redemptions.

Madoff is currently incarcerated in the Butner Federal Correctional Institution in North Carolina. He is scheduled for release in 2139.[1]

At the same time as Madoff was admitting that his investment business was built on one big lie, an Irish fraudster by the name of Breifne O'Brien was confessing something similar to investors in his property and shipping insurance empire. One of Dublin's best-known socialites with a taste for expensive cars and lavish homes, O'Brien had systematically defrauded investors out of at least EUR8.5 million by persuading them to put their money into non-existent property schemes in Paris, Manchester and Hamburg and a bogus linen shipping insurance scheme.

O'Brien used the funds instead to support his expensive lifestyle, buy properties for himself, including an apartment in Barbados, and a new Audi Q7 for his wife, the Dublin socialite and party planner Fiona Nagle.

In Dublin's relatively small and incestuous financial circles, it was enough to earn O'Brien the sobriquet of 'Ireland's Bernie Madoff'. In truth, his Ponzi was much closer in style and character to that of Felix Vossen. His victims were mostly good friends and close associates whom he had met while studying economics at Trinity College and entertained at the famous Sinatra Balls he threw annually at Dublin's Four Seasons hotel. They holidayed together, attended each other's christenings and were among the 300 guests at O'Brien's wedding, held at the family estate, Carrigrohane Castle outside Cork.

When investors sought to get their money out of O'Brien, he would either repay them using funds obtained from new investors or persuade them to roll their investments over into other non-existent property schemes. He forged documents and invented relationships with businessmen and professional advisers to embellish his credentials and prove his bona fides: all characteristics of the classic Ponzi and every one of them a tactic he could have borrowed from Vossen.

Like Vossen, O'Brien had the gift of the gab and an eye for whatever might make him a quick buck. Not long after graduating from Dublin's Trinity College he found himself, like much of the Irish diaspora, in London scratching a living from one entrepreneurial wheeze or another. He identified one such opportunity after visiting Twickenham for the England-Ireland rugby international and finding the stadium's plastic seating distinctly uncomfortable on the buttocks. The next time he attended a game there he turned up with a truck load of plastic cushions which he sold to willing fans for a tidy profit.

But, like Vossen, O'Brien was not very good either at what he claimed to be his area of expertise. Vossen was a poor share trader; O'Brien was no great shakes at property management, the business on which his Ponzi was built.

After returning to Dublin, one of his first business ventures involved a burger joint called Starvin' Marvin which he opened in the centre of the city in 1993 with two friends he had met at Trinity. As part of the agreement with their landlord, they were required to take out the lease on the entire building, even though the diner only occupied the ground and first floors. O'Brien's job was to let the apartments above the diner. But he failed to find a single tenant and within a year the business collapsed under the weight of the rent it was being forced to pay.

When news of his Ponzi emerged at the end of 2008, after O'Brien admitted he did not have the funds to repay investors, fraud officers confiscated his Aston Martin DB7. But it took a further six years for O'Brien to come to court as he mounted an unsuccessful legal attempt to prevent the prosecution taking place, on the grounds that it had been prejudiced by the adverse publicity he had attracted. He finally pleaded guilty to 14 sample counts of theft and deception between 2003 and 2008 and was sentenced to seven years in jail in October 2014. The charges related to five named investors but there are thought to have been many more victims. Of the EUR8.5 million he stole, only EUR420,000 has been recovered. O'Brien is understood to have been released on licence early in 2018.

***

There are a number of hallmarks of the classic Ponzi scheme. First and foremost is the promise of unusually high returns. These are designed to encourage investors to keep their funds in the scheme and not seek redemptions.

Then there is the use of vague but authoritative-sounding terminology to impress investors, allied to claims that the scheme relies upon a secret or proprietary investment strategy.

Very often, victims will be well-known to the perpetrator as part of a deliberate ploy to blur the lines between personal friendship and professional relationships.

Prompt payment of dividends will often be offered to investors who insist on such at the outset, to create the impression amongst others that the fund is healthy and solvent.

Investors will receive simple, periodic statements showing the purported increase in value of their funds but they will also experience difficulty and delays in getting money out of such schemes.

Investor money will often be put into unregistered investments sold by unlicensed sellers.

The perpetrators of the scheme will often attempt to minimise withdrawals by offering new products or investment propositions which involve funds being rolled over or tied up for a longer period of time in return for guaranteed high returns.

A combination of these characteristics was present in the frauds orchestrated by Ponzi, Madoff, O'Brien and Vossen. And what unites them, of course, is that they all collapsed when they were no longer able to withstand the level of redemptions being demanded by investors.

The trigger for the run on Ponzi's scheme was the hugely damaging press coverage it received, led by the *Boston Post*.

In Madoff's case, the catalyst was the 2008 global financial crisis which panicked investors into wanting to liquidate their positions. For Vossen, a culmination of coincidental factors conspired to bring his fraudulent scheme to the tipping point.

In the same way that Vossen's fraud brought shame and disgrace to the family name, Madoff's Ponzi has had tragic consequences for his family. Bernie's son Mark took his own life on the second anniversary of his father's arrest. His other son Andrew died of lymphoma four years later. Neither son ever visited their father in prison. Mark left a suicide note for the family lawyer Charles Flumenbaum lamenting that 'no one wants to believe the truth'. Andrew, too, blamed the return of the cancer which eventually killed him on the damage the scandal had caused him. It had, he said, killed his brother quickly and it was killing him slowly.

Madoff's apology to all those he hurt also bears more than a passing resemblance to the valedictory email Felix Vossen sent shortly after he had gone on the run. This is what Madoff said: 'I have left a legacy of shame, as some of my victims have pointed out, to my family and my grandchildren. This is something I will live with for the rest of my life. I'm sorry. I know that doesn't help you.'

There will always be willing perpetrators – and easy victims – of fraud, not least because it is hard to detect and difficult to prosecute. Unexplained Wealth Orders, used for the first time in Britain in 2018, have added a further weapon to the armoury of investigators and prosecutors, enabling them to root out and confiscate proceeds of fraud, particularly those amassed by oligarchs and laundered through the UK.

But even though they could be costing the UK economy alone £37.5 billion a year, the number of frauds that result in prosecution, much less jail sentences, remains tiny according to BDO, the professional services firm that collects annual data on the crime. It calculates that as few as one in 50 cases of fraud results in prosecution. Very often individual victims are reluctant to come forward for fear of exposure and ridicule, while corporate victims may prefer to settle cases privately.

It is safe to assume, therefore, that Felix Vossen will not be the last practitioner of the Ponzi. Indeed, at this very moment, someone, somewhere is almost certainly being parted from their money because they have been seduced into investing in something which is too tempting to resist. But also, too good to be true.

ORIGINAL DOCUMENTS

2015/10013685
Felix Vossen
Seite 41/51

Anhang A

Nr.	Geschädigte	Betrag	Datum	Bank	Bank-domizil	Konto-Nr.	Kontoinhaber
1	Vossen Norbert u. Cornelia	EUR 1'000'000.00	21.04.2009	CS	St. Moritz	734651-02-4 EUR	Felix Vossen
1	Vossen Norbert u. Cornelia	EUR 1'000'000.00	26.02.2010	CS	St. Moritz	734651-02-4 EUR	Felix Vossen
1	Vossen Cornelia	EUR 570'000.00	14.05.2013	CS	St. Moritz	734651-02-3 EUR	Felix Vossen
1	Vossen Cornelia	EUR 130'000.00	21.05.2013	CS	St. Moritz	734651-02-3 EUR	Felix Vossen
1	Vossen Norbert*	EUR 750'000.00	20.08.2013	CS	St. Moritz	734651-02-3 EUR	Felix Vossen
1	Vossen Norbert u. Cornelia	EUR 700'000.00	23.09.2013	Barclays	Gross-britannien	83101614	Exponential Media Ventures I Ltd.
1	Vossen Norbert u. Cornelia	EUR 800'000.00	01.11.2013	Barclays	Gross-britannien	83101614	Exponential Media Ventures I Ltd.
1	Vossen Norbert u. Cornelia	EUR 600'000.00	30.07.2014	Barclays	Gross-britannien	83101614	Exponential Media Ventures I Ltd.
1	Vossen Norbert u. Cornelia	GBP 500'000.00	23.09.2014	Barclays	Gross-britannien	83101614	Exponential Media Ventures I Ltd.
2		USD 353'937.00	07.08.2008	UBS	St. Moritz	221-863666.70H USD	Vossen Capital Partners L.P.
2		USD 101'959.00	11.08.2008	UBS	St. Moritz	221-863666.70H USD	Vossen Capital Partners L.P.
2		USD 101'959.00	08.08.2008	UBS	Stamford Branch	0260007993	Vossen Capital Partners L.P.
2		USD 287'948.37	12.08.2008	UBS	St. Moritz	221-863666.70H USD	Vossen Capital Partners L.P.
2		USD 285'074.00	26.08.2008	UBS	St. Moritz	221-863666.70H USD	Vossen Capital Partners L.P.
2		USD 192'466.00	26.08.2008	UBS	St. Moritz	221-863666.70H USD	Vossen Capital Partners L.P.
2		USD 408'760.00	09.01.2009	UBS	St. Moritz	221-863666.70H USD	Vossen Capital Partners L.P.
2		USD 11'177.00	27.02.2009	UBS	St. Moritz	221-863666.70H USD	Vossen Capital Partners L.P.
2		USD 6'118.00	03.04.2009	UBS	St. Moritz	221-863666.70H USD	Vossen Capital Partners L.P.
2		USD 11'510.00	05.05.2009	UBS	St. Moritz	221-863666.70H USD	Vossen Capital Partners L.P.
2		USD 10'355.00	31.07.2009	UBS	St. Moritz	221-863666.70H USD	Vossen Capital Partners L.P.
2		USD 29'893.00	30.06.2009	UBS	St. Moritz	221-863666.70H USD	Vossen Capital Partners L.P.

2015/10013685
Felix Vossen
Seite 42/51

Nr.	Geschädigte	Betrag	Datum	Bank	Bank-domizil	Konto-Nr.	Kontoinhaber
2		USD 14'443.00	30.10.2009	UBS	St. Moritz	221-863666.70H USD	Vossen Capital Partners L.P.
2		USD 904.00	11.02.2009	UBS	St. Moritz	221-863666.70H GBP	Vossen Capital Partners L.P.
2		USD 14'255.00	04.01.2010	UBS			
2		USD 5'486.00	03.01.2011	UBS			
2		GBP 500'000.00	01.12.2008	UBS	St. Moritz	221-863666.71G GBP	Vossen Capital Partners L.P.
2		GBP 150'000.00	21.04.2009	UBS	St. Moritz	221-863666.71G GBP	Vossen Capital Partners L.P.
2		GBP 700'000.00	04.08.2009	UBS	St. Moritz	221-863666.71G GBP	Vossen Capital Partners L.P.
2		GBP 300'000.00	21.08.2009	UBS	St. Moritz	221-863666.71G GBP	Vossen Capital Partners L.P.
2		GBP 250'000.00	24.08.2009	UBS	St. Moritz	221-863666.71G GBP	Vossen Capital Partners L.P.
2		GBP 200'000.00	14.12.2011	UBS	St. Moritz	221-863666.61T GBP	Vossen Capital Partners L.P.
2		GBP 300'000.00	15.12.2011	UBS	St. Moritz	221-863666.61T GBP	Vossen Capital Partners L.P.
2		GBP 57'100.00	26.02.2014	CS	St. Moritz	734651-02-1 GPB	Felix Vossen
3		GBP 200'000.00	11.05.2007	UBS	St. Moritz	221-863666.62Z GBP	Vossen Capital Partners L.P.
3		GBP 50'000.00	06.03.2008	UBS	St. Moritz	221-863666.62Z GBP	Vossen Capital Partners L.P.
3		GBP 100'395.00	01.09.2008				
3		GBP 110'000.00	22.10.2008	UBS	St. Moritz	221-863666.62Z GBP	Vossen Capital Partners L.P.
3		GBP 100'000.00	31.12.2013	CS	St. Moritz	734651-02-01 GBP	Felix Vossen
3		GBP 100'000.00	22.05.2008	UBS	St. Moritz	221-863666.62Z GBP	Vossen Capital Partners L.P.
3		USD 218'456.48	01.07.2010				
3		GBP 50'000.00	06.08.2013	CS	St. Moritz	734651-02-01 GBP	Felix Vossen
3		GBP 50'000.00	03.01.2014	CS	St. Moritz	734651-02-01 GBP	Felix Vossen
3		GBP 50'000.00	03.01.2014	CS	St. Moritz	734651-02-01 GBP	Felix Vossen
3		USD 147'040.00	08.07.2013	ZKB	Zürich	1100-1560.028 CHF	VCP Asset Management AG

2015/10013685
Felix Vossen
Seite 43/51

Nr.	Geschädigte	Betrag	Datum	Bank	Bank-domizil	Konto-Nr.	Kontoinhaber
4		USD 862'849.00	01.09.2004	CS	St. Moritz	734651-02 USD	Felix Vossen
4		USD 137'151.00	17.09.2004	CS	St. Moritz	734651-02 USD	Felix Vossen
4		GBP 500'000.00	19.10.2006				
4		GBP 250'000.00	14.07.2007				
4		GBP 250'000.00	15.07.2007				
4		GBP 10'000.00	06.05.2009	CS	St. Moritz	734651-02-1 GBP	Felix Vossen
4		GBP 250'000.00	13.08.2013	CS	St. Moritz	734651-02-1 GBP	Felix Vossen
4		GBP 500'000.00	09.02.2005	CS	St. Moritz	734651-02-1 GBP	Felix Vossen
4		GBP 500'000.00	19.10.2005	CS	St. Moritz	734651-02-1 GBP	Felix Vossen
4		GBP 275'000.00	20.04.2007	CS	St. Moritz	734651-02-1 GBP	Felix Vossen
4		GBP 25'000.00	05.10.2007	CS	St. Moritz	734651-02-1 GBP	Felix Vossen
4		GBP 500'000.00	11.07.2011	UBS	St. Moritz	221-859373.60E GBP	Felix Vossen
4		GBP 250'000.00	24.11.2011	UBS	St. Moritz	221-859373.60E GBP	Felix Vossen
5		USD 500'000.00	06.04.2005	CS	St. Moritz	734651-02 USD	Felix Vossen
5		GBP 350'000.00	27.06.2011	CS	St. Moritz	734651-02-1 GBP	Felix Vossen
5		GBP 500'000.00	29.05.2012	CS	St. Moritz	734651-02-1 GBP	Felix Vossen
5		GBP 250'000.00	11.12.2012	CS	St. Moritz	734651-02-1 GBP	Felix Vossen
5		GBP 100'000.00	27.03.2013	CS	St. Moritz	734651-02-1 GBP	Felix Vossen
5		GBP 250'000.00	17.10.2013	CS	St. Moritz	734651-02-1 GBP	Felix Vossen
5		GBP 100'000.00	01.11.2013	CS	St. Moritz	734651-02-1 GBP	Felix Vossen
6		GBP 350'000.00	11.07.2007				
6		GBP 80'000.00	24.12.2007	UBS	St. Moritz	221-863666.67E GBP	Vossen Capital Partners L.P.
6		GBP 60'000.00	26.02.2009	UBS	St. Moritz	221-863666.67E GBP	Vossen Capital Partenrs L.P.

Anhang B

Datum	Konto-Nr.	Kontoinhaber	Bezugsort	EUR	CHF	GBP
08.07.10	734651-02-4	Felix Vossen	Zürich, Paradeplatz	100'350.00		
26.07.10	734651-01	Felix Vossen	Zürich, Paradeplatz		50'000.00	
18.10.11	734651-01	Felix Vossen	Zürich, Flughafen		25'450.00	
29.02.12	734651-01	Felix Vossen	St. Moritz		2'000.00	
16.06.12	734651-02-1	Felix Vossen	Zürich, Flughafen			26'151.82
03.07.12	734651-02-1	Felix Vossen	Zürich, Paradeplatz			25'250.00
21.09.12	734651-02-1	Felix Vossen	Zürich, Paradeplatz			4'040.00
04.03.13	734651-02-1	Felix Vossen	Zürich, Flughafen			10'100.00
04.03.13	734651-02-1	Felix Vossen	Zürich, Flughafen			15'150.00
15.05.13	734651-02-1	Felix Vossen	Zürich, Flughafen			15'150.00
15.05.13	734651-02-1	Felix Vossen	Zürich, Paradeplatz			25'250.00
28.05.13	734651-02-1	Felix Vossen	Zürich, Paradeplatz			60'360.00
11.06.13	734651-01	Felix Vossen	Zürich, Flughafen		22'000.00	
11.06.13	734651-02-1	Felix Vossen	Zürich, Flughafen			5'050.00
29.09.13	734651-02-1	Felix Vossen	Zürich, Flughafen			20'200.00
08.10.13	734651-02-1	Felix Vossen	Zürich, Paradeplatz			40'240.00
25.10.13	734651-02-1	Felix Vossen	Zürich, Paradeplatz			5'050.00
30.01.14	734651-02-1	Felix Vossen	Zürich, Paradeplatz			5'050.00
29.04.14	734651-02-1	Felix Vossen	Zürich, Paradeplatz			25'250.00
29.10.14	734651-02-1	Felix Vossen	Zürich, Paradeplatz			20'200.00
01.12.14	734651-02-1	Felix Vossen	Zürich, Paradeplatz			10'100.00

Datum	Konto-Nr.	Kontoinhaber	Bezugsort	EUR	CHF	GBP
20.01.15	734651-02-1	Felix Vossen	Zürich, Flughafen			10'100.00
27.02.15	734651-01	Felix Vossen	Zürich, Paradeplatz		22'000.00	
04.03.15	734651-01	Felix Vossen	Zürich, Flughafen		11'000.00	
04.03.15	734651-02-2	Felix Vossen	Zürich, Flughafen	14'140.00		

Anhang C

Datum	Konto-Nr.	Kontoinhaber	CHF	EUR	GBP	USD
29.04.2014	305116.104	VCP Investment Advisors AG				10'000.52
29.04.2014	305116.104	VCP Investment Advisors AG				7'793.31
25.11.2014	253051162	VCP Investment Advisors AG		5'050.00		
25.11.2014	25305116	VCP Investment Advisors AG	45'000.00			
01.12.2014	253051164	VCP Investment Advisors AG			8'534.50	
20.02.2015	253051163	VCP Investment Advisors AG	50'000.00			
27.02.2015	11351586.2003	Felix Vossen		92'460.00		

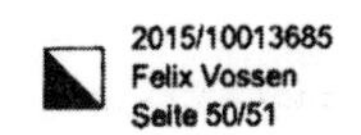

Anhang D

Datum	Belastungs-Konto-Nr.	Begünstigte	GBP
12.05.09	734651-02-1	Virtus Trust Ltd., Guernsey	75'017.18
17.07.09	734651-02-1	Alderham Ltd., Guernsey	53'002.84
17.07.09	734651-02-1	Virtus Trust Ltd., Guernsey	55'277.84
16.10.09	734651-02-1	Virtus Trust Ltd., Guernsey	50'042.47
01.03.10	734651-02-1	Virtus Trust Ltd., Guernsey	50'042.75
04.05.10	734651-02-1	Alderham Ltd., Guernsey	50'017.58
28.08.12	734651-02-1	Alderham Ltd., Guernsey	180'203.27
07.11.13	734651-02-1	Virtus Trust Ltd., Guernsey	5'922.30

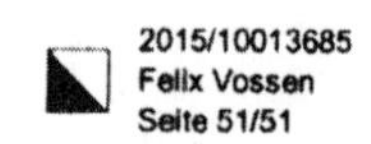
2015/10013685
Felix Vossen
Seite 51/51

Anhang E

Credit Suisse

Datum	Belastungs-Konto-Nr.	Begünstigte	GBP
26.09.2014	734651-02-1	VCP Investment Advisors Ltd., GB	360'003.29
30.09.2014	734651-02-1	VCP Investment Advisors Ltd., GB	40'003.29
23.12.2014	734651-02-1	VCP Investment Advisors Ltd., GB	90'003.31
23.02.2015	734651-02-1	VCP Investment Advisors Ltd., GB	129'703.62

Banque Cramer

Datum	Belastungs-Konto-Nr.	Begünstigte	GBP	USD
11.04.2014	305116.104	VCP Investment Advisors Ltd., GB		85'647.42
28.04.2014	305116.104	VCP Investment Advisors Ltd., GB		85'932.20
06.06.2014	305116.104	VCP Investment Advisors Ltd., GB		34'357.41
29.07.2014	305116.102	VCP Investment Advisors Ltd., GB	300'029.32	
10.09.2014	253051153	VCP Investment Advisors Ltd., GB	60'033.21	
12.01.2015	253051164	VCP Investment Advisors Ltd., GB	100'032.54	
09.02.2015	253051164	VCP Investment Advisors Ltd., GB	100'035.42	

Vossen Capital Partners LP
Seefeld Strasse 69
CH-8008 Zurich
T: +41 43 488 37 41
F: +41 43 488 35 50

Client ID	Account Number	Client Name
CLID065	221-863666.68M	

Performance Report from 01 January 2012 to 31 March 2012

	Number of Units	Net Unit Price	Value
Opening Balance	1,211.40	$242.4382	$293,689.64
Deposits	0.00	$0.0000	$0.00
Withdrawals	-83.40	$262.8193	-$21,919.13
Subtotal	1,128.00		$271,770.51
Gross Return			$48,104.37
Total Fees			-$11,123.68
Net Return			$36,980.69
Closing Balance	1,128.00	$273.7156	$308,751.20

	Jan 12	Feb 12	Mar 12	Q1	YTD
VCP Net Unit Price	256.6748	269.1849	273.7156	273.7156	273.7156
VCP Net % Return	5.87%	4.87%	1.68%	12.90%	12.90%
S&P 500 Index	4.36%	4.06%	3.13%	12.00%	12.00%

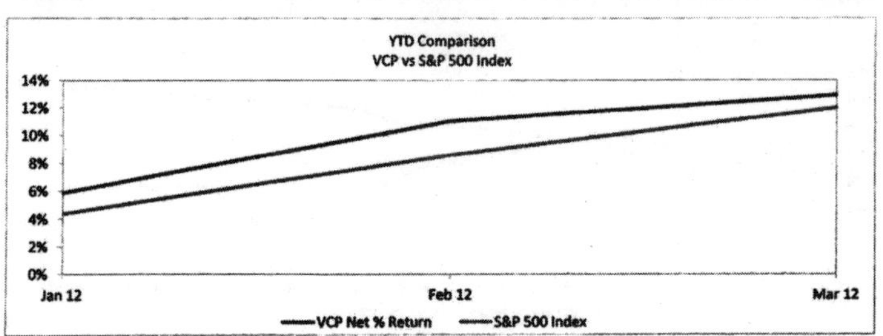

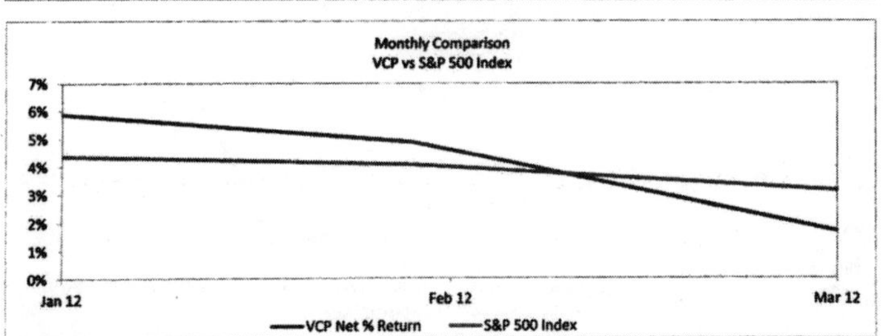

Schedule of Transactions

Date	Description	Number of Units	Funds Deposited	Funds Withdrawn	Fees
31/01/2012	AMF				569.23
31/01/2012	Performance Fee				4,311.56
31/01/2012	Bank Transfer	15.29		3,924.65	0.00
31/01/2012	Bank Transfer	27.27		7,000.00	0.00
29/02/2012	AMF				539.00
29/02/2012	Performance Fee				3,655.58
29/02/2012	Bank Transfer	14.84		3,994.48	0.00
29/02/2012	Bank Transfer	26.00		7,000.00	0.00
30/03/2012	AMF				565.53
30/03/2012	Performance Fee				1,277.66
30/03/2012	Custodian Fee				205.12

All figures quoted in US Dollars.
The net return is calculated using a time-weighted return measure after deducting all advisor fees, commissions and exchange fees.

Issue Date 05/07/12 Page 1 of 1 Q112.65.221-863666.68M

Vossen Capital Partners LP
Seefeld Strasse 69
CH-8008 Zurich
T: +41 43 488 37 41
F: +41 43 488 35 50

Client ID	Account Number	Client Name
CLID065	221-863666.68M	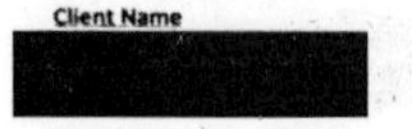

Performance Report from 01 October 2011 to 31 December 2011

	Number of Units	Net Unit Price	Value
Opening Balance	1,211.40	$236.3407	$286,303.12
Deposits	0.00	$0.0000	$0.00
Withdrawals	0.00	$0.0000	$0.00
Subtotal	1,211.40	$236.3407	$286,303.12
Gross Return			$10,721.69
Total Fees			-$3,335.18
Net Return			$7,386.51
Closing Balance	1,211.40	$242.4382	$293,689.64

	Jan 11	Feb 11	Mar 11	Q1	Apr 11	May 11	Jun 11	Q2	Jul 11	Aug 11	Sep 11	Q3	Oct 11	Nov 11	Dec 11	Q4	YTD
VCP Net Unit Price	207.5678	211.0549	215.5081	215.5081	216.4132	222.0616	225.3037	225.3037	226.5727	233.3976	236.3407	236.3407	237.4829	240.6982	242.4382	242.4382	242.4382
VCP Net % Return	1.23%	1.68%	2.11%	5.10%	0.42%	2.61%	1.46%	4.54%	0.56%	3.01%	1.26%	4.89%	0.48%	1.35%	0.72%	2.58%	18.24%
S&P 500 Index	0.83%	4.66%	-0.10%	5.42%	2.85%	-1.35%	-1.83%	-0.39%	-2.15%	-5.68%	-7.18%	-14.33%	10.77%	-0.51%	0.85%	11.15%	0.00%

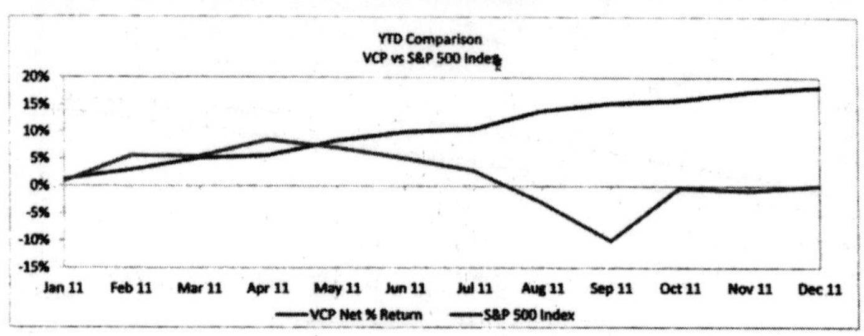

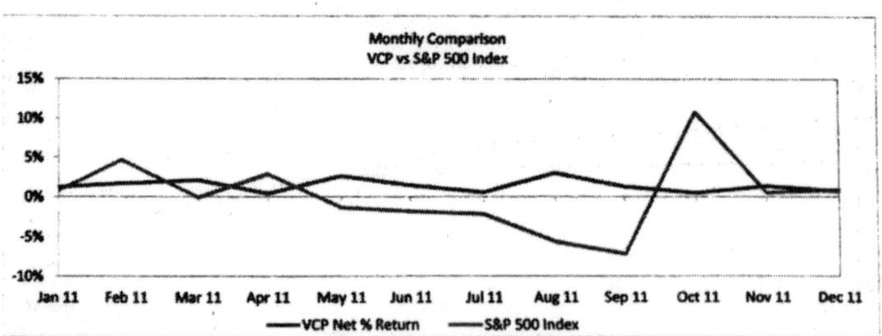

Schedule of Transactions

Date	Description	Number of Units	Funds Deposited	Funds Withdrawn	Fees
31/10/2011	AMF				435.65
31/10/2011	Performance Fee				345.92
30/11/2011	AMF				423.91
30/11/2011	Performance Fee				973.75
30/12/2011	AMF				440.03
30/12/2011	Performance Fee				526.96
30/12/2011	Custodian Fee				188.96

All figures quoted in US Dollars.
The net return is calculated using a time-weighted return measure after deducting all advisor fees, commissions and exchange fees.

Issue Date 05/07/12 Page 1 of 1 Q411.65.221-863666.68M

Vossen Capital Partners LP
Seefeld Strasse 69
CH-8008 Zurich
T: +41 43 488 37 41
F: +41 43 488 35 50

Client ID	Account Number	Client Name
CLID065	221-863666.68M	

Performance Report from 01 July 2011 to 30 September 2011

	Number of Units	Net Unit Price	Value
Opening Balance	1,211.40	$225.3037	$272,932.90
Deposits	0.00	$0.0000	$0.00
Withdrawals	0.00	$0.0000	$0.00
Subtotal	1,211.40	$225.3037	$272,932.90
Gross Return			$18,164.33
Total Fees			-$4,794.11
Net Return			$13,370.22
Closing Balance	1,211.40	$236.3407	$286,303.12

	Jan 11	Feb 11	Mar 11	Q1	Apr 11	May 11	Jun 11	Q2	Jul 11	Aug 11	Sep 11	Q3	YTD
VCP Net Unit Price	207.5678	211.0549	215.5081	215.5081	216.4132	222.0616	225.3037	225.3037	226.5727	233.3976	236.3407	236.3407	236.3407
VCP Net % Return	1.23%	1.68%	2.11%	5.10%	0.42%	2.61%	1.46%	4.54%	0.56%	3.01%	1.26%	4.89%	15.26%
S&P 500 Index	0.83%	4.66%	-0.10%	5.42%	2.85%	-1.35%	-1.83%	-0.39%	-2.15%	-5.68%	-7.18%	-14.33%	-10.04%

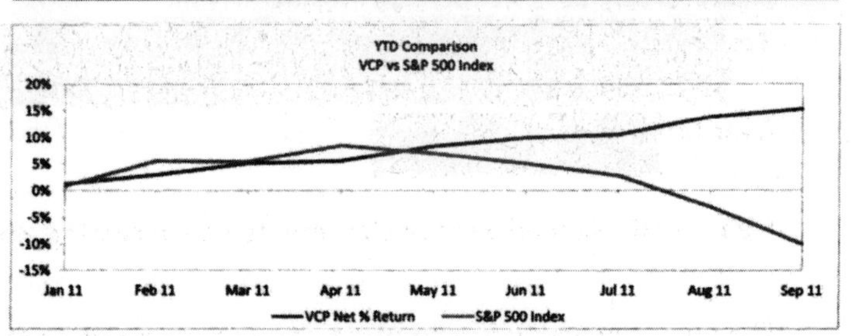

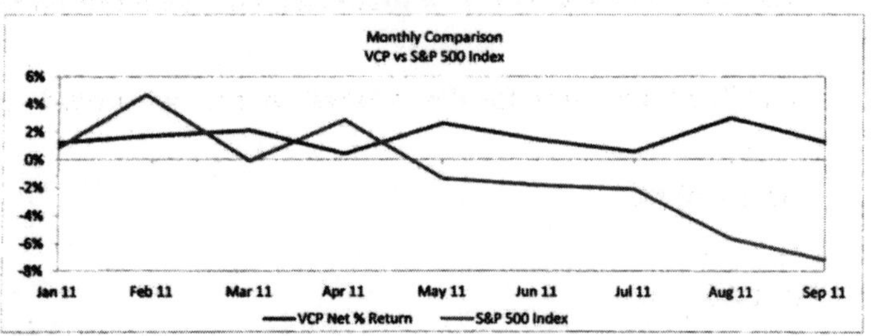

Schedule of Transactions

Date	Description	Number of Units	Funds Deposited	Funds Withdrawn	Fees
29/07/2011	AMF				415.89
29/07/2011	Performance Fee				384.32
31/08/2011	AMF				428.41
31/08/2011	Performance Fee				2,066.94
30/09/2011	AMF				419.66
30/09/2011	Performance Fee				891.31
30/09/2011	Custodian Fee				187.58

All figures quoted in US Dollars.

The net return is calculated using a time-weighted return measure after deducting all advisor fees, commissions and exchange fees.

Issue Date 05/07/11 **Page 1 of 1** Q311.65.221-863666.68M

From: Natalie Casanova <natalie.casanova@vcp-assetmanag

Subject: Statements | Quarterly Payment

Date: 26 July 2012 at 13:16:39 GMT-4

To:

Dear Mr

Please find attached a set of statements now including your

The quarterly payment was processed and went out on the :

I really do apologize for the inconvenience. I will update you

Best wishes,

Natalie

DIRECCIÓN GENERAL DE LA POLICÍA

Jefatura Superior de Policía de la Comunidad Valenciana Gabinete de Prensa

Nota de prensa

En el momento de la detención portaba una gran cantidad de dinero en efectivo en euros, francos suizos y libras esterlinas

La Policía Nacional detiene en Valencia a un hombre por apropiarse de 15 millones de francos suizos

- **Se le ha intervenido diversos documentos falsificados como tres pasaportes, francés, griego y holandés, así como una carta de identidad italiana y un permiso de conducir griego**
- **Se ha incautado 82.310 francos suizos, 13.010 libras esterlinas y 5.905 euros**
- **En su domicilio se ha localizado once teléfonos móviles, seis ordenadores portátiles, 244 gramos de al parecer cocaína y útiles para su elaboración y manipulación**

23-febrero-2016- Agentes de la Policía Nacional han detenido Valencia a un hombre de 41 años, de origen alemán, como presunto autor de los delitos de falsificación documental, resistencia, salud pública, blanqueo de capitales y reclamación Judicial. El ahora arrestado tenía en vigor una orden internacional de extradición por los presuntos delitos económicos y financieros y contra la propiedad al apropiarse de 15 millones de francos suizos a través de la creación de un entramado de empresas para la captación de inversiones en Suiza e Inglaterra. Durante el registro en su domicilio se intervino dinero, droga, y diversa documentación falsa.

Los hechos ocurrieron cuando agentes de la Policía Nacional patrullaban por la avenida de Peris y Valero de Valencia observaron a una persona que al percatarse de la presencia policial, evidenció signos de nerviosismo, por lo que tras darle el alto, éste se identificó con un pasaporte francés para a continuación intentar huir, siendo alcanzado a escasos metros del lugar por los policías.

Correo electrónico
Valencia.prensa@policia.es

G.V. Ramón y Cajal, 40
46007 VALENCIA
TEL.: 963 539 503
FAX: 963 525 504

www.policia.es

En un primer cacheo, le localizaron un permiso de conducir griego y una carta de identidad italiana los dos con su fotografía, así como una gran cantidad de dinero en euros, francos suizos y libras esterlinas.

Los policías averiguaron la vivienda donde residía que estaba régimen de alquiler, y tras solicitar el correspondiente mandamiento de entrada y registro intervinieron dos pasaportes falsificados, uno griego y el otro holandés ambos con su fotografía, así como un pasaporte alemán que resulto ser legítimo. Además han intervenido once teléfonos móviles, seis ordenadores portátiles y material informático, 244 gramos de al parecer cocaína y útiles para su elaboración y manipulación.

La totalidad del dinero intervenido asciende a 82.310 francos suizos, 13.010 libras esterlinas y 5.905 euros.

Una vez con su autentica identidad averiguaron que tenía en vigor una Orden Internacional de Extracción emitida por las Autoridades de Suiza por un delito económico y Financiero contra la propiedad, habiendo creado en el país transalpino e Inglaterra un entramado de empresas para la captación de inversiones, apropiándose de 15 millones de francos suizos.

En la operación han participado agentes de la Jefatura Superior de Policía con la colaboración de del grupo de localización de fugitivos de la Comisaría General de policía Judicial.

El detenido, sin antecedentes policiales, ha pasado a disposición judicial.

Valencia, 23 de febrero de 2016 j **@polprvalencia**

*** Se remiten fotografías**

Correo electrónico
Valencia.prensa@policia.es

Esta información puede ser usada o en su integridad sin necesidad de citar fuentes

G.V. Ramón y Cajal, 40
46007 VALENCIA
TEL.: 963 539 503
FAX: 963 525 504

Página 2 de 2

www.policia.es

IN THE HIGH COURT OF JUSTICE
QUEEN'S BENCH DIVISION

Claim No. HQ15X01859

Before The Honourable Mr Justice Lewis

Dated 13 March 2015

HIGH COURT OF JUSTICE
13 MAR 2015
INTERIM APPLICATIONS COURT
QUEEN'S BENCH LISTING

(1)
(2)
(3)
(4)
(5)
(6)
(7)
(8)
(9)
(10)
(11)
(12)
(13)
(14)
(15)
(16)
(17)
(18)
(19)

Applicants

and

(1) FELIX VOSSEN
(2) VOSSEN CAPITAL PARTNERS L.P.
(3) VCP ASSET MANAGEMENT AG
(4) VCP INVESTMENT ADVISERS AG
(5) VCP ANALYTICS GMBH

Respondents

1

ORDER

PENAL NOTICE

IF YOU (1) FELIX VOSSEN AND/OR (2) VOSSEN CAPITAL PARTNERS LP AND/OR (3) VCP ASSET MANAGEMENT AG AND/OR (4) VCP INVESTMENT ADVISERS AG AND/OR (5) VCP ANALYTICS GMBH DISOBEY THIS ORDER YOU MAY BE HELD TO BE IN CONTEMPT OF COURT AND MAY BE IMPRISONED, FINED OR HAVE YOUR ASSETS SEIZED.

ANY OTHER PERSON WHO KNOWS OF THIS ORDER AND DOES ANYTHING WHICH HELPS OR PERMITS THE RESPONDENTS TO BREACH THE TERMS OF THIS ORDER MAY ALSO BE HELD TO BE IN CONTEMPT OF COURT AND MAY BE IMPRISONED, FINED, OR HAVE THEIR ASSETS SEIZED.

This Order

1. This is a Freezing Injunction and Order for Disclosure made against (1) Felix Vossen, (2) Vossen Capital Partners LP, (3) VCP Asset Management AG (4) VCP Investment Advisers AG (5) VCP Analytics GmbH and (the "Respondents") on 13th March 2015 by Mr Justice Lewis on the application of [redacted] Others ("the Applicants"). The Judge read the Affidavit of Lee Ranford dated 13 March 2015.

2. This Order was made at a hearing without notice to the Respondents. The Respondents have a right to apply to the Court to vary or discharge the Order – see paragraph 19 below.

3. There will be a further hearing in respect of this Order on 20th March 2015 ("the Return Date").

4. Unless otherwise stated, references in this Order to "the Respondent" means any or all of them, and this Order is effective against any Respondent on whom it is served or who is given notice of it.

Freezing Injunction

5. Until the return date or further order of the Court, the Respondents must not:
   a. Remove from England and Wales any of his assets which are in England or Wales up to the value of £45,000,000; or
   b. In any way dispose of, or deal with or diminish the value of any of his assets which are in or outside England or Wales up to the same value.

6. Paragraph 5 of this Order applies to all the Respondent's assets whether or not they are in his own name and whether they are solely or jointly owned. For the purpose of this Order the Respondent's assets include any asset which he has the power, directly or indirectly, to dispose of or deal with as if it was his own. The Respondent is to be regarded as having such power if a third party holds or controls the asset in accordance with his direct or indirect instructions.

7. This prohibition includes the following assets in particular:
   a. Any money standing to the credit of any bank account including the amount of any cheque drawn on such account which has not been cleared, including, but not limited to, the following bank accounts, which it is noted that the Respondents have used:
      i. Felix Vossen

      8001 Zurich

      Account: CH5304835073465102001

      Credit Suisse AG 8 Paradeplatz

      Zurich

      ii. VCP Asset Management AG
      Waag Gasse 4
      8001 Zurich
      Zuercher Rantonal Bank

Bezirksgericht Zürich
9. Abteilung

Staatsanwaltschaft III des Kantons Zürich
23. Nov. 2017
Geschäftskontrolle

Geschäfts-Nr.: DG170153-L / UD

<u>Mitwirkend:</u> Vizepräsident Dr. S. Aeppli als Vorsitzender, Bezirksrichterin lic. iur. K. Eichenberger und Ersatzrichter lic. iur. R. Faga sowie Gerichtsschreiberin MLaw S. Zollinger

<u>Urteil vom 22. November 2017</u>
(Dispositiv)

in Sachen

<u>Staatsanwaltschaft III des Kantons Zürich</u>, Büro C-4, Unt.Nr. 2015/10013685, Weststr. 70, Postfach, 8036 Zürich,
Anklägerin

gegen

<u>Felix Burghardt Norbert Vossen</u>, geboren 11. April 1974, von Deutschland, Produzent, ohne festen Wohnsitz in der Schweiz, z.Zt. im vorzeitigen Strafvollzug in der JVA Pöschwies, Haft gemäss Anklageschrift, **Zustelladresse:** JVA Pöschwies, Roosstr. 49, 8105 Regensdorf,
Beschuldigter

amtlich verteidigt durch Rechtsanwalt lic. iur. Reto Steinmann, MSG Rechtsanwälte & Notare AG, Vorstadt 32, Postfach 4755, 6304 Zug

betreffend Betrug etc.

<u>Privatkläger</u>

2015/ [illegible] 13[illegible]85	Datum	Visum
Eingang [illegible]	23 [illegible] 2017	[illegible]
Eingang STA/S[illegible]	[illegible]	[illegible]
Ausgang GL/A[illegible]	23.11.17	[illegible]

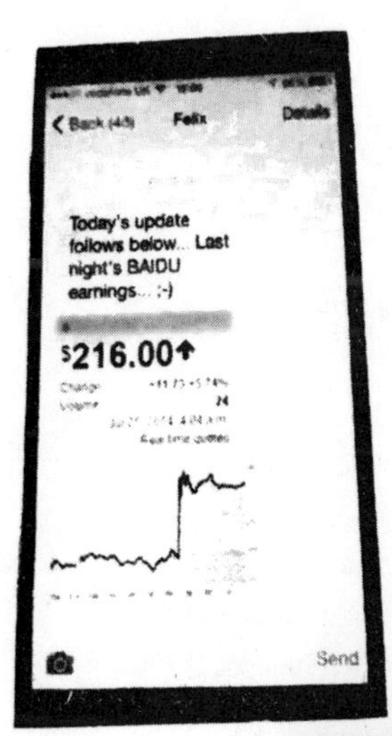
Back (43)
Felix
Details
Today's update follows below... Last night's BAIDU earnings... :-)
$216.00
Send

Felix
Details
And best performance tonight goes to... Twitter!!! :-)
$50.23
Send

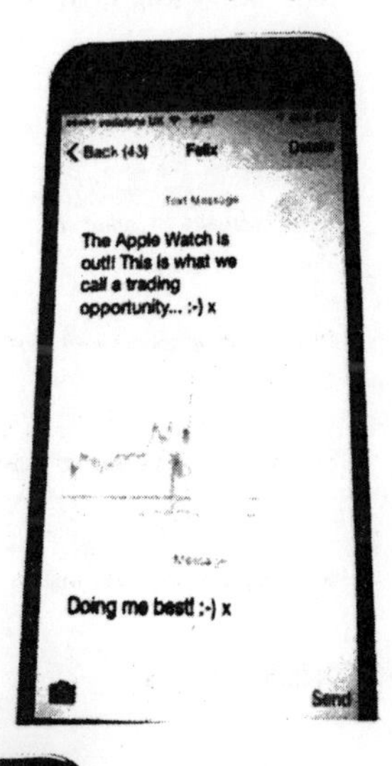
Back (43)
Felix
Text Message
The Apple Watch is out!! This is what we call a trading opportunity... :-) x
Doing me best! :-) x
Send

Back (43)
Felix
Details
This thing just won't quit...
Send

Back (43)
Felix
An this is why I love earnings season... :-)
Facebook Inc. C
$75.26
Change
Volume
5,833
Real time quotes
Send

Valuation Q4/13

From: Natalie Casanova (natalie.casanova@vcp-assetmanagement.ch)

To: [redacted]

Cc: robert.gassner@vcp-assetmanagement.ch; felix.vossen@vcp-assetmanagement.ch

Date: Wednesday, 15 January 2014, 17:54 GMT

Dear [redacted]

It is a pleasure to 'meet' you.

Please find attached your most recent valuation up to the end of the fourth quarter of 2013.

I will email your password separately in a moment.

Kind regards and best wishes,

Natalie Casanova

Natalie Casanova
Leiterin Kundenbeziehungen

VCP Asset Management AG
Waaggasse 4
CH-8001 Zürich

T. +41 (0) 44 210 0880
F. +41 (0) 44 210 0890
www.vcp-assetmanagement.ch

Confidentiality Caution and Disclaimer: This e-mail and any attachments are intended solely for the use of the individual or entity to which they are addressed and may contain confidential and/or privileged material. Access to this e-mail by anyone else is unauthorised and any review, retransmission, dissemination or other use of, or taking of any action in reliance upon, this information by persons or entities other than the intended recipient is prohibited. If you have received this e-mail in error, please notify the sender immediately and delete this e-mail from your system.

Q413.APS.92.1300-7073.208.TN.pdf
127.5kB

Quarterly Report

12/31/2014

221 - 863666.70H

1300 - 7073.208.TN

V•P

Overview

Net of Fees | US Dollar

12/31/2010 - 12/31/2014

Activity Summary

	Quarter to Date	12/31/2010 to Date
Beginning Value	11,412,478	6,583,792
Net Contributions/Withdrawals	-93,783	-2,259,547
Realized Gains	93,783	1,470,048
Unrealized Gains	457,443	6,075,628
Income Received	0	0
Ending Value	11,869,921	11,869,921

Change

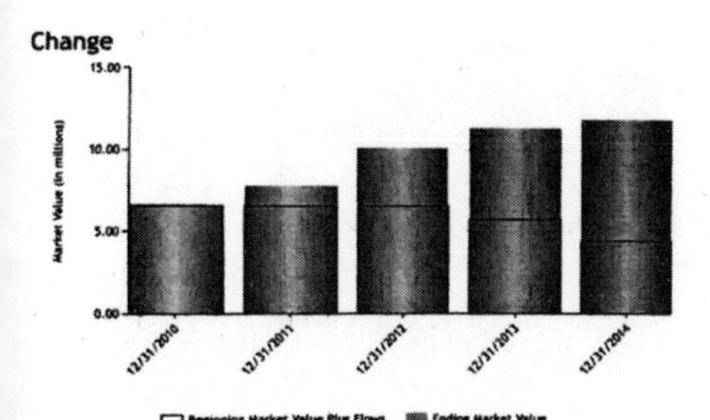

Allocation as of 12/31/2014

	Market Value	% Assets	Yield
VCP US Equity IV	11,869,921	100.0	
Total	11,869,921	100.0	0.0

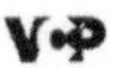

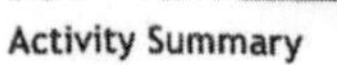

Overview

Net of Fees | US Dollar
12/31/2010 - 12/31/2014

Activity Summary

	Quarter to Date	Inception to Date
Beginning Value	929,806	804,422
Net Contributions/Withdrawals	-23,446	-47,818
Realized Gains	23,446	47,818
Unrealized Gains	21,464	146,848
Income Received	0	0
Ending Value	951,270	951,270

Change

Allocation as of 12/31/2014

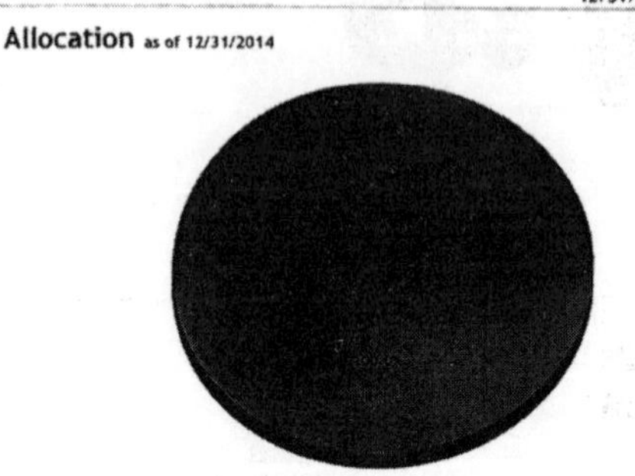

	Market Value	% Assets	Yield
VCP US Equity IV	951,270	100.0	
Total	**951,270**	**100.0**	**0.0**

Performance Overview

Net of Fees | US Dollar
12/31/2014

Performance History

	Month To Date	Quarter To Date	Year To Date	Latest 1 Year	Latest 3 Years
VCP US Equity IV	1.99	4.83	18.66	18.66	85.76
Overall Performance	**1.99**	**4.83**	**18.66**	**18.66**	**85.76**
Index					
MSCI	-1.71	0.66	2.93	2.93	44.57

Time Weighted Return 12/31/2010 to Date

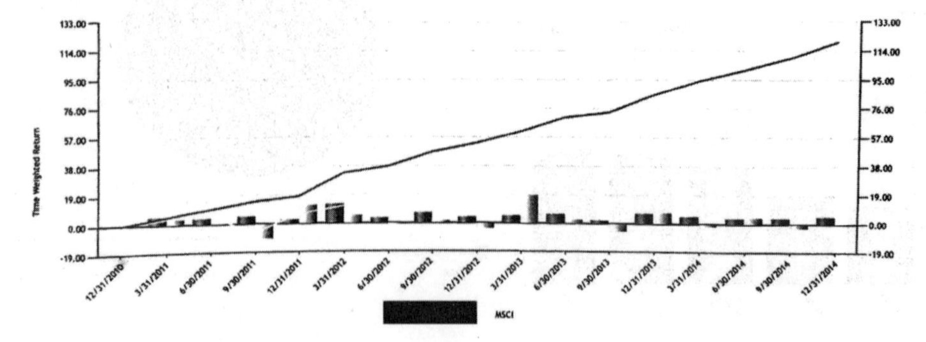

V•P

Performance Overview

Net of Fees | US Dollar
12/31/2014

Performance History

	Month To Date	Quarter To Date	Year To Date	Latest 1 Year	Latest 3 Years
VCP US Equity IV	1.99	4.83	18.66	18.66	
Overall Performance	**1.99**	**4.83**	**18.66**	**18.66**	
Index					
MSCI	-1.71	0.66	2.93	2.93	44.57

Time Weighted Return 10/31/2013 to Date

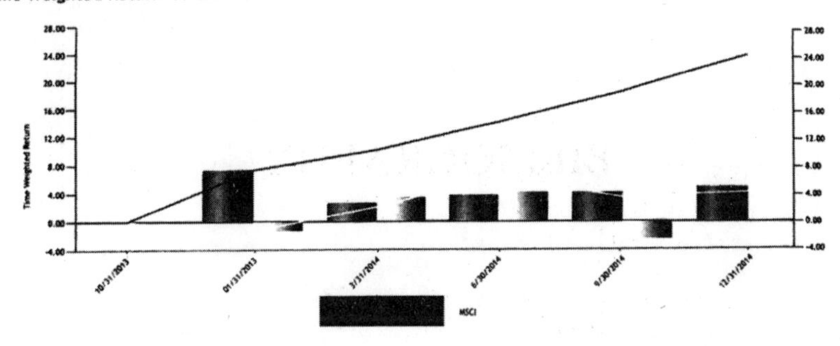

V•P

Household Overview

Net of Fees | US Dollar
12/31/2014

Performance 12/31/2010 to Date

Time Weighted Return

128.00
112.00
96.00
80.00
64.00
48.00
32.00
16.00
0.00

12/31/2010 6/30/2011 12/31/2011 6/30/2012 12/31/2012 6/30/2013 10/31/2013 12/31/2013 6/30/2014 12/31/2014

Activity Summary

	Month To Date	Quarter To Date	Year To Date	Latest 3 Years
Beginning Market Value	12,685,642	12,342,284	12,470,349	7,784,424
Net Additions	-117,229	-117,229	-1,470,048	-1,470,048
Gains/Losses	252,778	596.136	1,820,890	6,506,815
Ending Market Value	12,821,191	12,821,191	12,821,191	12,821,191
Time Weighted Return	**1.99**	**4.83**	**18.66**	**85.76**
Index				
MSCI	-1.71	0.66	2.93	44.57

Performance Summary

Portfolio	Market Value	Month To Date	Quarter To Date	Year To Date	Latest 3 Years
Household	**12,821,191**	**1.99**	**4.83**	**18.66**	**85.76**
	11,869,921	1.99	4.83	18.66	85.76
	951,270	1.99	4.83	18.66	

V•P

Appraisal

Net of Fees | US Dollar
12/31/2014

Quantity	Symbol	Description	Unit Cost	Local Currency Total Cost	Local Currency Price	Market Value	Reporting Currency Market Value	Reporting Currency % Assets	Yield
US Dollar(FX = 1.0000)									
26,356	VCPUE4	VCP US Equity IV	148.76	3,920,719	450.36	11,869,921	11,869,921	92.6	
2,112	VCPUE4	VCP US Equity IV	355.47	750,753	450.36	951,270	951,270	7.4	
				4,671,472		12,821,191	12,821,191	100.0	0.0
		US Dollar Total		4,671,472		12,821,191	12,821,191	100.0	0.0
Total							12,821,191	100.0	

BIBLIOGRAPHY

The Confidence Game, Maria Konnikova, Canongate Books, 2016

Offenders, Deviants or Patients (Third Edition), Herschel Prins, Routledge, 2005

The Psychopathy Checklist (Revised 2nd Edition), Robert D Hare, Toronto, Ontario, 2003

The Psychopath Inside, James Fallon, Penguin, 2013

Diagnostic and Statistical Manual of Mental Disorders (Fifth Edition), American Psychiatric Association Publishing, 2013

The Rise of Mr Ponzi, Charles Ponzi, 1936

Ponzi: The Incredible True Story of the King of Financial Cons, Donald Dunn, First Broadway Books, 2004

The Man Who Broke the Bank at Monte Carlo, Robert Quinn, History Press, 2016

Ponzi's Scheme: The True Story of a Financial Legend, Mitchell Zuckoff, Random House, 2005

Bust, Dearbhail McDonald, Penguin Books, 2010

ACKNOWLEDGEMENTS

My thanks to Ellie for her sterling investigative work in Spain, to Irene for all her help with the Valencia police, Katarina for translation, Marie for her tremendous assistance with all things German, Phoebe for her brilliant insights into psychopathy, Jon for his literary connections, Charlie at Viney Shaw for keeping the faith, Jon and the team at Amberley and, especially, to Fi for her patience, support and proof-reading skills.

Finally, thanks to all those victims of Felix Vossen who were brave and honest enough to tell their stories. Some of their names have been changed to protect their identities.

Michael Harrison, 8 March 2019

INDEX